Third World – Second Sex

Other Books by Miranda Davies
Third World – Second Sex (ed.) (Zed Press, 1983)
Half the Earth (compiled with two other women) (Pandora 1986)

Third World – Second Sex
Volume 2

Compiled by Miranda Davies

Zed Books Ltd.
London and New Jersey

Third World – Second Sex, Vol 2, was first published by
Zed Books Ltd., 57 Caledonian Road, London N1 9BU, UK, and
171 First Avenue, Atlantic Highlands, New Jersey 07716,
USA, in 1987

Typeset by EMS Photosetters, Rochford, Essex.
Cover design by Andrew Corbett, based on a design by
Jan Brown designs.
Printed and bound in the United Kingdom
by Biddles Ltd., Guildford and King's Lynn.

Second impression, 1990.

Library of Congress Cataloging-in-Publication Data

Third world, second sex 2.

Bibliography: p.
1. Women—Developing countries—Social conditions.
2. Feminism—Developing countries. I. Davies, Miranda.
HQ1870.9.T48.   1988   305.4'2'091724   88-5552
ISBN 0-86232-752-2
ISBN 0-86232-753-9 (pbk.)

British Library Cataloguing in Publication Data

Third world—second sex 2.
1. Women—Developing countries—Social conditions
Davies, Miranda
305.4'2'091742   HQ1870.9

ISBN 0-86232-752-0
ISBN 0-86232-753-9 Pbk

Contents

Preface

Seven years ago, when I was starting to collect material for the first volume of *Third World – Second Sex*, I hoped that it would contribute to a useful understanding and appreciation of what I later referred to as 'the revolutionary emergence of a new feminist consciousness amongst women in the Third World'. A number of women activists in Africa, Asia, the Middle East, the Pacific, Latin America and the Caribbean I knew distrusted the label 'feminist' and I wondered briefly if it was rash to use such a sweeping term. However, as this second compilation shows, the waves of protest and the development of new autonomous projects and organisations dedicated to women's liberation in these regions have not died down. In fact they are growing all the time.

My aim in putting together another book of articles and interviews by Third World women has been to record this progress by providing a channel for more women to communicate, in their own words, their concerns and experiences of organisation.

This volume introduces a number of new countries, including Algeria, Thailand, Brazil, South Africa and Papua New Guinea, as well as pointing to further issues. Some, like sexuality, international prostitution, and women and media, were barely touched upon in the first edition of *Third World – Second Sex*. Other themes, notably the role of women in national liberation movements before and after revolution, though no less important, received more attention in Volume 1.

I have also compiled a much more substantial resources section, listing all of (but not only) the women's networks and organisations without whose co-operation the book simply would not have been possible. I am particularly indebted to Isis International with whom I worked in Rome last year. As well as allowing me free access to all their documentation, Isis gave me permission to reproduce several articles from their own publications. In addition I am grateful to three London-based groups – SWAPO Women's Solidarity Campaign, the Philippine Resource Centre and the Anti-Apartheid Women's Committee – all of whom made available their material and patiently replied to my queries.

By again concentrating on the issue of organisation, that vital link between theory and practice, I hope this book provides not so much a depressing reminder of some of the specific forms of oppression which mar the daily lives of Third World women, as an exciting reflection of their courage and dynamism in striving to build a new and better future for themselves, their families, and women everywhere.

Miranda Davies
London
July 1987

Introduction

In confronting a broad range of issues, largely based on concrete experience, this volume of writings and interviews by Third World women is an important contribution to the theory and practice of the feminist movement worldwide.

The task of women in the so-called developing world is doubly difficult: to break loose from the bonds imposed upon them by their patriarchal traditional societies, and at the same time avoid the trap presented by developmental and modernising processes in which new forms of exploitation are embedded.

Female workers employed in the Free Trade Zones of Asia, Africa and Latin America nowadays produce garments for the fashion markets of the West, as well as other consumer products such as electronic goods, their super-exploitation (for instance, working for US$1.50 a day in Sri Lanka) justified as a means of generating both local employment and export earnings for the host countries. Similarly, as we see from the situations in Thailand and the Philippines cited in this book, tourist industries draw in women as waitresses, entertainers and prostitutes. Even the 'export' of women, mainly Asian, to more affluent countries as servants, and increasingly brides, is part of this trend. It may be that these women, in breaking away from their tradition-bound families, dream of achieving some sort of economic independence by entering the labour market or marrying abroad, only to find themselves victims of new forms of exploitation, oppression and degradation.

The explosive spread of feminism and feminist consciousness has been supported by a new body of creative work, much of it focusing on these kinds of issues, by women at both academic and activist levels. Women anthropologists and sociologists have taken a fresh look at the societies they study and the methodologies they have been taught; have uncovered the male biases in their disciplines and revealed the mainsprings of gender oppression. Women economists have examined the role of women as workers and housewives in the process of capital accumulation, and women historians continue to unearth our 'hidden history'. Together they have demonstrated how, in every patriarchal culture, women have been oppressed and controlled by ideologies that justify and legitimate their subjection. The detailed studies of micro-level situations undertaken by feminist activists from the Third World reveal the myriad ways in which women are exploited, and provide invaluable sources for feminists in their day-to-day campaigns.

Resistance to feminism is strongest where women attempt to attack those features of social practice or family life that subordinate them. Divisions within the women's movement also strengthen this resistance; many women still believe that women's struggles end when some of them have achieved parity with men in existing economic and political structures. Those feminists aware that all forms of oppression are linked to the subordination of women and that the potentialities of reformism are limited, continue the struggle on all fronts. They have made their own agendas and challenged the notions of duty, morality, family, religion and nation which have been used to subordinate them. The way women work, through existing political parties, the electoral process, legal and professional bodies, is clear from many pieces in this book. Yet, while participating in general struggles, women, confronted by issues basic to them as women, need to organise themselves separately.

Among other issues, *Third World – Second Sex 2* discusses problems encountered by women who are drawn into the labour force in developing countries. Women entering the labour market often face job discrimination on grounds of sex and find themselves relegated to lower-paid jobs. Moreover, as trade unions have been traditionally male-biased they rarely take up the specific demands of women workers.

Before women can become part of the industrial work-force on equitable terms or, indeed, obtain an 'equal' place in society, they need access to education on an equal basis with men – an issue raised by social reformers even in the colonial period. The right of women to education is now recognised in most countries. But, as this book demonstrates, learning and education is often a means of 'socialising' women into accepting the values of a male-dominated society. It can offer women the prospect of so-called equal opportunity in learning, in job-related education and entry into the labour market; it can also teach them their place in society. On a positive note, as we see here from experiences in Vietnam, Tigray and India, the education process can become a powerful tool for liberation.

The struggle against the still-dominant patriarchal social structures that place women's sexuality at the disposal of men is another focus of women's struggles, both in the Third World and in the West. The issues of sexuality, sexual oppression and domestic violence remain crucial problems yet to be resolved by the feminist movement. Articles in this book carefully delineate the difficulties inherent in even addressing these problems, let alone in analysing their causes to try to reduce or eliminate their impact.

It is no exaggeration to say that feminism has overcome national boundaries to form its own alert signals and network systems. If women go on strike as did the Polytex garment-workers in Sri Lanka, if a women is sentenced to be stoned to death for adultery in the name of Islam, if there are 'dowry deaths' in India, if women in peace movements in Europe are arrested, the alarm goes out, signalling to women's organisations everywhere the need to protest and to mobilise solidarity and support.

In this context the media are important. In common with all other institutions connected with the propagation of ideology, the media are instrumental in perpetuating subordination. Yet, as some of the following pages illustrate, there are many subtle ways in which they can be used to serve feminist objectives.

Feminism today has cut across class, nationality, ethnicity, religion and caste. There is hardly any sphere of activity it has not touched: mobilising support, arousing controversy and forcing governments, political parties, religious bodies and trade unions, among others, to face the issue of women's rights and women's liberation.

Societies and economies today are at diverse stages of development; women's struggles take many forms and confront a wide variety of issues. But, as *Third World – Second Sex 2* sets out to prove, the spread of the feminist movement worldwide has brought a new dimension to these struggles. No longer are they isolated actions by groups of women fighting for their rights, but a continuing widespread challenge to those national and international structures of oppression which continue to exploit women at every level.

Kumari Jayawardena
Colombo, Sri Lanka
July 1987

Part 1: Women, Politics and Organisation

1 Bound and Gagged by the Family Code

Marie-Aimée Hélie-Lucas

Marie-Aimée Hélie-Lucas is an Algerian feminist and founder member of the international solidarity network, Women Living Under Muslim Laws, based in France (see resources section). In the interview below, recorded in 1984 during the Fourth International Tribunal on Reproductive Rights in Amsterdam, she talked to Sophie Laws of the British radical feminist magazine, *Trouble and Strife*, about the situation of women in Algeria and the alarming implications of a law known as the Family Code. For fear of reprisal from the Algerian authorities, the interview was later published in *Trouble and Strife* (No 5, Spring 1985) using the pseudonym Nadine Claire. However, Marie-Aimée asked for her real name to be used here. She has also written a postscript in order to clarify and update some of the comments she made in 1984.

Marie-Aimée: I would like to start with this new law, which is known in Algeria under the name 'Family Code', (not the legal name of it, that is 'Law on Personal Status') a title which is also used in Tunisia and Morocco. After Independence, in 1962, we were still under extended French law on personal status, because we could not change all the laws at the same time. Under Ben Bella, who was the first president (1963–65), we already had a proposal of a family code, introducing some amendments to the Constitution about equal rights of all citizens, which we felt even at that time to be quite backward as far as women were concerned. Women were already discriminated against, under the pretext of the Koranic influence in the country. We had two other proposals, under Boumedienne, who was the second President of Algeria: the three proposals were stopped by Left individuals (both women and men) who were close to the presidents. What happened in 1982 was that a fourth proposal was issued, under Chadli, and we couldn't find out what it contained. This was also the case with the three previous ones, but they were circulated among a few people so that at least privileged people could have a look at them; this was also why Leftists could use their personal influence to stop them.

But this fourth proposal was kept entirely secret – I'll give you two examples to show you to what extent it was kept secret. We had friends who were ministers – they had only two sessions to discuss this proposal. They told us that a copy of it was given to them when they entered the room, and taken back when they went out of the room. And they accepted this! This gives you an idea of the climate of fear in

Algeria. We also have six women Deputies (MPs), so we went to them as well and asked them if we could look at the proposal, before it was passed without our knowledge. They also refused – the same things were happening to them. All the Deputies were given copies when they entered the room, and the copy was taken back. And they also accepted this. This is really anti-constitutional, because they are supposed to refer to us, they are supposed to represent us.

Anyway we couldn't get hold of this proposal so two weeks before we knew that it was going to be passed, we had to steal it. Then we duplicated 25 copies on an old alcohol machine, because that's the only way for it not to be traced by the police; they can find a modern machine. We tried to put these 25 copies in various strategic places where people would react. Only one copy reached the target: veteran women, women who fought in the Liberation struggle and who are legally organised. We have no free association at all, so it's very difficult to organise, it's always illegal, but those women are allowed to have their own meetings. So it was very important to reach this group.

They understood the situation, and they called a demonstration, the first women's demonstration for 20 years, since Independence – exactly 20 years. Usually any kind of demonstration is just crushed, but this time we had in the front line six women who had been condemned to death under the French, so the police didn't beat them. It was a good tactic. The women veterans also wrote to their Minister, the Minister of veterans, saying that they hadn't fought for such a result. They also wrote to the Minister of Justice and to the President. The State was frightened – the President stopped this proposal. We thought it was a big victory, and anyway the first one since Independence. Then what happened was that everything was very quiet, after 1982, and then we heard that this proposal (or another like it) was still there, and could be passed at any time.

Three feminists had been arrested in October, last October (1983), along with many other political prisoners. But these three had been arrested because they were feminists, and their only action had been to distribute copies of this proposal, and call for people to read it carefully and not let it be passed. They had been arrested then, and we heard about it in March, which means that it was kept secret – there were no trials, no nothing. So we started an international campaign. The President of Algeria received thousands of letters and telegrams from all over the world, because we could reach feminist groups in all continents. They were released after one and a half months' campaign. It was a big success.

And then immediately after their release, when everybody was relaxed and happy, the Family Code was passed. So now we are under this law, and I want to tell you what it is. These details are from the fourth proposal – the actual law that was passed may be slightly different, but the spirit won't have changed. It is said that it is inspired by Koranic law, but as we all know, religion is always used by the ruling class.

Family Code against women's rights

We have no right to marry, for instance: we have to be *given* in marriage, according to the tradition, by a man of our family to the other family. It was stated that the aim of marriage is *reproduction*, which also means that somebody can be divorced or repudiated (I will explain what that is) on the grounds of infertility. Repudiation is when the husband just sends his wife away – she is no more married to him, but she is not divorced, and stays like this. If her family takes her back, then at least she is fed, but if not, she is on the street. And with the cultural change in Algeria, it's more and more likely that more and more women will be on the street, and not back in their families. So it's certainly a big problem.

Sophie: *Before this family code was passed, could men repudiate their wives in the same way?*

Yes, of course, they could, but it was not *legal*. It was done for years, but the Constitution of Algeria guarantees equal rights, so it was anti-constitutional. But now this law is in contradiction with the Constitution. And we are going to fight it on legal grounds too.

We have no right to divorce at all. Only the husband can divorce. We have no right to work, we must get permission from our father or our husband to work. And this is a very good example of the fact that it is not Koranic law, because in the time of the Prophet, I doubt very much that anything was said about wage-earning, since it didn't exist at that time! So this is not only anti-socialist (and we pretend to be socialists), but it is also very much against women. Now when a couple divorce, or rather when a husband divorces his wife, the children are given to the woman, to the mother. But you cannot really say that she has responsibility for the children. A boy is given to her up to the age of nine or ten, and the girl until marriage. But she is only working as a maid in keeping the children – the husband can take them back whenever he feels she is not raising the children properly. She has got to stay close to him geographically, so that he can check on her every day. Which means that she cannot go to another city, she cannot build a new life, she has to be under his eye all the time. This is not having responsibility for the children. I could go on with this type of example, but it is useless.

There are laws of inheritance, too, which are Koranic laws – two women equal one man in many respects. This is also true in giving legal evidence.

The situation of women from 1962 to now has been increasingly bad, getting worse every year, and now it is even legal. So a lot of action will probably be taken in Algeria. It started in 1981, with the first feminist gathering that we have ever had. It was just plain information on the situation of women, on health, education – on three items. And this was already threatened by the Rightist forces that are now called Fundamentalist, that we call the Muslim Brothers. They threatened us that they would come and throw acid in our faces during this meeting, which fortunately they didn't do, but they were in the room, interrupting all the time. We couldn't rent a public place to hold this meeting, we had to be very tricky. Some of us had to register with a union, and then rent a room through the union. It was very complicated, and we have never been able to do it again. The second gathering of feminists was held in Oran, a different town, and it was held within the University, which means it wasn't really public. We have all these difficulties.

What we are planning to do now – it actually started off from sharing some information with Indian women. There are huge minorities of Muslims in India, and they are living under Muslim law, not the constitution of India. A young woman of 24 years old is now, presently, taking the Indian government to court saying that the law which is applied to her in her area is in contradiction with the Constitution, which is the case in most of the Arab countries. I don't know if she will win or not, but the action is very important. So we are planning to meet with other women living under Muslim law wherever they are, and have common action, or at least information about what's going on in our countries.

Thirty thousand abandoned children

Another thing which is very important and which is not talked about up till now is that we have lots and lots of abandoned children. Twenty years ago this didn't exist at all – it's a new phenomenon, which is appearing in all African capitals. I don't know about elsewhere, but I know about Africa – it began about ten or fifteen years ago. Usually, at least in my country, there were very few illegitimate pregnancies. What would happen was that either the mother was killed when she was pregnant, or she was killed after the delivery, and the child too. But on the other hand there was a traditional way of dealing with this: she would be hidden in her family, the males of the family would pretend that they didn't notice anything, she would more or less hide, but it was with their tacit consent, somehow. Then she would deliver, and anybody in the family or in the vicinity, or a friend, would take the child and say 'well I am the mother', and that was it. Well, this could work for, let us say, 100 cases a year, throughout Algeria.

It doesn't work now: we have 30,000 abandoned children in Algeria today. And this does not include the babies who die in the first three months. And I have to tell you that in the city of Algiers (which has the best health services of the whole country), there is official data from the Ministry of Health, that 35% to 85% of abandoned children die in the first three months. And this is in Algiers, in the capital. It is a huge percentage. They die of what is called in French 'hospitalisme du nouveau-né', hospitalisation of the new-born, which is lack of maternal care. Not that they are not fed, not that they don't have blankets or clothes, but they just let themselves die because nobody wants them. So you have to add this number, I don't know what the total for Algeria would be, to the 30,000 abandoned children. And if we want to have an idea of the number of unwed mothers, then we have to add again: those who commit suicide, and it's a huge number of women between 14 and 25 who commit suicide; those who commit infanticide, and they are also numerous; those who have illegal abortions; those who manage to find a family, deliver in secret and give the child away – and all sorts of other cases. So we have to face the fact that we have a lot of unwed mothers.

The position of our government is that it doesn't exist. Which means that these children are now put in a crèche until the age of three or four, then in an orphanage. And if you look at these children, I have been into all these places, they are mentally disabled. It is not that they were born like this – it's an acquired mental disability. So it means that they cannot be adopted by anyone later – at the age of four or five, they don't sit, they don't walk, they don't speak.

Because they get so little care?

Yes. And before 1972, they didn't even have these crèches, they were in hospitals, in huge rooms. Nobody was appointed to feed them, so anybody who passed by, either the woman who sweeps the floor, the doctor, the midwife, some patients would try and give some bottles, just at random. And they were put in beds with walls made out of material, so that they couldn't even see anything. They were put in their beds, facing the ceiling. And how could they survive? That is how they got mental disabilities. You could see huge rooms with 200 babies. This is a bit better now in the crèches, but still . . .

No right to adopt

So one of the struggles of Algerian women is to get something like adoption. This Family Code forbids adoption – it is said that it is anti-Koranic. It *isn't*. What is said in the Koran is that if you adopt a child, don't give it your name, for fear of incest, later incest. And don't let the child inherit, because you will hurt your natural children. But apart from these two recommendations nowhere is it said that adoption shouldn't be done. And in actual fact the Prophet himself had adopted children. And in the tradition it was very easy – you would just state in front of two witnesses that 'This is my child' and he or she was your child. Not having your name, but who cares? There is a huge difference between this situation and what the State is doing now, a system of fostering under the name of Kafala, which is to give some of these children to families to look after them. But now we have to go through the State to have the charge of those children and this means that the State, the Minister of Justice, is the legal tutor of these children. And this would never be transferred to the so-called adoptive parents.

They would never have any rights over the children?

No. Which means that at any point, the State can take the children back. So if you don't 'behave properly', if you are not a 'good citizen', if you have any kind of political activity, this is a continual threat. This is not adoption, not at all, and women are fighting for the rights of these children.

It has been known for some years, since around 1980, that we had all these children, really thrown into the garbage, somehow. Sweden proposed to take all of them, regardless of their disabilities, and just take care of them. Of course Sweden got a very nationalist answer – these children are our property. Well fair enough, I am not so much for adoption of Third World children in the First World – but on the condition that *we* take responsibility for our children. If we don't, then we have no rights over them.

It was mentioned in the first feminist gathering, of 1981, that Sweden had offered to take these children, and our women reacted the same way: 'These children belong to us, and even if they die here, that's where they should die, instead of living elsewhere'. And I heard from an official of the Ministry of Health: 'Better be a dead Algerian than a living Swedish citizen'. This nationalist reaction has to be denounced now, for it is really too much, what is happening to those children.

Especially that now with this new law, we have no more hope for legal adoption. Of course some families will take some children, but there is no security, not for them or for the children.

This is also something which is in the new Family Code, that it is only this type of Kafala which is allowed, and no adoption. And this is linked, this number of unwed mothers and abandoned children is linked to the policy of the Algerian State about contraception.

Contraception rights and population control in Algeria

We can examine the two decades since Independence separately. In the first decade, because of our so-called socialist and anti-imperialist stand, we were strongly against population control, and it was clearly stated by the second President of Algeria, Boumedienne, when he first opened the national Steel Company, in 1968, that the way to development is not population control, it is industrialisation. Fine, so we had to agree with this, as militants, but at the same time, we were signing our death warrants, as not only were we not allowed to practice but even to have *knowledge* on contraception. We were under the extended French law of the end of the First World War in France, which was a pro-natalist law, from 1920 or something like that. And it was really strongly forbidden to have any access to contraception. So in those ten years what happened was that women had an enormous amount of children. It was at the end of the war, so couples were coming back together, or new couples were formed. It was obviously in the interest of the State to replace all those men who had been killed. After ten years the population growth rate of Algeria was the highest in the world – 3.5%, because we don't have a high infant mortality rate. It was the highest, with Pakistan and a few other countries. The average number of living children per woman was 7.9. I went through the files of hospitals and clinics, and the number of pregnancies was *normally* about 13, 14. And I quite frequently came across cases of a number of pregnancies close to natural fecundity: 19 pregnancies.

So this is the situation, with a high instability in marriage, a lot of divorces and repudiations.

So women being left with many children?

Yes, or not necessarily left, but the children scattered, and it creates a lot of social and psychological problems. These unwed mothers and abandoned children are a consequence of this policy.

Meanwhile, in this first decade, the new class was building itself, under the cover of socialist bureaucracy. And now in the second decade they appear as a class, wanting to reproduce themselves as a class, and taking the means to do it. Which implies in the population policy that they changed completely from this anti-imperialist stand of encouraging population growth to a class approach to the problem. They are threatened as a class, which means they don't want all this lumpenproletariat to grow around the cities. Half the population of Algeria is now under 14 — a huge number of young people who cannot be provided with education.

And they will be on the labour market, and have no jobs, of course. And all this is a threat to this new class which I think now could be described as becoming a 'normal bourgeoisie', that is, owning some means of production, which they didn't do previously, because everything was state-owned. But there are more and more private investments in Algeria, and the self-managed sector is narrowing. Even the land, I think, will be given back to private property at some point.

Do they let in foreign capital?

Not yet. That will be a further step. But the change is very evident, and in population policy, which is where women are very much concerned now, the first step was January 1981, the new law of finance. Up to '81, we were under a type of French law, which meant that as far as taxes are concerned, if you are single you pay more tax than if you are married, and the more children you have, the less tax you pay. From one day to another, this was reversed. Which means that large families are penalised. So now, if you are single you pay less tax, and the more children you have, the more tax you pay.

Before 1972 we had only one clinic providing contraception, and it was an experimental university clinic, so it was not under the law because it was meant for research, at least we said so. We put a lot of energy into having this clinic as a first step, because we felt it was our right to have contraception. But now we are going to be *given* contraception, and in a way which is not at all satisfactory and does not respect women any more than they were respected in the previous stage. From '72, the beginning of the second decade, some more clinics were opened, inside the Maternal and Childcare clinics. Now we have about 500, which is nothing for Algeria, with a population getting on for 20 million people, with a lot of young people, so it will create a lot of problems. But there are more and more signs that contraception and even abortion is going to be enforced on women, because of this fear of the growing lumpenproletariat. Contraception is already legal, passed in 1978. And we agreed with this, we had to fight to get it, but at the same time we can see that this is done against us. We now have a law allowing 'therapeutic' abortion, which is good too, but again this is a first step, because they are going to have free abortion, which in itself is perfect, except that it is going to be enforced upon poor women. That is extremely clear. I have heard officials speaking openly of their fear of the people, and openly stating that abortion is the best thing – and sterilisation.

Does Islam say anything against contraception?

Not at all. We even have statements of high authorities, of colleges of doctors of the faith to state that abortion is forbidden, but that contraception is not forbidden. We had this, from the very beginning, during this decade when we couldn't obtain contraception. So you see Islam is used whenever it is suitable, but . . . when it suits *us*, it is not used.

Where would they get pregnant?

About unwed mothers. They are the product of all this. When I first started to study this I thought that they would probably be young women coming on the labour market, entering the so-called modern sector, but it was not the case. These women are from poor, but very traditional families; they are kept inside the families, and they hardly go out, maybe ten minutes to get bread somewhere, or go to visit the family, and they are closely watched. Of course, they are from the outskirts of the city, because we have a strong immigration from the countryside to the city, everywhere, and no work, so the whole patriarchal family collapses. Fair enough, we are very happy about it. But what happens is that some of the traditions are still maintained, but some of the rigid moral behaviour collapses. And this is not necessarily to the advantage of women. We have to face the fact that there must be, to a great extent, rape and incest, within the family. They can't go out, so where would they get pregnant?

They are mainly two groups: a group between 30 and 40, of divorced women, or widows – I won't talk about them now. But the younger group, from the age of 16 to 24 – when I talked to the medical doctors in the hospitals of Algiers, something very interesting was said to me. Of course it's not statistical data, but it's interesting anyway – they would say 'half of them are virgins, in this group', the young group. And another would say 'oh, at least half of them were virgins', and then another still, which means that there is some truth in this. They probably get pregnant after one very incomplete intercourse. This is also confirmed by the fact that some cases were known in the bourgeoisie, of young girls being pregnant and the parents knowing it, and begging the doctors to perform a caesarian on the girl, so that the hymen would still be intact. Which means that they *were* virgins. It's important, because doctors agreed to do it, and this was only 'for the sake of the girl', so that she can be married afterwards, hiding that she had ever been pregnant. Then she would undertake her so-called first pregnancy, without telling anybody, not even the doctor, that this was happening in a uterus that had been cut. Facing death – instead of social death, physical death. Because being pregnant is social death.

I have heard of many cases in hospitals, of lower-class girls who beg until the last minute for a caesarian for this reason. So all this is very complex, but there is a lot to think about, especially about the destruction of the extended family, and what is happening in such cases. The destruction of the authoritarian patriarchal family is *not* necessarily something which benefits women. In that case, it doesn't.

If there is nothing better? And the women have no power to create anything better?

Not for the time being. A young girl like this could not work. We don't exist outside the family. Even renting a room, for somebody like me, would be quite impossible. Nobody would rent me a room, unless somebody from my family, a male, came and said, 'oh yes, we all agree that she should have a flat'. And women who are living alone, there are some, are usually from a wealthy family that can afford to back them, in all respects. Especially on the moral side, and the social side.

So these girls usually hide their pregnancies until the last minute, in the family, bandaging themselves. And we usually have long, wide dresses, which are quite comfortable to hide pregnancies under. They would then get help from a woman friend or relative, who would say, 'oh, I'll take her to help me at home for three weeks if you don't mind'. And then in those three weeks she would be put in hospital, deliver, abandon the child and then come back, and it will be unknown. And that's the only way.

One last point I want to tell you about, about this virginity. It is really social death – you can't get married, you can't tell anyone, if you are no more a virgin. This business of caesarians shows what it means, and I quite understand, as their whole life is affected. We always had special women of the villages, who would sew back a hymen, but the number is increasing, so now we have huge numbers of Algerian women going to France, and maybe to other countries, and they have managed over years to convince Left groups to help them. And I'm sure it's very complicated for a Left, Western doctor to accept the idea of sewing back the hymen, because it's outside of what they can understand. And it's something nobody would like to do, but anyway they are doing it, and thanks to them those women can go back and pretend nothing ever happened. It also means the destruction of the personality of Algerian women, as we really have split personalities, having to do such things. But at least some people in the Left in Europe manage to understand that there is no other way, at present.

How do you feel about working with women outside Algeria?

I personally believe in internationalism, also among women's groups, but I am not representative of the opinion of Algerian women and Third World women in general, because you will usually find a lot of racism amongst us, towards you people. You see, accusing the West, and imperialism, is fine, but I don't see how we can get any solution except by identifying the Left forces, however limited their awareness is of our situation, of the evils of international capitalism.

I think we should work with Left people and with women, wherever they are. And if we are not satisfied with what they think, we can explain, instead of attacking them, because we don't identify the principal enemy by doing so. We destroy our own possibilities and forces, in the long run. That's why I wanted to talk to you – it took me ten years to decide that I would do it, because I also was nationalist enough to think that I should not speak outside. But I cannot speak *inside*, so what is the effect of my good will on what happens to Algerian women? When we started that campaign outside Algeria to free those three feminists, we did succeed, because I know where the weaknesses of the Algerian regime are: they don't want this to be exposed outside. I think on very limited points we can have common actions, for sure. We need a lot of information that you get very easily and we can't, so we need a lot of cooperation from the West. And I'm sure we can also give a lot of information, not only for our own sake, which is what I'm doing now, so that the regime would be frightened, and wouldn't dare apply this law that they've just passed. And I hope that this type of attempt can help the forces inside Algeria, women's forces, to fight this law.

But on the other hand I'm sure that we can also give information that would be useful to you – I don't think it's a one-way process at all. But believing in this kind of internationalism, acknowledging all the differences of interest and in wealth and class and whatever . . . this I don't deny, and I think we have to work on it . . . this is absolutely not typical. I haven't always been like this, either – I have been very blindly nationalist in the past.

Postscript: November 1986

Two-and-a-half years after giving this interview, there is both little to add and a good deal to comment upon: little to add about the situation within Algeria, but a lot to say about the development of women's organisations and about my own position on 'blind nationalism', internationalism and exchange between so-called north–south.

The situation of women in Algeria is no different in so far as the Family Code is now enforced with few modifications from the outline I was commenting on in 1984. The right to work no longer has to be submitted to the authorisation of fathers, husbands, elder sons or any other male tutor; otherwise the text remains unchanged.

Nevertheless, talking with women from other countries, I have come to realise that the Code itself is open to misinterpretation by foreigners: for instance, it recommends that a bride consent to her marriage. This shouldn't be read too quickly, the next paragraph informing us that her consent may be expressed by 'any sign'. So many young brides weep at their wedding, this could easily be interpreted as an indication of joy or emotion rather than the poignant anguish or terror which it so often is. In addition, she doesn't even have to sign the marriage contract, so the 'signs' of her consent can be interpreted by the male tutor at home.

The Family Code is written in a style similar to that of sacred texts (from the Koran to the Bible) in that one can find many contradictions from one paragraph to another. This means that each and every so-called protection or right given to women can be challenged using another paragraph of the law. Similarly, each and every limitation restricting male supremacy is later given back to men: polygamy and repudiation are finally left to a man's 'true' application of the moral prescriptions of religion; he just has to be a good Muslim and, as such, won't misuse sacred or legal texts in order to unfairly treat the women under his control.

Obviously, social behaviour in any country is not only determined by laws, but when new laws come to restrict the rights of citizens, calling on traditions and culture to justify the inequality they promote, we can certainly say that it is a sign of the times; more so, when one becomes aware of the fact that in several Muslim countries, new 'family codes' have recently been passed, which ALL restrict, at different levels and degrees, the rights of women; when one learns that Ministers of Justice of the Arab countries meet regularly to unify such Codes on Personal Status, led by the most reactionary factions, and that Ministers of Justice of Muslim countries in South Asia also meet to unify Codes on Personal Status, one has to face the fact that justice for women is threatened all over the Muslim world.

This comes at a time when fundamentalists are taking over in all the major religions, including Islam, and in an international situation where Islamic countries are generally accused of many evils, from promoting terrorism to preparing the third world war. This interpretation leaves no room for differentiating between the suffering people and the governments which oppress and mystify them. In fact, racism and anti-Islamism give ground to the rightists, and sometimes fascist governments which unfortunately lead Muslim countries to mobilise the people against external enemies, and get rid of their internal popular opposition. (It evidently also helps the governments of the non-Islamic countries to build their own internal rightist forces mobilised around racist slogans, but this is not what we are supposed to discuss here.)

By the same logic, women are caught in between two legitimacies: belonging to their people and loyalty to their female oppressed group. We are made to feel that protesting in the name of women's interests and rights is not to be done now. (It is never, has never been the right moment: not during the liberation struggle against colonialism, because all forces should be mobilised against the principal enemy: French colonialism; not after Independence, because all forces should be mobilised to build up the devastated country; not now that racist imperialist Western governments are attacking Islam and the Third World, etc.) Defending women's rights 'now' (this 'now' being ANY historical moment) is always a betrayal – of the people, of the nation, of the revolution, of Islam, of national identity, of cultural roots, of the Third World . . . according to the terminologies in use *hic et nunc*. This narrow approach towards nationalism is very effective: the women's movement in our countries is not strong enough, numerically speaking, and, therefore, ideologically and theoretically too, to challenge an interpretation which so suits the dominant males, including those of the Left, who are the first to accuse us of betrayal, of 'imported ideologies', of 'Westernism' – using the very same terminology our governments use against the Left at large. It is thus very hard to persist, in total isolation, in denouncing the stepping back of most of our regimes on the women's question and to go on organising the struggle.

My deepest admiration and regard goes to those of us who stubbornly trace their way into this ideological jungle, to promote the cause of women.

Not only are we prevented from speaking for women, but also from thinking, and even dreaming about a different fate. Yes, we are deprived of our dreams, because we are made to believe that leading the life we lead is the only way to be a good Muslim, a good Algerian, a good Pakistani, or a good Sudanese; we are not even aware of the differences which exist from one Muslim country to the other, of situations which may be more favourable to women than others, of the intricacies of culture, traditions and religion. Let women from Muslim countries out of their national ghettos, let them see that infibulation practised in Africa is unthinkable in Asia, that the veil worn in Arab countries is not there in Africa, that none of these practices rely on religious principles, but that religion everywhere backs such practices whenever they allow more control over women.

Although in most cases we cannot organise inside our own countries, nor even speak without facing heavy repression, we are also made to feel that we should not speak outside, that we should hide, in the name of national loyalty, the crimes committed against women and against other oppressed sectors of the people. We are thus made to identify with 'the nation', 'the people', conceptualised as an atomised and undifferentiated mass, without conflicting interests, without classes, and without history – in fact we are made to identify with the State and the ruling class as legitimate representatives of 'the people'.

Unfortunately, there are all too many examples of such attitudes in women's groups in our countries. I recently heard, in Pakistan, comments on exiled Iranian women who, their detractors said, should not denounce in the West the fate of women in Iran, because this is used by rightists forces in the West against Islam, and against the image of the Iranian people. This leaves the question open: are the Iranian people in power? or oppressed? Were the Germans who denounced Hitler during the Second World War anti-Germans or anti-Nazis? In India, at present, using the riots and massacres led by Hindu fundamentalists against the Muslim community, Muslim fundamentalists have succeeded in persuading Muslim women activists to stop their campaigns against the Muslim Personal Law, for fear of such protest being used 'against their own community' therefore adding to the discrimination already suffered under the dominant Hindus.

Remember how long it took for communists from Eastern Europe to become 'dissidents' and speak out about the crimes of Stalin, and the evils of supposedly communist countries. What have they betrayed, apart from their exploiters? In Algeria, many of us, including myself, kept silent for ten years after Independence, not to give fuel to the enemies of the glorious Algerian revolution; by so doing we have merely given those in power time to organise and strengthen, allowing them, amongst other things, to prepare and enforce discriminatory laws on women.

The last sentence of my interview of 1984 ends with this confession: 'I have been very blindly nationalist in the past'. I will certainly admit that Western right-wing forces may and will use our protests, especially if they remain isolated. But it is as true to say that our own rightist forces exploit our silence. Therefore, I believe the question is irrelevant. We have everything to gain in being truly internationalist; in exchanging all useful information, and in solidarity and support. In this way, by building our strength, it will become more and more difficult to exploit our protests in a way which does not suit our purposes. This is the dream which lies behind the network 'Women Living Under Muslim Laws'.

Women and women's groups from 17 countries now write to each other, ask for documentation, compare so-called Muslim Laws in different countries, send appeals for solidarity, inform others of their strategies in very practical terms, such as writing marriage contracts which give the maximum space to women, building documentation for local groups and so on.

This is only a beginning. Through the network we have been able to find out about plans to unify Codes of Personal Status, both in the Arab countries and in the South of Asia; we start knowing about how young fundamentalists are trained, and where, and who is funding them; and we learn about progressive interpretations of Islam, from the times of the Prophet until recently, and about the fate suffered by some courageous men and women who have spoken in favour of an egalitarian interpretation of religion. We realise that in most of our countries there is no room for agnosticism or atheism; that religion is forced down our throats, because there is a constant ideological confusion between religion, culture and nationality; and that we should work towards a clear-cut identification of these concepts and a separation between religion and the State.

We are in debt to the early Western internationalist feminists who, 20 years ago, started inviting women from the so-called Third World to international feminist gatherings, granting some of us the privilege to not only be in contact with feminists from all over the Western world, but also meet other Third World women. It is through international meetings that we came to know each other and later found associations at regional or continental level.

Much later, it is also through international feminist gatherings, such as the 4th International Tribunal on Reproductive Rights, where the first Action Committee on Women Living Under Muslim Laws was founded, that women from Muslim countries came to know each other.

In spite of all the difficulties which have emerged during international feminist gatherings, between women from the West and women from the Third World, we have largely benefited from these opportunities. Western feminists often have supported us in the past, and we have been accused in our own countries of being brain-washed by 'foreign ideologies', as if our reality was not enough of a reason to protest.

Now that we start supporting each other from within the Third World, within the Muslim World, etc . . . it becomes increasingly difficult to limit our action to an imitation of the West; the support of women from the West is less vital. Speaking out against discriminatory situations in Algeria or crimes against women in Iran can be used much less frequently by reactionary forces outside our countries, because support comes from within as well as outside. Inside our countries and even within the women's groups, we leave ourselves less open to nationalist justifications for keeping silent.

I said in an earlier interview there are situations in which Third World feminists could support Western feminists, as well as the reverse. We have an example of this, in that in the network we are supporting a group calling itself 'the five mothers from Algiers' – five French women whose children were taken away from them after their Algerian husbands had divorced them. We have much experience of such situations, which are common in all Muslim countries. Fathers make use of their unchallenged customary rights of ownership of the children, reinforced by modern laws, to deprive them of any contact with either their mothers or the maternal family. The situation of these five mothers is typical of countless women under Muslim laws.

For the first time, European women are supported in their struggle against unjust laws by women from Muslim countries who suffer under the same laws and traditions. Their fight is ours; in many of our countries women try to organise against the consequences of discrimination in marriage, divorce, custody, maintenance . . .

Of course, there are still nationalist reactions amongst some women's groups who fear that, once more, their protest will be used against Algeria and Islamic countries at large, fearing that the case will be presented as: French women fighting Arab barbarism.

We will not support injustice and discrimination in the name of national identity. It is in our own interest that internationalism should prevail over nationalism, and that we should link our struggles from one country to the other for reasons of ethics, as well as solidarity, in the hope that more such struggles will begin and receive national, regional and international support.

2   No Return to the Veil

F. Rahman

Using its own particular and narrow interpretation of Islamic laws, the government in Pakistan has, in recent years, introduced legislation especially oppressive towards women. Pakistani women already faced an uphill struggle against a ferociously patriarchal system even before these latest retrogressive laws. In an article in the magazine *Inside Asia* (June–August 1985), F. Rahman, a member of the Women's Action Forum (WAF), assessed their impact and described the form which organised women's movements have taken in Pakistan since independence.

Underdevelopment, religious and social norms, and the patriarchal feudal structure which still dominates society in Pakistan have combined to define the role and status of women as inferior and subservient to that of men. Consequently, the contribution that women make to society has been undervalued, underplayed and often ignored. The struggle for their rights as human beings and citizens has been launched by women in the cities, where modernisation and capitalist modes of

16

production have drawn them into the mainstream of visible economic activity, and where the literacy rate of women is higher than among their rural counterparts (34% and 6% respectively). Economic and social constraints have further restricted the leadership of most women's organisations to the upper-middle and bourgeois classes.

Although the recent recognition of the women's issue developed in the 1980s, women have attempted to voice their concern about society's neglect of them since independence in 1947. Shortly after partition the All Pakistan Women's Association (APWA) was formed to rehabilitate destitute women by teaching them basic skills to enable them to be economically independent. APWA's role as a social welfare organisation in setting up industrial homes and adult education centres, and in providing shelter to women, was followed by other welfare organisations which concentrated on teaching skills in handicrafts, embroidery, sewing and knitting, and in marketing the products made by women. At this stage the women's issue was seen as one requiring the social uplift of women, and it attracted many housewives as well as working women. Prominent among them were women who had participated in the movement for Pakistan.

Organisation develops

The women's movement gained momentum in the 1960s when, under pressure, the Government passed the Family Laws Ordinance, restricting the right of Pakistani Muslim men to marry a second time. At the end of the 1960s the movement to overthrow Field Marshal Ayub Khan's military regime included women from both the organised and unorganised sections of society.

This pattern of collective struggle continued during the 1970s when the participation of men and women in the political process created a new sense of awareness amongst women. Their right to vote was used often against the wishes of their male family members. Large numbers of women rallied to the Pakistan People's Party, with its call for an end to exploitation and its promise of justice and equality for all. Women were being employed in factories in increasing numbers and trade union activity escalated, some unions consisting solely of women. Although the main issues at the time were related to economic benefits, such as better pay, the questions of discrimination against women for skilled jobs and harassment of female workers by management were also raised.

The 1980s have heralded a change in women's attitude to their emancipation. The need for an independent movement to recognise and improve the status of women in Pakistan has emerged from the experience of collective action. Culturally – and from the orthodox religious standpoint – the woman is recognised as only a mother, wife, sister or daughter, which places her in subservience to all the male members of the family. This unequal relationship prevails even when the woman is the bread-winner or an equal provider. Where collective action is undertaken by men and women, such issues recede into the background, even for the more enlightened sections of Pakistani male society. To highlight the actual condition of women, to discuss these at public forums and to demand changes in social attitudes to women, by legislation and other means, is possible only from a separate and independent women's platform.

Legal persecution

The need for such a platform has been reinforced by the retrogressive interpretation of Islamic justice by the present military regime. The systematic erosion of women's rights began with the Hadood Ordinance of 1979. This equated rape with adultery in the severity of punishment, while at the same time the inability to prove rape – which requires the witnessing of the act by four adult Muslim males – resulted in the woman being penalised for adultery (an easy thing to prove if she became pregnant) while the man escaped scot-free. Repeal of the Family Laws Ordinance (1961), the Child Marriage Act, and the Dowry Bill were also at the time under consideration. Increasing restrictions on women's participation in public, social and cultural activities, coupled with a policy of forced segregation, combined to awaken the more educated and enlightened sections of urban women to the realisation that whatever rights they had were being taken away under the pretext of Islamisation.

The need for an organised forum from which women's issues could be projected found expression in the Women's Action Forum (WAF), founded in Karachi in September 1981. This soon acquired a national character when WAF chapters were set up in Lahore and Islamabad-Rawalpindi in October of that year. WAF provided an independent platform for individuals and other women's organisations, and the women's struggle for recognition of equal rights and status in society was launched. At the same time WAF advocated cooperation with other organisations and groups on issues where the women's cause was even indirectly threatened, such as in supporting the restoration of democracy and upholding the 1973 constitution.

WAF's programme galvanised existing women's organisations into action. APWA and other social welfare organisations, together with professional women's bodies such as the Business and Professional Women's Club, which had until then been functioning within their narrowly defined spheres, all broadened their programmes to demand fundamental changes in and additions to the existing laws to improve the status of women. Organisations such as Tehrik-e-Khawateen and the Democratic Women's Organisation with more radical programmes, in that they believed that women's causes cannot be disassociated from the democratic struggle of the people, increased their activity among the middle and lower middle sections of urban women. More importantly, all the women's groups felt the need to co-ordinate their actions and to demand a better deal through joint activities.

Repression intensifies

In February 1982 a joint action by 11 women's organisations against the proposed Law of Evidence, which equated the evidence of two women to that of one man, led to a crackdown by the regime on the women's procession in Lahore, the Punjab provincial capital. Despite repeated protests by women, and by others such as lawyers, the law was promulgated in 1984. Similar demonstrations and protests against the ban on women's participation in the Asian games, the Proposed Law of Qisas and Diyat (which would fix the blood money for a woman at half that of a man), rising crimes and an increase in brutality against women, are evidence of a nascent women's movement in Pakistan.

The practice of victimising and raping women in cases of hostility and family feuds, and the mutilation of women on the slightest provocation, occur to such an extent, particularly in the rural areas, that every newspaper relates at least one gruesome story of this kind daily. Only a small proportion of such cases are reported for fear of social censure. Women's organisations have jointly and individually organised seminars, pickets and protest meetings to publicise the inhuman treatment meted out to their sex. The spate of articles and news items in newspapers and magazines on the rights of women as defined by Islam, on the United Nations Charter on Human Rights and on the actual rights which women have in Pakistan, are evidence that Pakistani women are becoming both vocal and active.

Recently, research highlighting and evaluating the contributions of women to economic development has been undertaken by women academics, women's groups and the Women's Division (a government organisation). Such studies show that in rural areas the contribution of women is greater than men's, with women working an average of 16 to 18 hours a day. Such research and surveys provide the much needed raw material for the vocalisation of women's status by the more militant and conscious women's rights groups. Even the government has been forced to pay lip-service to development projects for women in its budgets and plans.

Today, women in Pakistan are speaking out in the face of continued social, religious and political repression. Male-dominated society resents any expression of the woman's self-realisation as an equal, and continues to disregard her contribution to economic development; religious fanatics obsessed by woman's sexuality would confine her to the four walls of the house (*chardewari*) or to the anonymity of a shroud (*chaddar*). At a political level the freedom to associate and express has yet to be granted, and retrogressive legislation has greatly damaged the position of women. With these odds against them, it is necessary that the awareness of the scores of urban-educated women spreads to the consciousness of those hundreds of thousands living in the slums and villages, so that an active and powerful women's movement can mature and become effective.

3   Organising under Apartheid

Fatima Meer

The bulk of this article consists of extracts from the United Nations document, *Women in the Apartheid Society* (April 1985) by Fatima Meer. It ends with a short interview with members of the Federation of Transvaal Women, reprinted from the British Anti-Apartheid Movement Women's Committee Newsletter (No 20, May/June 1985).

Women are not organised along sexual lines in South Africa. Feminism is almost entirely absent from the social fabric, primarily owing to the race factor. White women share with white men in the exploitation of blacks. The wages and incomes brought in by their men and the social security provided by the State afford them comfortable to affluent lives. While sexual discrimination exists, it is offset by the fact that the status of whites is infinitely higher than that of the black men; this not only invalidates an anti-male movement, but underlines the fact that to preserve their existing privileges white women must close their rank with white men as a class.

Black women have an intuitive understanding of the exploitation and devaluing of their men which rebounds upon them. Their wages are too low to maintain both them and their families; they are drawn into the cities and thus often lost to them, and, in the final analysis, the government, not their men, prevents them joining their menfolk and seeking employment outside the homelands. Black women support and join black men, even when they appear to be attacking them, as when they raid the beerhalls: it is to shake them out of their 'collaboration' with the system by spending their money in municipal outlets.

Women's organisations in South Africa must be viewed in terms of this dichotomy which inhibits sex or simple class fraternities and reacts against feminist coalitions. Even when women focus on problems peculiar to women, they interpret them as due to some malfunctioning of the social process rather than blame the men.

Women have a far lower propensity to organise than men; this is because of their subservience, both imposed and internalised. Normally, black women need the permission and approval of fathers, husbands and other male guardians to step outside the family for practically any reason, and may themselves feel it against the nature of women to belong to groupings other than the kinship unit. In a sample survey of 1,000 black women (African, Coloured and Indian) in industrial employment in the Durban metropolitan area, the vast majority had to seek permission for doing virtually anything apart from their domestic duties and their wage labour.

Only 32 per cent belonged to any community or women's organisations, most belonging to religious organisations; 52 per cent belonged to trade unions, but few attended meetings. A small minority, 38 per cent, expressed a desire to join existing community organisations, 59 per cent (the African response being the highest) wanted to join a women's organisation, and 85 per cent believed there was a need for women to organise.

It is, therefore, hardly surprising that women are conspicuously absent from the executives of welfare, educational, political and labour organisations, that the South African Parliament has never had more than four white women at any one time, and there are no women on the recently 'elected' Indian and Coloured chambers of the parliament, and when active in public life, women tend to support and follow progress and policies introduced and implemented by men.

In some sectors, such as the garment industry, employees are overwhelmingly women, yet managerial and supervisory posts and the executive positions in trade unions are filled predominantly by men. Women undergird political campaigns and have often given them their most volatile expression, yet few hold executive positions. Their exclusion from the main power blocks and the sense of inadequacy this cultivates when in male company has driven the more enterprising and relatively less repressed women to form women's organisations. Many of these are in fact subordinate wings of male-dominated bodies, encouraged by the men to provide tea-making, fund-raising or some similar services.

While such organisations involve a minority of South Africa's women, the impact of some is considerable. They may be classified broadly as those serving the recreational needs and developing the skills of members, those focused on welfare work, and those overtly or apparently political and engaged in protest activities. Middle class and white women's organisations are usually of the first two types, whereas the last are predominately African.

The influence of religion

Religion, particularly Christianity, is an important factor in bringing women together. The more progressive denominations have in recent times succeeded in bringing about some racial integration.

The Christian Women's Movement formed in 1982 under the auspices of the South African Council of Churches is overtly anti-apartheid and faintly feminist in outlook. It has stated:

> Our vision and our dream is to work for the realisation of a new community of women and men in the church and for the total liberation of all people in South Africa. We have made a commitment to work for the eradication of apartheid and all structural inequalities in the church and society . . . Our struggle for equality therefore cannot be separated from the political liberation of all people.

On the feminist level it asserts:

> We are concerned about the church's reluctance to allow women to participate fully in the life of the church. We are recognised as fund-raisers and tea-makers but the gifts and skills we can bring to policy-making bodies of the church are seldom recognised.

This 'Movement' however has yet to make an impact on South Africa's women.

The church has cradled the most prolific African women's organisation, the Manyano. The Manyano bonds African women in the urban areas drawn from a diversity of tribes giving them an identity manifested in distinctive uniforms, self-confidence and security. In the depressed townships where men as the main bread-winners often have neither the means nor the will to respond to women's needs, and the State turns its back on them, the Manyano serves as a welfare pool. It organises *stokvels* or saving clubs, rotating among members the benefit of the capital accumulated each month to help with such emergencies as school and university fees, down payments and demands from creditors.

Non-political on the face of it, the Manyano has a potential for quick politicisation inherent in a non-tribal, Christian, but intrinsically African grouping. It funnels grievances which though unintellectualised are expressed 'intuitively' as rooted in racism. 'White people do these things to blacks'; 'They happen because whites make them happen'.

Manyanos have converted temporarily into protest groups against apartheid. They defended women's right to brew beer in the 1940s, resisted the extension of passes to women in 1913 and in the 1950s, and agitated against the expropriation of African-owned property and forced removals in 1954, as well as against statutory inferiorisation of African education in 1955. The Manyano remains the most authentic African women's organisation, and underpins women's activities in the overtly political organisations. The African National Congress Women's League (ANCWL), for instance, appears not only to have been modelled on the Manyano, but to a considerable extent supported by it. The success of the 1956 Pretoria pass demonstration was largely due to Manyano networks.

The Young Women's Christian Association (YWCA) is the other side of the coin of the African churchwomen. Where the Manyano represents the relatively uneducated, unskilled worker, largely in domestic employment, the YWCA represents the relatively educated and economically better-off African church-women.

The YWCA began incorporating black chapters towards the middle of the present century. By the 1940s, the African component was the largest, composed almost entirely of the Zengele (home-makers) clubs. But the large black membership provoked tension and eventually split the body into white and non-racial. The latter, largely African-dominated, is affiliated to the world body and is by far the more important.

The Young Women's Catholic Association has never taken a direct political stance, preferring to use other organisations for such purpose; its main contribution lies in the educational and welfare service it provides in the townships. It is a well organised national body with regional and local committees throughout the country.

There are numerous groups related to the white, Coloured and Indian churches; most are consciously ethnic. Some groups extend services to other communities, some are self-centred attending to their own needs, raising funds for new amenities, etc.

Hinduism and Islam inspire other women's groups; the first involves Indian women, the second Indian and Malay women. The groups are small and their interests range from the purely ritualistic and theological, to education and welfare. Women are largely responsible for running extra school classes in language and religion. The Women's Cultural Group, primarily Indian and Muslim in membership, organises lectures, has published a best-seller cook book, raises funds for welfare services for all races, and has established an educational foundation which provides bursaries for young black women. Radical forces within Islam are also challenging the Muslim women to take political positions.

Social groups

The better known, non-church linked, white-dominated women's bodies in South Africa are the National Council of Women, the Housewives League, the Business and Professional Women, the Women's Institute and the Toast Mistress. Most of these groups are affiliates of international organisations. Apart from the National Council of Women, all other organisations until very recently excluded blacks from membership. Today, most organisations allow for separate black affiliates. Their interests are centred around improving the competence of members in housewifery, gardening, crafts and public speaking.

The National Council of Women in South Africa, established in 1913, is an affiliate of the International Council of Women. In recent years, it has adopted a clear stance against apartheid. Its 47th conference in 1981 affirmed that 'South Africa is one country and one people' and rejected racial discrimination as 'morally unsound and a dangerous obstacle to the peaceful development of our country'.

Though racially integrated today, in earlier years it was not. In 1936, African women founded their own National Council of African Women, which by 1953, had four branches on the Reef and one each in Pietermaritzburg and Durban. The National Council of African Women, like the YWCA, differed markedly from the Manyano both in its Western orientation and in its upper-class membership. Considering itself as a parallel to the white 'Council', it emulated white women and tended to see African problems as due to ignorance and illiteracy. It was up to the African women and to the African people to liberate themselves from tribalism and take their position alongside the whites. The Daughters of Africa and the Zengele Clubs were similar in approach.

The oldest Indian organisation is the Indian Women's Association, operative since the time of Gandhi. Clearly political at the time of its founding in Durban and Johannesburg, and supportive of Gandhi's passive resistance campaign, it became a small group of middle-class Indian women in Durban, with educational and welfare interests.

Political groups and the mass protests

It is the political arena that has drawn the most volatile response from South Africa's women. White women, English and Afrikaner, have joined white men in their conflicts with each other and against indigenous blacks, and some have been enshrined as heroines in white annals. Generally, white women defend the apartheid system and resist change. The Women's Enfranchisement Association of the Union, established soon after the Union of South Africa came into existence in 1910, finally won the franchise for white women in 1930, but it did so mainly to stir up the white franchise against the blacks and in this way gain the necessary two-thirds majority to abolish the Cape native vote.

The most impressive white women's political group is the Black Sash, founded soon after the Nationalist Party took power in 1949, specifically to protest against the excesses of the system against human rights. This organisation has grown in stature and work and now runs valuable advice bureaux to assist black women.

The most spectacular records are those of the mass resistance of black women; African, Indian, and Coloured. In 1912, all campaigned against passes: Africans and Coloured as a single body in the Orange Free State against residential passes; Indians in Natal and in the Transvaal against provincial barriers and poll taxes.

The resistance in the Orange Free State was provoked by an 1893 law requiring all African and Coloured women to produce work permits on request by the police in order to establish their 'right' to be in the area. The women, supported by the men, pleaded for years with the authorities to abolish the law which humiliated them, and obliged young girls to leave school and seek employment or be removed to other areas. Their pleas ignored, they finally formed the Native and Coloured Women's Association and openly defied the law, marching on the local administration offices, dumping their passes and facing arrest. Over 1,000 were arrested. In 1918, the movement spread to the Transvaal: in 1923, the passes were finally withdrawn.

At the beginning of the century, Indian women in Natal and the Transvaal proved the efficacy of the new liberation dialectic of *satyagraha* that Gandhi introduced. The South African Indian resistance movement remained by and large an élitist protest, until the women *satyagrahis* from the two ashrams in Natal and the Transvaal, Phoenix and Tolstoy respectively, commuted it into a mass movement. In 1912, they defied the anti-Asiatic law, crossed the provincial border from both ends and provoked the miners of Newcastle to strike. One thousand workers thereafter began the epic march, led by Gandhi, across the Natal border into the Transvaal; the entire Indian labour force of Natal went on strike, bringing the industry to a standstill. Arrests and imprisonment followed, and the government was forced to modify some of the hardships against the Indians. The great figure of that struggle was not Gandhi, but the emaciated young Valiamma, who refused to surrender despite her fatal illness that developed as a result of repeated imprisonment. She died in the struggle.

In 1946, Indian women again took the lead in launching the second passive resistance campaign against the anti-Indian Land Act: at the end of that campaign, almost 2,000 Indians had been imprisoned for defying segregatory laws.

Persecution of African women 1940–60

The militancy of the African women has moved in a continuous stream throughout the century. Their movement has, however, been severely restricted by two elements: traditional patriarchy and the State's influx control legislation, since they are the last component of the South African population to be considered for even the most menial jobs. Yet, at least a third are the sole supporters of their families, because of the high incidence of children born out of wedlock (about 50 per cent of all African births) and because of the system of migrant labour and wages that ignore the needs of workers' families. Nationalist Party legislation enacted educational laws that condemned African children to servitude; laws that reduced African land-holdings took away land traditionally allotted to women; laws against urban 'squatting' resulting in women being arrested because they attempted to join their husbands, or to seek employment in the towns. In the face of such persecution, African women have taken desperate measures to force the authorities to concede to them the basic right to protect their children.

African women in urban areas began constituting a problem for the white system in the late 1940s and 1950s. The reserves ceased to be productive about this time and due to the declining fertility of the land, and increased population density aggravated by government legislation, they no longer provided an economic base.

Economic recession and mechanisation increased employment and piled an even greater burden on the homelands and the women living there. More women, therefore, began moving to the cities in search of work in order to relieve rural distress. But as they congregated on rented plots, restructuring family life in urban slums, the authorities declared such settlements illegal and subjected the women and their families to constant police raids and heavy fines; and, being 'illegal', civic authorities ignored them and provided no amenities. The situation continues today. In the 1940s on the Reef, the anger of the women burst bounds: they organised resistance and marches, and clashed with the police in numerous townships. They demanded houses and better living facilities.

A 1908 law prohibiting the domestic brewing of beer, a traditional right of African women, was another issue which enraged the women. In the urban townships, brewing and selling beer provided the women with a source of income and the family savings. Women boycotted the beerhalls, picketed the men and demanded that the municipalities use the profit from the beerhall sale to house and develop other amenities in the townships. Attacks on beerhalls and demands for reinstituting the right of women to brew beer continued during the 1940s and 1950s and subsided only after 1960, when the liquor laws were somewhat relaxed.

Poor and costly transport also provoked boycotts in which women played a prominent part.

In 1952, passes were extended to African women throughout the country. Up to 1918, when they had been withdrawn in the face of stringent resistance, they had been applied to African and Coloured women in the Orange Free State alone. The intention was to contain the women in the reserves, to leave them there to starve with their dependants. Spontaneous resistance to the imposition of passes throughout the country continued for eight years. Thousands of women were repeatedly imprisoned. In 1954, 2,000 were arrested in Johannesburg; 4,000 in Pretoria; 1,200 in Germiston; and 350 in Bethlehem. In 1955, 2,000 women marched to the Native Commission's office in Vereeniging.

The ANCWL, founded in 1943, played the most important role among women's organisations in consolidating these issues and in giving them national prominence. The League set up branches throughout the country and identified its membership through its own distinctive uniform.

Co-ordination of Congress women and support for national liberation

In 1952, women from the Natal Indian Congress (NIC) and the ANC joined forces and established the Durban and District Women's League. In doing so, they went ahead of their parent bodies, which operated in consultation but not as a single body. The League had taken stock of the manipulation of Africans against Indians in 1949, and saw its prime object as that of restoring mutual confidence. It therefore concentrated its activities in Cato Manor, the area worst hit during the disturbance. A crèche and milk distribution centre were established and League members were bussed out daily to administer and to teach. The League was actively engaged in the 1952 Campaign of Defiance of Unjust Laws. When passes were introduced for African women, it organised a vigorous protest movement culminating in a mass march on the Department of Native Affairs in Pietermaritzburg and the arrest of 600 women, mainly African, but including a significant number of Indian women and a few white members of the Liberal Party.

League representatives were among the founding members of the Federation of South African Women in 1954, and Natal sent a deputation of 156 members to the historic march of 20,000 women on Pretoria in 1956, organised by the Federation of South African Women.

In 1960, the League organised a protest march of the women and children of those detained in Durban during the emergency. Some 60 women with their children were arrested and charged, the charges being withdrawn after a short spell in prison and an appearance in court. The League organised a weekly vigil outside the prison to keep the public mind focused on the inequity of detention without trial. This was the last of the League's activities. The banning of its secretary in 1954 and the detention of its chairperson in 1960 had weakened the organising committee, but it was the banning of the ANC and key members of the NIC that spelt its demise.

Federation of South African Women

The Federation of South African Women was founded in 1954 in Johannesburg in an environment of seething discontent and country-wide protests against passes, inadequate housing, high transport costs, and inferior education. A number of regionally based African women's organisations had emerged and the ANCWL, considerably strengthened by the Defiance of Unjust Laws Campaign, provided a national unitary base. There was a need, however, to draw in women of all races throughout the country and the Federation was conceived for this purpose.

The initiative for the establishment of the Federation of South African Women came from the white women of the Congress of Democrats, and was inspired by the Women's International Democratic Federation established at about the same time. Its success was indisputably due to the activities of the ANCWL. If there were ideological differences, they never touched the rank and file. Even the fact that most members of the organising committee were white and that there was no general white membership did not produce any tension that was not contained within the structure of the organisation. With the ANC as its mainstay, with support from the women of the Coloured, Indian and white Congresses and from the Food and Canning Workers' Union, the Federation focused above all on the current issue of passes. Its activities, unlike those of the more local and spontaneous groups, were strictly within the framework of the law. In 1955, it led a protest of 2,000 women to Pretoria, and another in 1956 with the participation of 20,000 women. Apart from these two momentous events, and the constitution of a women's charter identifying the fundamental demands of South African women for complete equality in colour and sex, the activities of the Federation were relatively low key, supportive of the Congress Alliance and protesting against high rents and poor amenities.

The pass issue was particularly an African issue, concerning both men and women. In 1958 the ANC questioned the advisability of protests organised by women only and grew alarmed at the increased victimisation of African women. In 1960, both the ANC and the Pan Africanist Congress (PAC) of Azania took up passes as a national issue. The massacre of Sharpeville followed, emergency was proclaimed, and the two African organisations, as well as the Congress of Democrats, were banned. This development led to the end of the Federation.

In 1956, the arrest of five members of the Federation on a charge of treason, following the Federation's participation in the organisation of the Congress of the People, had already dealt a blow. It held its third and last conference in Port Elizabeth in 1961.

The weakness of both the Natal League and the Federation was that, organisationally, they were much too centralised and did not develop sufficient grassroots responsibility. More serious, however, was the fact that neither were independent women's organisations. Both relied on the ANCWL, which in turn was a unit of the ANC. Apart from other implications this had on their activities, inevitably both would collapse with the banning of the ANC, unless they organised in the underground, which neither did.

In 1972, Natal began organising the women anew on a non-racial political basis with the founding of the Women's Federation, Natal. There were, however, strong feelings against the inclusion of white women and when the Federation became national in 1975, it did so as the Federation of Black Women. The national three-day conference in Durban focusing on the black family drew 300 delegates representing over 100 women's organisations and groups. Ministries were organised into such key areas as education, franchise, housing, women's disabilities, etc. Branches began to be set up in rural areas, and a blueprint for a black women's magazine was mapped out. The Federation became actively involved when violence erupted in Soweto in 1976.

An open air mass-rally planned in Durban was stopped by the government placing a blanket ban on all outdoor meetings, a ban operative to this day. The President of the Federation was banned within six months of its founding and imprisoned without trial, together with five executive members. The Federation itself was banned following its second conference, and its monies confiscated.

The United Women's Organisation in the western Cape and the Natal Organisation of Women in Natal have been inspired by and trace their roots to the Federation of South African Women. They have been in existence for the past two or three years and are growing in organisation and membership. As their goals, they identify the elimination of race and sex discrimination, as well as the organisation of a joint general campaign for full and equal democratic rights for all in South Africa. The United Women's Organisation significantly includes a 'consumer committee', 'workers' support committee' and '9 August committee'. The Federation, which was never actually banned, has been revived and if the Government does not come down heavily on the present black organisations, as it is threatening to do, new developments on the women's front can be expected.

Whereas past political organisations drew membership from older married women, the new initiative is coming in the main from younger women. The focus remains broadly liberatory, but there is consciousness of ideological issues of feminism, class and race. While these have as yet not been significantly articulated, the chances are that they will give the new movement an intellectual dimension the organisations lacked in the past.

Exploitation is unbridled in a racist society because oppressors can isolate themselves from those they oppress. In a class society isolation can never be complete. The lines of class distinction are forever mixing and mingling, and the upper class can never hope to remain uncontaminated by the lower. Moreover, where the classes share common political rights, the demands of the lower classes for redress and a more equitable share in the accumulated goods and services cannot be ignored.

In South Africa, those in power as a white class have effectively quarantined the blacks into homelands and group areas. They can, therefore, tolerate to a very high extent the social aberrations wreaked by economic deprivation. The fact that blacks have no power to influence legislative procedures and obtain redress for their condition secures that quarantine.

But no quarantine lasts forever. The ghettos today seethe with discontent, resistance is high, and revolution is a matter of time. The women are a fundamental part of it, because they suffer the consequences of apartheid in a way men never can. They are trained to care, to bear responsibility and guilt, and when they cannot care, and cannot be responsible, then the guilt is too overwhelming to be locked within themselves; it explodes, is externalised, and placed where it rightly belongs, in the system that suppresses and oppresses. The liberated women become the driving force for societal liberation.

As long as racism continues and a people, not a particular sex, is the object of oppression, the women will continue to overlook their own discrimination and dedicate themselves to the liberation of their people.

Women organising locally

The Federation of Transvaal Women talk to the South African Students'-Press Union, SASPU National.

Why is a women's organisation necessary?

Women need to develop their organisational skills if they are to improve their position in South Africa. Women's organisations are needed so that we can learn from each other, develop confidence and be able to take leadership roles . . . we can discuss the special problems facing us as women.

What problems do you face in organising women?

Many women just don't have the time for meetings, after working in the factories for $9\frac{1}{2}$ hours a day.

Women have been seen as the tools in the home. So if you organise a meeting at seven in the evening, a woman will tell you: 'That's good, but I have to cook for the children and I have to do the washing . . . so I can't come.' Some men see women's role in political organisations like our Federation as a threat to themselves. They will say: 'If my wife goes out to fight about the rents, who is going to do the cooking at home?' Even among progressive activists, you find those same attitudes.

These are some of the things we have to look at practically. At the same time, we can't demand that women confront all these issues at once. It's a long and difficult process. In the rural areas these attitudes about women are even stronger.

Although we see South Africa and the Bantustans as one country, undivided, on a practical level we have problems because homeland leaders dislike any type of progressive activity.

What is your approach to organising women?

We've got to organise around the day-to-day issues that affect every woman in the street. Our programme emphasises local activity. We see the rural areas as our priority. Here our approach is not to be too ambitious but to start with practical issues.

What campaigns will you be involved in this year?

Because this year [1985] is the 30th anniversary of the Freedom Charter, we included it in our programme of action. It includes clauses of the Women's Charter, and the issues raised in it make it possible to organise women around issues like health, maternity benefits, equal wages and education. We have also resolved to endorse the Education Charter. We have thought deeply about issues like sexual harassment at schools, and unequal education.

How do you see the link between high profile campaigns which are explicitly political and day-to-day issues?

We see organising women in their own communities as political. Day-to-day issues create a climate for people to become involved in campaigns. This work around practical issues will help us build a solid base. At the same time, this serves a broader political function for women . . . they mustn't take a step back in the struggle . . . but must be alongside men.

Will you be taking up the issue of unemployment?

This is a key issue affecting women. They are the ones who get fired first when there's a recession and the last to get jobs.

A suggestion for dealing with unemployment is to establish self-help projects or bulk-buying schemes. While these don't solve the problem, they do help in mobilising women.

What are some of the plans for local activities?

There are quite a few ideas for practical projects. Tembisa women want to establish a first aid training project and other women want to start child-minding and literacy programmes.

Then there are issues women want to know more about, like the new marriages act. In Soweto a burning issue is the high tariffs at Baragwanath hospital and the fact that the dispensary closes at 6pm. It was felt Soweto women would have to initiate some action jointly with other groups and work out a campaign around this.

4 Feminism and Social Struggle in Mexico

Gisela Espinosa Damián

Gisela Espinosa Damián is a Mexican feminist economist who spent three years working with the excellent centre for popular education, CIDHAL (Communication, Exchange and Human Development in Latin America), based in Cuernavaca. She wrote this article in January 1986, shortly after coordinating a series of women's workshops on sexuality, together with Esther Madrid and Amelia Hernández, in a poor working-class neighbourhood on the outskirts of Mexico City.

Towards a new dimension of feminism

There is an old debate between Marxism and feminism, an old conflict between the class war and the war of the sexes which is playing an increasingly important part in the political life of our country.

For the overwhelming majority of the Left in Mexico, the struggle of women against the machinery of oppression is a problem which cannot be solved under present conditions, but can be solved only by socialism. The feminists for their part, especially in the 1970s, denounced and sensitised the people to women's specific oppression under capitalism, putting forward demands which were intended to transform the situation here and now.

In the 1970s, the feminist movement did not extend beyond a reduced sector of the petit bourgeoisie and was more or less separated from the general struggle of the exploited, at a time when the workers' movement – peasants, shantytown dwellers, academics and students – were going through a widespread ascendancy. Isolated, ridiculed and satanised, feminists militantly continued to denounce their oppression, familiarising society with a problem which is nowadays a daily topic of after-dinner conversation in universities and in political and social organisations.

The decade of the 1980s heralded a new opportunity for developing the women's struggle. For the first time in years, more than 1,000 women – peasants, women in poor urban communities, factory workers, office workers and housewives – met to discuss the specific problems faced in each sector, during the First National Women's Meeting, which took place in Mexico City in November 1980. At this first national meeting the seed was sown for a discussion of the women's problem on a huge scale, as well as the successes achieved in the meeting itself. A proposal was made to hold regional meetings in May 1981. The First Women Workers' Meeting was also held in Mexico City, attended by approximately 300 women from 30 working centres. As a result, a Women Workers' Committee was formed which, although unable to consolidate, enabled the women's problem to be discussed in several factories and institutions with groups of working-class women. In a parallel way, regional meetings of peasant women were held in the centre and south-east of the country. In November 1983, more than 500 women participated in the First National Meeting of Women of the Popular Urban Movement, in Durango. In 1984, a Women's Forum was organised; the participants were basically factory and office workers and militants from various political organisations. And in August 1985, the First Regional Meeting of Peasant Women of the National Committee Scheme of Ayala was held in Morelos; in the same month, the Second National

Poster for the First Latin American and Caribbean Feminist Meeting, Colombia 1980.

Meeting of Women of the National Committee of the Popular Urban Movement took place in the city of Monterrey. Finally, as a result of the earthquake on 19 September 1985, there emerged a movement of women whose wretched working conditions and high level of exploitation were revealed from the rubble of their workshops and factories: the dressmakers.

With greater or lesser resistance and decision, little experience and through a process undefined by any clear outline of the main idea of the work and action to be taken, democratic political organisations have become involved in the women's problem, in response to the drive and vitality of the women's movement.

The opening-up of the women's question among poor and working-class communities gave feminism a new dimension. If in the 1970s feminists were relentlessly denouncing the problem of the sexes, in the 1980s women from the exploited classes are seeking to incorporate demands and struggles, arising from their own particular forms of exploitation and oppression, into the popular movement in general, creating their own areas for discussion and new forms of organisation.

The integration of the feminist struggle, or rather the movement of women from the exploited classes into the broader democratic movement, is full of obstacles, not only because of the usual difficulties of new work with a previously unrecognised sector, but above all because the women's struggle itself reverses the established order and hierarchies in the family, trade unions, political organisations and at every level of social life. This process of change can be very threatening for the bourgeoisie and the State, but also for the exploited classes and organisations of the Left themselves. As a result, the relationship between Marxism and feminism, or between the class war and the war of the sexes, is riddled with conflict. This explains why the women's movement has encountered opposition not only from among the ruling classes but also in the home, in the community among *compañeros* in life, work and struggle.

For democratic and grassroots organisations, but above all for women themselves, creating a feminist project with a class outlook constitutes a challenge. Even when all women experience oppression, the form it takes changes from one sector to another: shantytown dwellers, peasants, workers, office workers, intellectuals, housewives, may all share a common base of oppression, but each sector experiences it in a specific way, consequently leading to different demands.

In spite of all the difficulties, the women's movement in Mexico today has exceeded the targets of the 1970s as much in its composition as in its content, and is beginning to establish itself as a mass problem in whose definition women from the exploited classes are taking part.

Women in the *colonias populares**

The *colona* women of the National Committee of the Popular Urban Movement are exceptional for the steadfastness of their work, the growth of their organisations

---

* Poor urban suburbs.

Front cover of Mexican popular education booklet on the menopause (CIDHAL 1982). Lower text reads: We women approach the menopause filled with fear, myths and trepidation. We've been made to believe that women are only destined to be wives and mothers. Society assumes we're good for nothing outside that role.

and the fighting spirit of their struggles. Since before the First Meeting in 1983, a process began in which *colona* women began to question their role in the family, the burden of their domestic work, their relationship with their partners, the sexist education of their children, their subordinate position in various institutions, their problems within the community etc. With differing and occasionally contradictory positions, they began to develop struggles and build up women's groups and coordination networks, in such a way that today they have consolidated the Regional Committee of Mexico Valley Women of CONAMUP and are planning to transform their oppressive conditions at every level.

It is not for nothing that women have always been the majority, the backbone of the popular urban movement. Even when men, women and children all experience the problems caused by badly built small houses, lack of public services such as water, electricity, drainage, pavements, schools, health centres and popular food centres, or the high cost of living which reduces the possibility of survival, it falls fundamentally to women to manage the income or rather the poverty. It is they who have to overcome and make up for the lack of any kind of services with their own labour. They get jobs as housewives or domestic workers, as cooks, nurses, teachers, washerwomen, in other words carrying out all the functions designed for keeping and reproducing the workforce. In this way, the sexual division of labour continues to have an economic purpose in our day.

For their partners and husbands, the search for or conservation of a paid job represents a difficult and complex problem, but at least it enables them to keep in touch with the outside world; women, on the other hand, are recruited to a private, domestic world, isolated in the home and separated by four walls from thousands of women who live in the same situation, each solving problems of finance, health and education on her own. For women, everything presents itself and is solved at home.

In practice the daily life of women in these poor urban neighbourhoods means long and never-ending workdays, their minds and bodies always worrying about cooking, washing, ironing, carrying water and looking after children – all made worse by the national economic crisis which forces them to double their physical and mental efforts in order to try to achieve a minimum subsistence. Under these conditions it is not surprising that, faced with a general lack of basic services, which forces them to work more intensely, it is primarily they who mobilise themselves to achieve them. Their material conditions and role within the family and society naturally place them as the motivating power and principal mainstay of the popular urban movement. Their participation in struggle stems directly from their own problems.

In the history of the popular urban movement and CONAMUP, there have always been many women who are pregnant or carrying children in their arms, striving to improve their own living and working conditions and those of the whole family. From outside, this struggle looks like a series of mobilisations, meetings, local regional and national organisations, but it also has an intimate history, a little-known prelude sealed by that moment when a woman decides to leave her home, not to do the cooking on time for one day, to leave the children with a neighbour, to face her husband's jealousy, the criticism from her mother-in-law, mother and in many cases the children themselves. In this private world it is difficult for women to break away and for the rest of the family to understand and accept that wives, mothers or daughters are capable of transcending the four walls of their homes.

These domestic chains are much more than the high cost of living and a shortage of services; they subject women to an oppression which, even though it may be explained in general terms by the social structure and ideology of the system we live in, and even when it manifests itself at all levels of social life, still generates its most important reproductive mechanisms in the domestic sphere in which women daily operate.

It is from this problem of women's everyday life that struggle emerges, intertwined with that of class, and it is this oppression which transforms itself into rebellion and becomes a creative force towards building a new society, even on the level of most intimate relations.

The role of sexuality

The social role of women begins at birth and ends at death, characterised by subordination and oppression, determined by sex. In this sense, sexuality is understood not only as genital relations but also as a social role incorporating a concept of the world and of life, and defining the form in which relationships with partners, children, themselves, and so on will take. It is a practice and an attitude, a system of values which operates in all our relationships. From the sexual problems of women, numerous experiences have taken place in different sectors, which tend to mitigate or resolve the social contradictions which emerge from the feminine sexual role. The struggle for sexual liberation, lesbianism as an option, the fight for free and voluntary maternity, legal abortion and against forced sterilisation and population policies imposed on Third World countries, and other less spectacular struggles such as that for nurseries or sharing children's education and housework – all are forms of rebellion or rejection of the social role which society has traditionally placed on women.

The experience I am going to relate provides a background in this context. It is the story of a sexuality workshop carried out with a group of women from Nezahualcóyotl City, who have a long history of struggle for homes and services. They are organised women who take part in the Regional Committee of Mexico Valley Women of CONAMUP.

Sexuality workshop

We arrived in Neza' in August 1984, at the 'October 18th' people's tenement, so named precisely because it was acquired on the day of the first National Civic Strike. Nine families live in this block of flats, where one room acts as the neighbourhood office. The women arrived gradually, the majority from the same block, others from nearby houses. Initially there was a group of ten or twelve women. We all introduced ourselves and began to talk about our most deeply felt needs. Various subjects were brought up, but sexuality proved to be one of the points of greatest interest so we decided to begin with that.

'Problems get smaller when you talk about them.' From the series *Esse Sexo Que E Nosso* (This Sex of Ours), Fundação Carlos Chagas, Brazil.

The women asked themselves three basic questions:

1. What is sexuality?
2. How do we teach our children about it?
3. What are the conditions of the system which force us to remain in 'this situation'?

They left 'this situation' undefined, and we decided to start from there, dealing with the subject of sexual ignorance and repression. At the beginning, it was a matter of the women starting with their own experiences, ideas and values, identifying a problem they experienced daily but did not know much about, and, without venturing into too much detail, raising doubts and contradictions about it.

We started this session with an activity which may seem rather simple, but for them represented a confrontation with themselves and with their own repression.

The technique consists of drawing the bodies of a naked man and woman and, when everyone has finished, showing their drawings for the group to give their opinions and discuss some of the questions raised. At first there was great resistance, some claiming they couldn't draw, others wanting their children to leave the office until, with much nervous laughter, they finally got down to it. Ninety per cent of the women drew asexual men and women without genital organs. When they showed them, the group began to voice their opinions:

'This woman's missing something'.
'What thing?'
'Something'.
'What?'
'Well . . . her breasts . . . her sex'.

By the time they had finished showing the drawings the tension had eased considerably. We then began a series of questions such as:

– How did you feel doing the drawing? Why? Why do we feel ashamed or find it difficult to draw sexual organs?
– What did our families tell us or reveal about sex?
– What did teachers show us? What does the Church say?
– Where or with whom do we talk about such things?
– How do we behave with our children?
– What information do we give them? What do we want to know and what do we want to change?

The answers included shame, taboo, 'forbidden things'. Someone said: 'It's shameful to speak about that'. Another woman said, 'We all feel a little shame, a little fear . . .'

They acknowledged that there was great ignorance of the body, the organs and sexual functions. One woman said, 'I didn't know what to do when I had my period. I was really afraid; I thought I had cut myself'. Another said, 'I didn't know anything, I thought I was really ill, I had no one to tell.'

There was also much evidence of blame mixed with shame. Someone said, 'When my breasts grew I put on two shirts and a sweater . . . I walked around trying to hide.'

Social pressure and values came out in the conversation: 'Fathers worry about girls losing their virginity. The honour and prestige of the family are ruined . . .' 'It's the men that give you worth . . .' 'Mothers don't explain anything to us because they are ashamed.'

The desire to change was timidly outlined: 'I think,' said one woman, 'that you have to teach boys and girls that sex is a natural thing, but . . . how?'

As they reached a few conclusions, problems began to identify themselves as collective: something which concerns all of us but which we experience in isolation. A woman said pensively and almost at the end, 'It's the same for all of us.'

This was the starting point, the most important steps forward being: 1) The feeling of facing a problem collectively and not simply as individuals, and the perception of this time and space as something of their own, offering the opportunity to discuss subjects which are traditionally kept quiet; 2) The identification of certain obscure aspects of their sexuality, their bodies, their ideas, relationships with their partners, children etc. As well as emotion and the desire to talk about that part of their history they also showed fear, the fear of 'telling' – resistance to talking about 'forbidden things' not only for the rest of society, but also for themselves..

After these first questions and problems had been raised, we structured the workshop to try to place different themes relating to sexuality in the life cycle, for instance discussing infancy meant highlighting the ways in which we are conditioned into certain sexual roles. We returned to this subject at different times. Under the heading 'Adolescence and Youth' we talked about menstruation and virginity; under 'Youth and Maturity': the relationship between couples, domestic work, contraceptives, maternity, abortion, sexual violence and, lastly, the menopause.

In handling these subjects we used various materials which gave basic information or which encouraged discussion, but obviously, the most important material came from the women themselves, with their ideas, experiences, problems and alternatives.

Regarding the contents of the workshop, the elements which had begun to reveal themselves in the first session continued to be expressed afterwards; most women, when remembering their pasts, relived the myths, fear, shame, ignorance, self-devaluation and repression, the feeling of being an object and submitting, out of a feeling of duty, to the family, husband, society and to their own prejudices.

So, for example, speaking of virginity they said:

– 'It's something sacred which must be looked after.'
– 'Men carry the family name and honour of the home, if they want to they can dishonour a woman and throw her out into the street.'
– 'When I lost my virginity I lost everything. I felt different, like an old woman who's no longer worth anything.'

The women themselves reproduce these ideas, although there are also those who view them critically:

– 'Is that little bit of skin worth so much?' someone asked. 'No, friend, a woman is worthy for her work and her feelings.'

'Who cares if we are virgins? We feel for our mother, our husbands, we can work and think without being virgins.'

Women have also adopted social values which they believe in and are prepared to defend.

There has never been agreement about the value of virginity for women.

In the relationship between partners, the dichotomy between one's needs and desires and one's obligation was much more pronounced.

Comments included:

- 'Sometimes your body's not up to it, but your husband wants to and . . .'
- 'Doing it without wanting to makes us feel as if we're being used.'
- 'We have to be with our husbands because we are married, sometimes we pretend so we don't have any problems.'
- 'I think that there's also rape in the home. When they force us to do it they see us as objects.'
- 'If I say no to him, he demands it and even hits me . . . I can't ask him to do what I like.'

Perhaps a quarter of the women were satisfied with their sexual relationship with their partner. Most found themselves forced, having to give in for fear of their husband's anger. Although patriarchal ideology and culture play a large part in this situation, there is also a question of money: the man takes the money home (in the majority of cases) the woman feels 'kept' and that she has a duty to reciprocate. The fear is not only of beatings or anger, but of abandonment, especially for women with children. And in fact there is a serious problem of survival and of social rejection when the husband goes away. Women's submission to their partner in a sexual relationship is based not only on the machismo of men, but also on a certain material and social need to guarantee the relationship, and thereby survival. Women are able to renounce pleasure and disregard domination of their own body because they also receive something in exchange, they receive a security which they cannot guarantee by any other means.

- 'If someone loves us we want to be with them. If they mistreat us, we are only there out of duty . . . but we are there.'
- 'Once we are married there's a division in ourselves, in our feelings and the use of our body.'
- 'We are not mistresses of our body because the system makes us think in a different way to how we want to do things.'
- 'Our body is the only thing that's really ours and yet we can't make decisions about it'.

Physical violence is another element in the relationship between men and women. More than half the women are beaten, and although many defend themselves with the same violence, the idea also prevails that if a woman 'behaves badly', it's right to beat her.

As regards motherhood, suffice it to say that out of 20 women, only one had taken the decision to be a mother, yet motherhood is commonly presented as women's destiny.

So it is that women are alienated in their relationship with their bodies, a situation reflected by ignorance, an obstacle to physical self-exploration, the denial of pleasure or naturalness with which dissatisfaction in a sexual relationship begins, the impossibility of deciding when and how many children to have. In this way sexuality becomes a continuous cycle of repression, obligation, violence, shame, fear, hiding . . . Faced with these problems, society has few answers and, worse still, creates the conditions to reproduce them, because to keep women repressed in such a way helps guarantee the reproduction of the system under which we live.

Progress, leading to organisation

The progress of the group had many ups and downs, tensions, fears, resistance and contradictions which were gradually resolved or repeated, depending on the subject and time. We cannot say that shame and fear were overcome at once and by everyone, nor that the women one by one questioned and overcame the problems of their sexuality under scrutiny. Neither do we believe that progress has been even: whilst the subject of virginity may deeply question the beliefs of some, for others it may be motherhood or the relationship with their partner.

The *colonas* gave free rein to their feelings on many occasions; they brought up complex problems within the family, letting go their anxiety and depression which, at times, came out all at once. But change is a slow, uneven process and many things needed time to be appraised or assimilated.

As a result of the workshop, the women began to ask themselves if the only struggle they could wage was against the State and the bourgeoisie; if a couple who struggle against the inequalities of the system can be so unequal in their private life, what kind of life are they fighting for? Slight changes began to occur in the family, in some aspects of the children's education, the relationship with the husband, in the attitude to housework. They also began to spread some of their criticisms or new ideas in the local community through small drama productions. Male interest in what was happening in the workshop grew. They wanted to come to meetings. For their part the women felt stronger and understood better. They wanted to talk together about their conclusions or about the things they wanted to change. The war of the sexes began to transcend the women's group itself and to yield results in their family lives and in the organisation. Personal problems began to change into political problems. After a year, consideration of the women's question and its problems in the private sector had begun to be a part of everyone's political duty. Here, at least, the class war and the war of the sexes have begun to intertwine and be seen as just one struggle – the struggle against all oppression and exploitation.

5 Women, Vote for Yourselves! Reflections on a Feminist Election Campaign

Virginia Vargas

Virginia Vargas is one of two Peruvian feminists who, at the very last minute, stood for Parliament during the run-up to their country's last elections in April 1985. A sociologist, among other activities she has worked for the Ministry of Education, is a founder member of the Flora Tristán Centre for Peruvian Women and plays a leading role in the Latin American and Caribbean Women's Studies Association (ALACEM). She was also part of the Peruvian delegation to the Non-Governmental Conference to mark the end of the Decade for Women in Nairobi.

In this article, reprinted from *Isis International Women's Journal No. 5* (1986) on the Latin American Women's Movement, Virginia Vargas describes her experience with Victoria Villanueva when both campaigned as independent feminist candidates under the umbrella of the broad socialist alliance, Izquierda Unida (United Left). Although neither was finally elected, the participation of two feminists in the electoral process marked an important step in the history of women's struggles in Peru.

Redefining our feminist position

The new wave of feminist activity which emerged in Peru in the 1970s, in the midst of great national upheaval, heralded the slow and painful transition we had made from an initial identification with the ideas and practices of the Peruvian Left towards an autonomous position, in terms of both ideology and organisation. Through a process of consciousness-raising and reflection we had managed to formulate our feminist position and evolve a way of working collectively and on a personal level toward the elimination of women's oppression. Moreover, we had reached this point without suffering any great internal ruptures.

The fruits of our efforts during those eight years can be seen in the opening up of discussion about so-called women's problems, leading to the integration of new themes into political debate, and the upsurge of new groups, alternative publications, feminist work-places, research, and literary and artistic output. Nevertheless, the development of the women's movement was far from even. Moments of progress would suddenly be met by apparent deadlock. There were tensions, notably between the need to consolidate our own internal work and at the

Poster for the Second Latin American and Caribbean Feminist Meeting, Peru 1983.

same time respond to the growing complexity of women's demands in the wider society. The tendency to cut ourselves off, taking refuge in what we had learned, may have given us valuable strength but it threatened to divorce us from the experiences of women outside. We also ran the risk of becoming increasingly isolated from the overall political struggle.

The need to break this inertia was especially urgent at a time when alternative political strategies were under constant discussion and when women, under pressure from the national crisis and hazards of daily survival, were developing new creative methods of organisation without necessarily considering their own specific

'Election Day' (*La Cacerola*, Uruguay 1984).

Man: I'm going to vote early. I'm so excited.
Woman: Me too. I'll be down there as soon as I can.
Man (hours later): Women always leave the important things till the last minute.

needs. It was time for us to expand our influence and build ourselves a more solid base in society; to transform ourselves into a visible movement capable of challenging political parties, institutions and the State.

A remote idea becomes reality

With the probability of forthcoming elections we gradually began to think about the electoral process as a possible opportunity for putting our increasing criticisms of the movement into practice. At this stage we weren't all thinking about forwarding our own candidates. However, we did share the alarming sensation that the electoral process highlighted the absence of a feminist perspective on themes of national importance, demonstrating our failure to reach a wider number of women.

First proposals for a list of women candidates in fact came from outside the women's movement. We had hardly even started formulating possible electoral strategies when certain newspapers and magazines were suggesting us as potential members of parliament. One publication went as far as naming one of us as the Minister for Women's Affairs in a hypothetical left-wing government. Meanwhile, the movement itself was engaged in various working groups, one of which focused precisely on this question of seizing political opportunity.

After some preliminary discussion about our position in relation to the electoral process enthusiasm for the idea of candidates soon began to take hold and it was decided to widen the debate within the whole women's movement, a step which led to some of the most valuable discussion we've had in recent times. Many questions came up: Weren't we meant to be an autonomous political movement? Did we really need to join the formal electoral process in ᵓ rder to establish our legitimacy? Why align ourselves to Izquierda Unida rather than APRA (the Popular Revolutionary Alliance of America)? Wouldn't this imply blatant conciliation with the patriarchal Left? Needless to say there was no one answer.

The degree to which we'd be able to retain our autonomy in such a seemingly 'natural' affiliation proved to be one of the main stumbling blocks to our discussion, giving rise to three main positions. The first argued that the movement already identified itself with the Left, so to join the parliamentary lists would simply legitimise the situation. The second maintained that the IU had never shown any genuine interest in incorporating women's demands into its programme and so upheld an absolute need for autonomy. There was also concern about the problem of not being able to shake off identification with a political party after the elections. Those who took up the third position shared much in common with the first and felt that emphasising the dilemma of autonomy versus cooperation tended to paralyse initiative by imposing too much of a theoretical scheme on reality. Progress is seldom made without risks and it was worth encountering hostility if access to such a privileged political platform would bring us closer to other women.

We never saw the electoral process as the one and only solution. The movement clearly had to develop through a system of multiple strategies, confronting different parties and candidates about their position on women, opening up a permanent platform for debate about feminist priorities and programmes, seeking alliances with candidates from all sides; in other words transforming ourselves into a permanent pressure group to ensure that women's issues remained an ongoing part of political debate. At the same time our candidates would aim to use the electoral space provided by the IU as a means of disseminating our ideas and, were we to be elected, of maintaining a permanent defence of women's rights in parliament.

Just as the feminist movement's wholesale identification with the Left might threaten our democratic tradition of embracing women with different political loyalties, so it was dangerous to interpret autonomy as simply deliberate isolation from political and social processes, or as a defence against fear of confronting the public world. True autonomy isn't about maintaining the cosy security of a small group, bent on preserving the purity of its doctrine. It's about taking risks and confronting patriarchal power at every level. Otherwise we simply end up using up our energies on isolated struggles which may be gratifying in themselves but have little impact on society, let alone the development of a global strategy towards eliminating women's oppression. In order to assert the movement's autonomy we needed to gather all forces in favour of women's demands, whatever negotiations and conflict this might involve.

All this discussion about the pros and cons of varying degrees of autonomy brought to light some of the most complex, controversial aspects of feminist theory and practice. How we organise, the ways in which decisions are made, the meaning of leadership, all add up to the tension between individual and collective interests/needs which tends to characterise the exercising of power. In this respect two unspoken questions haunted the early days of our candidacies: how to justify setting them in motion without consensus; and why we and not other women from the movement should be candidates.

In the end there was no consensus or vote taken to settle our proposals or define the strategy we were to follow. However, seeing that a significant sector of the movement clearly supported our candidacies, it was decided to form a committee in order to start publicising our campaign. Petitions were printed requesting 'signatures of support for two candidates from the feminist movement who are standing for parliament as independents on the lists of Izquierda Unida'. (At that time the IU embraced eight political parties and a significant number of independents.)

The collection of signatures was our first real creative action, not only because it wasn't done by any other candidates but because it involved a kind of mini-campaign of conviction, face to face, within families, between friends, in the popular sectors, in work places, in hairdressers, markets and many more areas. In less than a month we managed to gather over 5,000 names from both women and men. The petitions were then handed over to the electoral committee of the IU whose task it was to prepare the final list of candidates.

The movement was simultaneously working on what was to be the 'Platform for the Rights of Women', formulating a programme of demands designed as the basis of our electoral campaign. This programme also turned out to be a very useful tool for opening up discussion with different parties and political organisations on their position in relation to women.

The obstacles of working within Izquierda Unida

In general, relations between the feminist movement and political parties have been plagued with disagreements and contradictions. In the beginning, the Peruvian movement was very much linked to party militancy. As well as struggling hard for our autonomy, we were intent on raising the whole issue of gender and women's equal participation in political parties within the Left. But, although many party women led or at least joined this process, party leaders tended not to recognise the autonomy of the women's movement and felt threatened by criticism of their beliefs and organisational practice.

As a result we candidates were regarded with great mistrust. People within the IU found it hard to understand how we could have an independent political viewpoint from our male comrades. Individual political parties resented us as late arrivals and reproached us for our permanent criticism of women's position; and party militants viewed us as disloyal competition in territory that didn't belong to us. Only a few independents really lent their support, defending our candidacy and demanding that we be incorporated right up until the last minute. Our names as candidates were finally incorporated one hour before the time ran out for registering Parliamentary lists at the National Board of Elections.

The system of preferential voting used for the first time in these last presidential elections allowed for the personalisation of electoral preferences. Voting was on three levels: for president, two national senators and two provincial deputies. It was also possible to combine different lists for each level. Under the umbrella of the IU we were allocated 29th place for senator (out of 60) and 31st place for deputy for Lima (out of 40). The general low support for the IU severely reduced our chances.

As official candidates we found ourselves entering a kind of vacuum in which we weren't strictly representing either the women's movement or the IU. Neither were we entirely independent. We didn't want to compromise the autonomy of the movement; we wanted separate space so that its activities could carry on as usual, although we still needed its strength and solidarity. In this atmosphere of ambiguities and insecurity we launched our campaign.

The design of the campaign united all that was most creative about the feminist movement. Even those who hadn't agreed with the candidacies lent their experience and imagination, carried forward by the theme 'Women, Vote For Yourselves: Feminists in Parliament'. Flyers dealing with themes such as sexuality, violence, work and organisation, such as had never been seen before in an electoral campaign, gave weight to the famous 'Women, Vote For Yourselves'. The texts read as follows:

1. Because we have always been the targets of violence: ill-treated at home, assaulted in the street, harassed at work, raped . . . We reject war and destruction. Because we have always been the source of life we defend and want to change it. Because together we can fulfil our dreams. Feminists for Parliament! The Only Hope For Peace!

2. Because we women have the capacity for organisation we have created hundreds of community eating places, opened nurseries and kindergartens for

children. Because day after day we confront our country's crisis with intelligence and because we can change Peru. Feminists for Parliament! For the Organisation of Women!

3. For the fair recognition of housewives' work; because we should have access to better jobs; for equal wages for women and men; for a social security system that includes us all; and for laws to protect working mothers. Feminists for Parliament! For Equality at Work!

4. For the right to know and control our own bodies; for free access to contraception and family-planning methods, for our own choice in sexuality; for a health system to meet our needs. Feminists for Parliament! For Health as a Woman's Right!

Nevertheless, as we had suspected, our candidacies turned out to be an island within the dynamic of the IU. The predominant debate was profoundly masculine with only vague isolated references to women, usually bathed in clichés aimed at trying to maintain a certain modernity without having to make any significant compromises. Feeling trapped and angry, we quickly decided not to participate any more in these campaign meetings. Instead we would dedicate ourselves to our own campaign, based on our own strengths, on our feminist platform and our scarce economic resources.

So, what happened to all of us?

An electoral campaign is a serious event. More than anything, it's a 'time for politics' in the institutional sense and not a 'time for living' which is probably what most wore us out. Fuelled by endless eloquent phrases, promises never intended to be fulfilled, the most inhuman means of destroying opponents and, above all, the ability to sell an image to the media as much as to the electorate, electoral logic has no let-up. We felt quite lost.

We found a basic conflict between this utilitarian concept of politics, aimed at influencing a mass of people without taking into account any of their individual diversity, and our own search, albeit hesitant, for a political approach anchored more in the specific identity of each social being.

Our approach also had its limitations. By concentrating on the day-to-day experiences and perceptions of women our feminist discourse let specific issues, hitherto forbidden, such as sexuality, the implications of domestic work, violence, reproductive rights, organisational autonomy etc., cover up the wider political dimension. No matter how much women (and the few men who were willing to understand) related to these themes and identified with the political aspects of their own personal grievances, given the tremendous burden of daily survival there simply wasn't time to overcome their fear of the unknown and redirect that knowledge into new methods of concrete action.

Despite our efforts we also encountered the opposite problem of our approach being too general. Again, in such a short time, how could we possibly demonstrate the unique diversity of women?

As women (irrespective of class) we tend to respond and adapt to whatever relations of power we happen to be engaged in. In the course of our daily lives we learn to develop many ways of complicity or resistance, including learning how to prioritise our demands. Similarly in relation to the electoral campaign we needed to reflect on the contradictions between our passive role as participants in the formal political system and the rebellious spirit which underlined our feminist demands. Unfortunately we lacked both the time and the necessary previous experience to embark on such a slow process. Instead we mainly had to rely on the impact of our slogan 'Women, Vote For Yourselves'.

The women who voted for us were basically those with whom we already had a direct relationship or else women with whom we managed to build much stronger relations during the campaign. This was especially clear in the case of working-class women. When it came to middle-class women we benefited more from the influence of all those years of feminist communication through the mass media, alternative publications, seminars and cultural activities.

In spite of the force of our slogans, which had the potential of reaching all women, our creativity became lost. One way or another, against our will, we fell in with the electoral dynamic of responding to the exigencies of the least organised sectors of the working class, concentrating our energies on thousands of small actions and meetings which, however positive our reception, were too limited to achieve the wide influence we needed. There were few opportunities to put forward more global strategies aimed more at the middle classes who, given the complications of the preferential voting system, were a far more likely public.

In the end only two women from the IU were elected. Both became provincial deputies, not for their position on women but for the clout of their political parties. But in spite of all the problems it was an invaluable experience. We did succeed in planting a feminist viewpoint in an area quite unprepared for, let alone interested in, women or feminists. We learned a lot about our own limitations as well as the limitations of the formal political process. Although the continuing development of our discourse and practice may bring us closer to women, it's very difficult to reach any kind of 'total' perspective. But we're learning. Having opened up the way we must try new strategies for gaining power for women. Our next attempt is bound to be more successful.

6   Women and Politics: Reflections from Nairobi

Based on a report by **Amal Jou'beh**

Amal Jou'beh went to Nairobi as a representative of the Palestinian Union of Women's Work Committees (see chapter 12 on Women Behind Bars). This article, reprinted from the Union's Newsletter (Autumn 1985) is based on her report.

In July 1985, two representatives of the Union of Women's Work Committees went to Nairobi, Kenya, to participate in the International Women's Forum, a gathering of 14,000 women, individuals and representatives of non-governmental organisations from all over the world.

At the same time, the third United Nations Conference on Women was meeting to review the progress made by member nations through the Decade of Women, 1975–85, and to agree on resolutions for the future. The Forum thus complemented the official conference, by offering opportunities to discuss each and every issue affecting women worldwide. It was the third Forum, but the first to which the UWWC had sent delegates; they formed part of a Palestinian group of 12 from inside the occupied territories; another 30 Palestinian women came from other countries.

There was little prearranged structure to the Forum, but six topics were suggested in advance: equality, development, peace, health, work, and education. Before the Forum opened, key issues, which were crucial to women of Palestine and all other oppressed people, had already surfaced. These were:

* Can the situation of women be separated from the political and economic context in which they live?
* Can feminist issues be considered in isolation from national issues?

The organisers of the Forum, among whom representatives from the United States and other developed Western nations were disproportionately powerful, insisted that the Forum be 'non-political', that it should discuss issues specific to women and leave politics aside.

Changing the whole context: women's struggle in the Third World

It is true that women's movements in developed countries have waged campaigns

لجان العمل النسائي في المناطق المحتلة

on specific issues important to women's lives – rape and wife-battering for example – and have discussed these issues at times in isolation from the whole situation in society. Whether this approach is the most productive for women in developed countries is an important question, but for women in developing countries, it is clearly less pressing to tackle such specific phenomena than to try to change the whole context in which they live. Women who live under political, economic or racial oppression believe that their oppression as women is part of their oppression as people. They have the right to approach their struggle from this direction.

The UWWC knows that the liberation of women in Palestinian society is essential, and that an effective national liberation struggle depends on the participation of women as well as men. Their priority at present, however, must be to get rid of the Israeli military occupation. On the one hand, the occupation itself is one of the major impediments to women's progress; on the other, many of the specifically feminist concerns of Western women can be realised only once a certain level of self-determination and development has been reached. Women's health and health-care in the occupied territories, for example, are seriously affected by gender discrimination, but this issue is difficult to tackle when all health provision is in the hands of an occupying power. Similarly, women's fight for equality rests in part on establishing an enabling framework of laws and welfare provisions; an impossible task for a stateless people.

In Nairobi, the UWWC delegates found that many Western women still tend to look at developing countries in a fragmented, individualistic, 'orientalist' way. They focused on some particular abuse of women, such as wife-beating or polygamy, and saw this as an essential determinant of women's situation. Palestinian women tried to explain that the context in which such abuses occur – the structural political violence or economic violence – is even more important than the abuses themselves, and that until this framework is removed, the particular manifestations of women's oppression cannot be overcome.

The attempt to impose a Western, non-political concept of 'women's issues' is a kind of cultural imperialism, and a political act in itself. It aims at forcing Third World women to accept the status quo and acquiesce in their national subordination. The oppressiveness of the demand to 'stay out of politics' is not always accidental. The hypocrisy with which it can be used was evidenced at Nairobi by some United States delegates, who tried to use this 'non-political' forum to further their government's political aims. They put pressure on some Palestinian delegates to enter into talks with Zionist women. Such talks, however non-political their subject, would have served very well the United States' political ambition to be the 'peace-maker' in the Middle East.

No politics means no Palestine

As far as Palestinian women were concerned, the effort to depoliticise the Forum – to concentrate on details and ignore their context – was a flagrant attempt by the pro-Israeli lobby to exclude discussion of Palestinian national questions. Many illustrations could be given. For instance, at the planning stage, the organisers prevented the name 'Palestine' from appearing in the title of a planned workshop on the grounds that it would introduce a distracting political note into the subject to be discussed. To judge from the Israeli press in the months leading up to the Forum, Israel was particularly afraid of the introduction of politics. The Forum might, Israel feared, become the stage for a concerted attack on Israeli policies.

But Israel's own political intentions were clear: it hoped to use the Forum to justify its occupation of the West Bank and Gaza, and to this end had prepared reports purporting to show that the situation of Palestinian women had improved under Israeli rule.

To quiet the Palestinian voices that would be raised to contradict these findings, the military authorities prevented several of the most experienced and effective Palestinian women from leaving the country to appear at the Forum.

Nevertheless, the Palestinian women were well able to present their case, to counter Israeli propaganda, and at the same time to call attention to the centrality of politics in their experience as women. The Israeli delegates were not well-informed, and their occasional resort to disruption and emotional displays did not make a good impression. The support that Palestinian women received, especially from Third World women, was overwhelming. According to one participant, women were 'queueing up at the microphone' at every opportunity to show solidarity with Palestinian women and denounce Israeli policies. Black South African and Nicaraguan women in particular came to Nairobi with carefully prepared accounts of Israel's contributions to their own sufferings, and their support was especially valuable in light of the current focus of world attention on their countries.

Thus, although owing to US pressure, the motion that 'Zionism is racism' was defeated at the official UN conference, in the Forum Palestinian women felt that they presented their situation effectively and added to an already sizeable body of supporters worldwide.

UWWC at the Forum

What did the UWWC delegates themselves achieve? As only two, in such a huge gathering (there were 30 to 40 workshops each day, over 1,000 in all), it was obviously impossible for them to take advantage of all the opportunities to learn about other women and their problems and solutions. They had to plan carefully, and to focus their energies.

The first task was to make the situation of Palestinian women known to as wide an audience as possible, through formal and informal means. The UWWC held a well-attended panel discussion on 'Palestinian women under occupation' and presented papers on the history of the women's movement in Palestine, and on education. Palestinian delegates also spoke on health in the occupied territories, refugees, the parallels between Zionism and apartheid, prisoners and Israel's involvement in the spread of nuclear weapons.

The second task was to answer all pro-Zionist statements about Palestinian women. The UWWC coordinated with other Palestinian women to ensure a presence at every Israeli-sponsored event.

The Forum was an opportunity for the UWWC to strengthen and build new links with many sympathisers from all over the world: women's movements in the Arab world; delegates from the socialist countries; Third World liberation movements; and progressive women from Western countries. Particularly friendly contacts were made with women from Panama and Tanzania. The UWWC delegates found that women involved in Third World liberation struggles were eager to exchange ideas and experiences of how women's struggles for personal and social liberation could be incorporated into and add their strength to national struggles. The Palestinian women's movement is widely respected for its effective mobilisation of women in the dual struggle for social and national development.

The UWWC delegates were impressed by the extensive knowledge women from other countries had about the Palestinian–Israeli conflict: they felt that Palestinian women now must learn as much about the struggles of other women.

Finally, the delegates used the occasion to publicise the work and programme of the UWWC. The delegates left Nairobi satisfied that they had played an effective and successful role, enriched with the knowledge they had gained of other women's lives and struggles, knowledge they will share with women in the occupied territories. Valuable friendships with women's groups abroad will be developed in the future, and the task begun at Nairobi, of showing the world the true nature of women's oppression and struggle under military occupation, will be continued.

Part 2:
Women at War

7 Guatemalan Women Have Always Participated — Reflections from *Compañeras* in the National Liberation Movement

Latin American Working Group (Canada)

Women have a long history of organisation in the popular movements of Central America and are ever more active today, both in terms of pursuing women's issues and the overall struggle against repression and injustice. The interview and article below describe the participation of women in Guatemala, where a military coup in 1954 has been followed by more than three decades of brutal repression, culminating in the present civil war.

The interview, recorded in Canada in 1983, is reprinted from the dossier *Central American Women Speak for Themselves*, published by the Latin American Working Group in Ontario; Maria Lupe's testimony was originally published in *Compañero*, the magazine of Guatemala's Guerrilla Army of the Poor (EGP). More recently, an organisation called IXQUIC has been formed in Mexico in order to 'deepen knowledge of the situation of women in Guatemala and promote solidarity with their cause'.

Talking to a *Compañera*

When did women first become involved in the popular struggle in Guatemala?

The Guatemalan people have been involved for a very long time, for many years, in a silent struggle. From the beginning, working in every way, women have always been there.

Because of the conditions in our country, many women have become deeply political. Women in Central America in general have been changing because of the life, the conditions and their own determination to change the situation. As a result, women are changing the situation of women by actively participating inside the struggle. Even unconsciously, women are doing a great deal of work, are part of the struggle and part of the decision-making. But, this implies more work, risks and sacrifices. Women are prepared to become involved in these many different roles because they know if they do not, they will never have the possibility of changing society or their conditions.

Symbol of IXQUIC.

Can you talk about some of the early work carried out by women?

As I said, Guatemalan women have always participated in the 'process', the struggle, and have been active at every level. To give a couple of examples of women who were involved very early on and who took part in the armed opposition when not many were involved – we remember Rogelia Cruz. Rogelia was named Miss Guatemala one year, but afterwards took part in the armed oppositional organisation. She was captured and found later showing signs of terrible torture. Her breast was cut off, she had been beaten with a rifle. It was the first example of really brutal torture by the army. Of course that has become quite common now.

Nora Paiz was involved in the armed struggle, through the FAR (the Revolutionary Armed Forces) – also in the early stages, starting around 1963. She was killed, I believe around 1966, with the poet Rene Castillo. They were coming back to the city, back down from the mountains and were caught and both were . . . burned alive . . . yes, burned alive.

During the 1944–54 period, popular organisations flourished, and also women's participation. Their participation is probably most evident with the teachers, because at that time, the teachers took a very prominent role in the opposition to the dictator Ubico . . . just before the ten years of democracy Guatemalans experienced.

In fact one of the teachers – Maria Chinchia – is recognised as a kind of heroine, remembered because she was very brave in facing the army. She went out into the streets leading protests; she was in the front lines when she was killed in 1944. For facing Ubico in that way, she is considered to be especially brave.

And also in that period there was a women's organisation. I think that it was part of the popular movement spreading throughout the country.

The major point is that women have never been outside the struggle, for its entire process. From the beginning, they have worked at every level. They participate now, and they will participate even more after the victory, during reconstruction. This participation will guarantee them an important role in the future.

The other case I want to mention is that of Yolandita – the teenager who worked at the National Confederation of Workers (CNT) when there was a shortage of lawyers after the repression. She had been working there since she was 13 years old. At that time she decided to quit school in order to be more involved in the student movement. But at the same time she decided to work at the CNT with the workers.

'Men and women: all out to help in the mechanics workshop'. Drawing from *Out of the Ashes: The Lives and Hopes of Refugees from El Salvador and Guatemala* (El Salvador and Guatemala Committees for Human Rights/War On Want Campaigns, London 1985).

She made this decision after her father and 7-year-old brother were killed in 1975, when she was 12. Her father was political and had been starting to get involved in the unions. After that, she decided to work with the workers at the CNT and at the same time to work in the organisation of secondary students – she wanted to link those struggles.

To experience what it was like to be a worker she quit school when she was 15. She worked in a factory making paper boxes. She didn't tell the management about her age when she applied, otherwise she wouldn't have been accepted; nor her last name, which was known. But they were willing to accept anyone as long as they were prepared to work for minimal wages. She worked for 80 cents a day. Also because of the chemicals they had to use, her hands were raw and had sores most of the time. She stayed there until she was fired for organising the women – there were mostly women in the factory. So, she came back to work at the CNT, more deeply, definitely to work with workers, and not with the students any more.

After the repression in 1980, she worked at the CNT with peasants and urban workers. She participated in the *toma* (takeover) of El Calbario Church. There were lawyers to cover certain actions, but never enough, so she began doing things related to legal work. Later, in October 1980, she was at the Palace of Justice, protesting because a peasant had been killed in the *toma* of the church. She was giving out pamphlets along with a 17-year-old boy. A member of one of the paramilitary organisations happened to be there and she was caught. This became an international case, which probably helped save her life. She was put in jail for 15 days, and tortured and raped several times – the first to rape her was the Chief of Police, Manuel Valiente Tellez. She was also tortured with the *capucha* (a hood often put over the heads of torture victims).

Because of all the international pressure, she was released. Someone told me that from Sweden alone, 5,000 telegrams were sent. She was 16-years-old at the time. After that . . . (her mother still worked as a lawyer at the CNT) . . . she was released, but she was blinded because she got an infection in her eyes and ears from DDT they used in the *capucha*. Then she had to go into hospital, and later left the country for a time, although she was still in the struggle.

She recovered her sight. She is very strong because of all her experience in working with peasants and the workers and students. The peasants she worked with – who really love her – when they found out she was blind, raised some money through the union and gave it to her to buy a braille watch. She said, 'Thank the *compañeros*, but I will not be needing a braille watch. Because I'm going to be OK. I will be needing other things but not a braille watch'.

Today she is about 19-years-old. Her consciousness is very high and she is still working very hard. And she has been struggling since she was 13. Her mother sent out a tape about her case and wanted it to be known in the outside. She also said to tell people that they are still struggling with the same love as before.

You see, the struggle of our people is not because they *hate* the army; it is because they *love* the people.

Can you explain how Guatemalan women see their struggle as women, particularly in the context of increased repression?

At the time when all the unions and labour federations were coming together in the CNUS (National Committee of Trade Union Community)* women certainly didn't see their struggle as an isolated one. They saw themselves along with others who were exploited – not just as a women's particular issue. That same attitude or

---

* An umbrella organisation of more than 100 union, peasant and other organisations, formed in 1976 to strengthen the labour movement's demands and to give support to labour groups undergoing increased police repression.

position was true at all levels of work and in the mass organisations. It's not that women didn't experience their exploitation or oppression as women, but we realised that there had to be a change in that system which was oppressing us. We realised we would have to go to the roots of the problem. Women wouldn't be able to do that just through a women's organisation, or isolated from the rest of what was going on.

It's not a question of setting aside women's rights. And it's not as if we don't have women's demands – or that we will be the last sector to demand our rights. At the same time as we are participating at different levels within the struggle, we are getting clearer about our own role and we are beginning to break down traditional patterns . . . patterns which we had for so long that we as women didn't even know that we were oppressed. Now, because of our participation, women are able to understand their oppression as women. From now on it won't be so hard for women to put forward their own demands.

We also don't see it as just a question of waiting until the right time, because women are already doing this in their daily practice. These patterns are things that have to be broken, not after the victory, but every day and at all levels. These patterns involve both men and women, and both men and women will have to change them.

Some sectors of Guatemalan women have been affected by the women's movement in North America . . . but it's important to distinguish which sectors. I couldn't say for example, that Indian women in Guatemala have been affected by the North American women's movement. Not even by Guatemalan women, and certainly not by middle or upper classes of women. I agree that women who have the opportunity and exposure to the North American women's movement have been affected, but unfortunately for many, it seems to be a snobbish thing. I couldn't say that it has touched most Guatemalan women very deeply.

I think it is especially important to look at the participation of Indian women . . . a participation that is less in mass organisations and more in the armed opposition. Indian women didn't generally follow a pattern of working in mass organisations and then go into armed struggle. They have gone right from their oppression to joining the armed struggle.

The issue of Indian women's participation is very complex. In Guatemala, Indians have largely been able to conserve their own culture and traditions. Within the framework of exploitation, they have been very exploited. But at the same time, they are closed societies and have retained a deep sense of community. They don't allow *ladinos* or foreigners, as a general rule, to come into their communities. Within this context, women have their own roles.

Customs, traditions and culture are extremely important to the Indian women as well as men, of course. You may have heard about how some of these women are now changing their traditional clothing for uniforms in order to take up armed struggle. You have to realise the extent to which they have developed their consciousness in order for them to do that – something very, very deep has occurred, especially in some of the rural communities. Their disposition to give up one of the things that is most precious to them in order to take up the struggle is very significant, and this is just one expression of the commitment of many Indian women.

How has your own consciousness about women's struggles developed?

From my own experience, I know that if I had never had experience and involvement in the popular struggle, I would have never developed an awareness of women's oppression. I would have remained like so many women, especially in the cities, who never participate and don't know what is going on, or even what their rights are. It was my participation in the whole process, you might say, that opened my eyes to women's exploitation as such.

I can remember some of the things that began to open my eyes. I began to realise how much harder it is for the peasant women, the *campesinas*, than for the men and also for women in the cities, than for their working husbands. For example, I can remember seeing women in the Highlands with babies on their backs, taking care of sheep, and taking care of other children. Then they would have to take their lunch to their husbands. Women would have to make the clothing and also they sell some things to bring in a little extra income into the family. At the same time, they have to take care of all the children. Look how much they are doing! I mean, the man has to leave the home early in the morning and go to the fields to work. But the infrastructure and all the support is the women.

In the case of women in the factories, I can remember being particularly struck by seeing pregnant women in the textile factories, working night shifts without a chair to sit on, without anything to make the work a bit easier for them. But they would be there, working just as hard as the men.

In many cases, of course, both the man and woman will be working, but the burden of the housework and the children will be on the woman. So she will have a double day. If she's involved in unions or other political work, then she will have a triple day.

Desertion has also been a problem, just as in Nicaragua and El Salvador. The problem has been more common in the cities than in the countryside, although it is also evident there. It occurs in the middle and upper classes as well, but in these cases, women will have some means of economic support. Their children are recognised, or they can go to court to fight for an allowance.

The other thing you will see quite commonly is domestics having children as a result of being forced to have relationships with their bosses. In many cases, the women will have the children and then give them to the grandparents to care for. They will go back to work, and then frequently will have another child. Of course, when she can she sends money home for the children.

To understand Guatemalan women, I think it is very important to recognise that we come from very different perspectives and contexts. Our social, economic and political situations are very different.

That makes a very great difference between women in Central America and women in North America. For example, one of the important issues there is abortion. That is not by any means a central issue for women in rural communities in Central America. I imagine that women in the refugee camps who have lost their children will want to have more children. Because the situations are so different.

The perception of women's organisations is different, too. I think that AMNLAE in Nicaragua has played a very positive role in terms of women's demands, and possibly will play an even more important role in the future. Slowly, I think, they are getting women's demands through the government . . . the Law of Nurturing and sharing of housework are two good examples.

We have to think about how Guatemalan Indian women, who have participated in the struggle, will be able to fit back into their communities after the victory. What will happen to their relationship to the women who didn't have the same level of participation? It will be very interesting. It's almost certain that they won't go back to accepting the old traditional roles. But at the same time, they will go back to their communities and work in the reconstruction.

I think it is important for Western women to understand why we don't have the same demands, or *revindicaciones*. What could we ask for now in terms of being equal? In many senses, for women it would mean equal repression and we already have that.

In North America, if the social conditions were to greatly change, or if there was a major issue that was really important for women in terms of threatening their whole status, or their lives – then that issue would become the most important for them. At the same time, we in Central America can't expect that the same issues or demands we have will be what is most important in North America. The demands cannot be the same in both North and Central America. That is not to say that there cannot be solidarity, for there must be.

It is possible that there might be organisations such as AMNLAE at some point in El Salvador, Honduras, Costa Rica and Guatemala, but our situation will be dealt with in a different way, among other things, because of the Indian people. For the first time in our history, we are respecting the Indian people. It would hardly be respecting them if we tried to impose our ideas about women's organisations on them, without taking into account the Indian culture and all their traditions. Guatemala will be a different situation.

Testimony of María Lupe

María Lupe, a non-Indian *campesina* woman, is one of the first *campañeras* who joined the Guerrilla Army of the poor (EGP) in the early 70s, during the beginning of the guerrilla war in the jungles of the department of El Quiché.

In the past my husband and I were very poor. We worked for the rich plantation owners. I took care of the workers, cooking and doing the laundry, from one in the morning till ten at night. Since there was no electric generator, everything was done by hand. My husband earned 50 cents a day, I got only my food. Later we bought a little house and rented some land, but things went badly for us and we fell into debt.

Twelve years ago we decided to go see if they would give us land in the North, in the Ixcán, but it was even harder for us there. There was nothing there; the store was a four-day walk away. For four months we ate only corn *atol* (gruel) and *tortillas*; one of the children there died from malnutrition.

I was pregnant with my third daughter, and had malaria through most of my pregnancy. I was also malnourished. The baby was born after seven months. She was very small and I almost lost her. Then the government officials came, and they gave us a plot of land. More settlers arrived and it got a little better. They came from everywhere, from the coast, from the East and from the North.

After we had been there two years the first *compañeros* from the EGP arrived. I remember that at that time we didn't even have corn. Not knowing them, I was afraid, and besides one of the government people had already told us that the guerrillas would come to rob us and to rape our daughters. Even one of my boys, who has joined with them now, went to hide the radio.

All of the *compañeros* helped to build a house. It was the first time that we saw collective work. Afterwards they explained that they were poor, and that they were fighting so that all of us, the poor people, could live better. They said that the poor would win. How will they win? I thought, if the towns are so far away . . . Now I see how the struggle has developed everywhere.

We begin to collaborate

We were one of the first families to begin to collaborate. I liked raising chickens and pigs. We sold them at a good price to the guerrillas in addition to the ones we gave them. Later we passed information to them and shopped for them.

All the families collaborated, although sometimes it was only the women or only the men who would talk to them. Then they had to convince their partners. Sometimes they didn't agree. Many times the husbands didn't want other men to pay attention to their wives, because of jealousy. Then other *compañeras* would talk to these women. We women organised around food. Everyone would bring it to my house, then I would take it to the mountains where the *compañeros* were training.

After a year, government spies appeared, and later the army. There was a lack of secrecy, and everyone knew we collaborated. My *compañero* and my oldest daughter, who was 12, went to train in the mountains. My daughter learned how to read and write there. They stayed three months, then returned. But within a week they had to join up once and for all because the army was investigating them and was going to go after them. (At that time the guerrillas executed Luis Arenas, a very repressive landlord who was called the Tiger of Ixcán. The EGP became public and repression increased.)

I remained alone with six children. We continued to collaborate. We got food and information from people in the entire area. It was rare to find anyone who didn't know about the *compañeros*. About 20 families began to help each other and to work collectively.

Women struggle to do political work

Workshops were held for the organised people. They were separate for men and for women. One of the *compañeras* would give a talk. We talked about discrimination against women, and why we could not mix with the men because they didn't trust us. We learned about the discrimination of husbands against wives in addition to the exploitation of the poor by the rich. A husband tells his wife to stay at home, not to do certain things. Often the wife, because she is not aware, thinks that it is natural.

The first thing we tried to change was wife-beating. It was hard to stop. While we were talking, the *compañeras* would be explaining to the men that women are not slaves, and should not be hit. But we have been able to stop it; it no longer happens. Also we had to struggle so that women would be allowed to do political work. Sometimes, for example, they would have to go out at night, but the men did not want to let them go. Later they realised it was because they didn't trust them. My husband and I never had that problem.

I was the first woman to join the Organization. The army was pursuing me, and was about to come and get me. I had left the girls with another *compañera*, but she wasn't able to take good care of them, so I had to go down to the village, where the army knew me, to get them out of there. We did it as an operation and I took the girls to the mountains. We lived for months like that, in a camp. Sometimes I would stay there alone with the girls and all we would see was monkeys.

In the camp I did everything: training, studying, going out to other villages to talk to the people and do the shopping. If the *compañeros* went shopping alone in a village, the people didn't trust them. When women went along the villagers could see that women were also involved and carried their own guns as well as the men. We talked to the people. We spoke to the women, and the men spoke to the men.

We also struggled with discrimination. When the *compañeros* came to a house they always helped with the cooking. The women were surprised that the men could do that, but we explained to them bit by bit that both men and women could do everything. I helped in the fields, in the planting. I explained to people that I had not done these jobs before, but that I had learned out of necessity. They could see that women also could work in the fields. Whenever we came to a place, we always helped with everything.

In the camp there were *compañeros* from all over: from the mountains and the jungle. At that time there were few *compañeras*, maybe four, now there are many more. They never let me participate in any actions because I had to be able to go into the village with the girls; the other *compañeras* participated. I liked the training, although some *compañeros* said that women couldn't take as much as men. Sometimes that is true, but at others it isn't. In the mountains everything is different, it is more collective, one travels in groups of 30 or 40 while others remain in the camp.

Children join

We organised the care of the five girls – the littlest one was three and the oldest was 12 at that time – among the *compañeros*. The bigger ones were already helping and participating in the meetings. They went to the training with their wooden carbines; that's what they played with, and all of them learned to read. There were no other children, as the *compañeras* left them with their families in the villages.

A lot of people say you shouldn't talk in front of children. But children learn what

67

is explained to them. We would tell them that they were not to talk loudly because the army would come. They can be taught discipline at an early age. We explained that other children are also left without their parents, and that after the victory we will all be together.

We explain to them that we are poor, that we can't buy what we want. And they understand. One day my six-year-old girl came to tell us that there was a spy there, and none of us had seen him. He had come to kill a *compañera*.

In the villages the children carry food, information, and keep the secret of the Organisation. They can join up at 12. During the time I was active, few children had joined because the repression was not as great. It is because of the repression that we join up. Now they say there are a lot of children who have joined.

Now I have a year-old grandchild. Both my daughter and her *compañero* have joined up. He didn't see the baby until eight months after its birth. I have three children in the Organisation: 16, 20, and 22 years old. Another daughter is 12 and she already wants to join. She says she wants to be free and have something to defend herself with.

8 Women in Namibia: The Fight Goes On

SWAPO Women's Solidarity Campaign (UK)

During a brief visit to Britain in June 1983, Pendukeni Kaulinge, Secretary of SWAPO Women's Council, spoke to women from the SWAPO Women's Solidarity Campaign in London about the situation of women refugees from Namibia. She also told of her own involvement in the armed liberation struggle which, in 1987, continues to escalate against ongoing South African aggression.

The interview is preceded by a short introduction reproduced from a booklet entitled *Namibia: Women in the Struggle* which was published in 1984 by the SWAPO Department of Information and Publicity, based in Angola.

> Since Namibian women are the mothers, the sisters and indeed the wives of all Namibian men who are fighting for the liberation of their fatherland, it goes without saying that the Namibian woman cannot but be an integral part of the struggle for the liberation of her country. In other words, she cannot detach herself from the plight, the fight, the hopes and the aspirations of the Namibian nation, a nation which is locked in a bitter and horrendous battle for its liberation.
>
> As mothers, Namibian women are forced to bear direct and immediate witness to the reality of malnutrition, illiteracy, and unemployment of their children. They are also obliged to confront, in the context of the struggle for liberation which Namibia has been going through for the last two decades, the torment of persecution, torture and death of their children, husbands, relatives and all their loved ones. In short, the Namibian woman is an inseparable part of a nation that is undergoing the most trying period of its historical development. She cannot but be a full participant in the arduous historical process in which Namibia is currently involved.

Namibian people's resistance to colonial domination dates back to the last quarter of the 19th century, when thousands of women were killed alongside their men during the German military campaign to conquer Namibia and subject its people to German imperial domination.

This fact, seldom remembered by historians, constitutes a sobering reminder that Namibian women have been at the centre of resistance to foreign domination as long as Namibia has fallen victim to imperialism. It is certain that when the definitive history of anti-colonial resistance is written, the evidence will be overwhelming as to the extent of Namibian women's sacrifice for the independence of their country.

The picture is much clearer when it comes to the role played by contemporary Namibian women and which they continue to play in the struggle for national and social liberation.

Women in the People's Liberation Army of Namibia (Namibia Support Committee, London).

When the movement for national liberation emerged in Namibia during the latter half of the 1950's, Namibian women stood side by side with their male compatriots. It is, for instance, a well-known fact that on December 10 1959, the very day when the UN General Assembly adopted its historic resolution proclaiming the universal right of man to live in freedom, socio-economic justice and security, Namibian women came out in hundreds and took to the streets of Windhoek in protest against the segregationist policies and practices of the South African colonial administration in Namibia.

The historic December 10, 1959 uprising in Windhoek, which resulted in the death of 12 and wounding of 50 of the African demonstrators, was sparked off by a forced removal of the African population from its residential area which was close to the centre of the city, to a new township, 'Katutura', situated a long distance away from the city centre of work and business activity.

Women played a predominant role in that popular anti-colonial uprising – an uprising which heralded the birth of the South West Africa People's Organisation (SWAPO) four months afterwards. Among those killed and wounded by the racist South African police and para-troopers, was a score of African women. It is against this background that December 10 is commemorated by the Namibian people and their friends as Namibian Women's Day in recognition of the heroic role played by the women and in memory of the sacrifices they made, together with their male compatriots, for the rights and freedom of the people and the independence of Namibia.

Following the renewed upsurge of mass political activity against the colonial regime in the country at the beginning of the 1970's, thousands of Namibian women threw their active political weight behind the vanguard liberation movement, SWAPO. This was particularly true with reference to young Namibian women, who as students, nurses, teachers and secretaries defied oppressive orders and brutal floggings to pour out in their thousands to join mass political rallies which SWAPO of Namibia organised throughout the country. They saturated the ranks of the militant SWAPO Youth League (SYL).

By the middle of the 1970's hundreds of Namibian women enlisted themselves into the guerrilla ranks of the People's Liberation Army of Namibia (PLAN) in order to fight arms in hand for the liberation of their beloved country. Today many of them can be found at various levels of structures of their people's liberation army. There are women commanders, radio communication operators, military nurses, battlefield medical assistants, combatants, political commissars, etc.

In the operational zones, Namibian women continue to play an important role in providing food and information on the movements of enemy troops to the heroic combatants of PLAN. For this vital support given to the freedom fighters of SWAPO, Namibian women are being killed in cold blood, tortured and raped by racist sadistic soldiers of the South African army of occupation in the country.

Other Namibian women continue to carry out clandestine political work in the urban areas, and for this daring anti-colonial activity, many women such as Ida Jimmy and Getrude Kandanga have been subjected to long-term imprisonment in the capital of Windhoek.

The repressive activities of the South African army in the rural war zones have resulted in the destruction of many peasant villages, leaving many rural women homeless and propertyless.

Design by Emma Mathews (Namibia Support Committee, London).

Against this background, tens of thousands of Namibian women have been forced to leave their country and to seek political asylum in the neighbouring countries of Angola, Zambia, and Botswana. In order to alleviate the depressing conditions of exile life, SWAPO Women's Council (SWC) the feminine wing of SWAPO, has worked out programmes for learning, for productive labour and cultural creativity. There are literacy campaign courses, and formal correspondence courses at both primary and secondary levels. A significant number of women are involved in this learning activity. Some are involved as teachers and others as learners. Vocational training in the fields of weaving, tailoring, driving, typing, etc., is being conducted in order to keep exiled women busy preparing themselves for a fruitful and productive future in their country after independence.

Crop production as well as the raising of chickens and pigs are among the productive activities in which exiled women are involved for the purpose of both providing for their own consumption and acquiring experience for the future.

Significant also is the number of Namibian women who are on scholarships abroad. They are engaged in their thousands in secondary and advanced programmes of education.

Interview with Pendukeni Kaulinge

Q: *What is life like for women in the refugee settlements?*

A: Well the lifestyle of women living in Kwanza Sul, Angola, differs from those living in the settlements in Zambia. In Angola, the conditions are rather difficult. These women who have lost almost everything they own apart from their lives, are living in a very depressive situation. A woman has little to do, she does not have a space in which to move about, she lives in a tent. She has to fetch water sometimes or get wood from somewhere. She has to look after her child, or maybe if she is pregnant, friends will help her. So our women really do live under difficult conditions and expect a lot from SWC.

We have put up projects for them but these are not really enough because so many – 95% – are illiterate Therefore, last year, we sent a group of mainly women to Zimbabwe for literacy training, to become teachers. They have just completed their training and are doing their practice in the settlements in Zambia. We hope that if this programme gets off the ground our women will pick up something from it and we will be able to integrate them.

Now women in Zambia are well off, not in the European sense, but they at least have possibilities. They have land and can cultivate crops; the food is there and if they need something like fruit or vegetables, they can go out into the villages and buy it. Many of them are working, but they have told us that it's not enough. They want something to occupy them throughout the day, so they are suggesting that maybe we could try to get them some pigs, some goats, so that they are occupied the whole day. They also have classes in the afternoons. These are only small, but we find that if a woman starts studying after a few years she will be able to go on to secondary education somewhere else, increasing her potentialities.

So there is a general problem of morale for women who leave Namibia?

The women who arrive in Angola, many of them if not all, are those who sneak out, literally, sometimes leaving their children and usually their husbands. Many of them leave, really not because they feel they have to work and fight against the South African regime, but they just cannot stand the pressure from the SA troops all over the country. Sometimes they are informed by someone that the police are watching them, 'you be careful, you are in danger', so they have to sneak out at night, and because the troops are all over the place they have to abandon everything. Even if they are leaving their children, they have to send them in all directions so as to arouse no suspicion. Therefore, when they arrive at the settlements they are tired and their morale is really low. We have to try to raise it by trying to explain how we have come to find ourselves in such a situation. It takes only a few months before they begin to wake up, they understand and try to accept the reality.

In what ways are women politically involved inside Namibia?

Women inside the country are the backbone of our struggle. Our fighters are very integral of course, but the women, even if they are very old, are the informers of our soldiers; the suppliers of food to our soldiers; the mobilisers of each other; they are just everything. Their active participation has cost so many of them so much, because when the Boers realised that it was the women who were providing all this information and food they created a special squad, dressed like our soldiers and asking, 'We are hungry Mama, can you help us please?' They send these squads to the houses during the day and if they are helped at a particular house, a group of people from the same squad will come during the night either to kill the whole family or only the women. They try so hard to scare our women from helping our fighters, they even rip pregnant mothers open so that others will be deterred. But this does not work. When the SA regime announced that all boys from the age of 16 were to be called up for military training, our women stood up in a very big protest. They held rallies from town to town explaining to others why we could not allow our sons to fight against their brothers and sisters. This was one of the factors that led to the arrest and detention of Comrade Ida Jimmy. [A leading member of the SWC in Namibia, she was released in October 1985 after five years' imprisonment, interrogation and torture for speaking at a SWAPO rally.] Even though the SA repressive machinery has become so huge, they also use hidden tactics. So our women inside Namibia are playing a very important historical role.

How did you leave Namibia? Did your family know you were planning to go?

I had made some plans: I dropped hints to my mother, who loved me so much, so as to prepare her that maybe one of these days I was going to leave. She was very suspicious: 'You are going to leave the country?' 'Oh, I'm not sure.' I left whilst I was doing my secondary education at a school some distance from my home. I arranged dates with my brother and on my return to school I just organised myself totally; I wrote letters which I hid under my pillow. It was a Friday afternoon and I called a friend and told him to call the principal of our school and pretend to be my father wanting to inform me that one of my relatives at home was dying.

This comrade did as I requested and the principal said that as it was Friday I could leave but be back by Monday. I told my school friends that I had had bad news from home and would see them next week. So we left this impression.

We walked from Oshigambo – we did not want to be given any transport in case people suspected why we were carrying suitcases. It took us six hours to reach the place where we were to wait for our transport to the border. When asked where we were going, we said to a wedding in the south. From the border we walked until we were safely inside Angola and took a bus to the borders with Zambia.

Namibian women on the move (Namibia Support Committee, London).

What was the spirit in which you left? Did you feel any sadness?

Oh no, I didn't. I used to recall the words of my mother: 'Whose mother would be helped if you were to say you wouldn't go because your mother cried?' No mother is happy that her sons and daughters are leaving, but I didn't feel bad because I was so determined. I knew I was going to go back. I had this notion that one day I would return home, my mother would see me and my father would see me with the fruits I had brought back.

Unfortunately they are now both dead, by the hands of the KOEVODT, this squadron which goes around the houses asking for food and identifying the families which help the freedom fighters. My family provided food. So they came at night for my father and my mother insisted on going too to see what would happen to her husband. It was a few metres from our house when they started shooting at my father and my mother was screaming so they shot her too, to shut her up.

Did you join the People's Liberation Army immediately on reaching the settlements?

Oh yes, by the time we left we were just asking for a gun. Because we realised we had come to that conclusion. Things were so bad and we were tired of being beaten up for just speaking. What was the use of talking? So we demanded that we should be given arms to fight the Boers.

Did you have problems with the male comrades when you asked to take up arms?

No, I can just say outright, no, from the beginning. Because the whole situation of being a soldier demands unity. Therefore the male comrades were feeling that, these sisters of ours who have this courage, we mustn't give them any feeling that they are not a part of this group. And I can say that the way we use the word 'Comrade' sometimes, when we talk about it in the streets, I think we do not know the meaning of it. But to be a soldier, this is when you really know she or he is my comrade. It's automatic. In battle, when someone falls or is bleeding you feel: I *have* to protect the life of this comrade, irrespective of sex. If I know that my comrade is beaten about by so many enemies, I have to make sure that I do my best. I can even say that sometimes these comrades forget entirely about sexual differences. When women have their natural problems [periods] a boy will tear up his uniform just to give aid to this comrade.

So the bond between our fighters, men or women, is very strong and that's why I am so confident that there is no way after independence that our men will say, 'Now you go back to the kitchen', because many of us have gone through the same process and we have realised each other's abilities.

Are there women of all ages in the settlements?

There are lots of very young women, many of whom have completed their primary education. With this group you can do anything; our main concern is those elderly women who cannot even write 'A'. They are the ones for whom we feel we must do a lot. We do not want them to return as they are, as they left the country. We have to help them, so we put them in separate settlements from the younger ones, who can do everything for themselves, partly to avoid those lazy ones wanting to be helped by the older women.

The younger women have grown up fully committed, but the older women have a different sense of struggle. As far as they are concerned they've never accepted foreign occupation. It is a pity they cannot write, because they have the experience of colonialism. How do they convey the folk history?

The distance between the two settlements is big, but the older women talk to the younger ones, telling of how they used to live, how they used to suffer, and support their husbands when they fought. One feeling they have in common is that something must be done. Even the very elderly. I remember one woman comrade in the SWC, she's around 70. That woman is so dynamic, when she speaks, telling how they suffered under the Boers you feel your whole body literally shaking. Sometimes I feel like taking her along when I go to meetings, just to tell the world, really she is so great. They have this strength still. Despite their physical frailty, they say: 'We cannot see these kids living under the same conditions that we did.' It's very encouraging for us.

We have the ongoing campaigns around sanitary towels and literacy, but how do you see the role of women in the West who wish to help?

You are trying to give us material assistance and political support. But our situation is so complicated. If you have not seen how the people are living yourself, you can have no concept of the problems we have, they are so many. I think the best thing you can do is just to explain our problems. People in the West must know what is happening in Namibia, because I feel that we are very much ignored by the media. If you can, intensify these campaigns, let the world know, let the world understand.

Women need clothing, blankets, shelter . . . just about everything needed by a human being. They need tents; people on the Angola side live in tents so that when the enemy is seen around that area, they can shift to another place.

Aren't people living in fixed areas?

No, we are constantly moving, and therefore the need for tents is very high, and they don't last long; after six months you find them already developing holes. And it always seems to rain when we move which makes things very difficult as the trucks become stuck in the mud.

I know you have received our message about sanitary towels. This time it is very serious, the senior women in our office are buying toilet paper as there are no sanitary towels available in Angola. We are asking for more from aid agencies so we can send someone to either Lusaka, Zambia, or to Congo-Brazzaville, to buy large quantities, but we have a problem finding hard cash.

I like the idea of us making sanitary towels in the settlements. It might end this problem, but where would we get a constant supply of materials? If we talk in terms of cultivating cotton this is something for the future. But what do we do right now?

9   ANC Women Speak

Outwrite

One of the most prominent organisations opposing apartheid is the African National Congress (ANC). Banned in South Africa more than 20 years ago, whilst in exile the ANC has called for armed struggle and is now being consulted internationally as the major political opposition to the ruling apartheid regime.

The following extracts are taken from an interview with two representatives of the ANC Women's Section which first appeared in the British feminist newspaper, *Outwrite* (No 41, November 1985).

What is women's participation in the ANC?

Women in the ANC are still in the process of struggle to advance themselves, to take up more areas of responsibility within the movement.

The ANC delegation to the Nairobi end of decade conference was quoted as saying: 'It would be suicidal for us to adopt feminist ideas. Our enemy is the system and we cannot exhaust our energies on women's issues'.

I think that to a lot of our comrades, feminism has a negative, Western feminist context. The organisation is very seriously committed to the emancipation of women but cannot see that as a separate struggle from our overall liberation struggle. We think that our actual liberation will be meaningless if it doesn't encompass women's emancipation, but for our women, the only way to really achieve that is to participate now as much as possible in the forces that are changing society.

What power has the women's section to actually change ANC policy?

The women's section has a strong voice within the movement and has taken up issues, like our child-care centre in Tanzania which was set up to make it possible for women to resume their duties and activities as soon as possible. There has been a slow and painful process with men starting to participate in that kind of thing. I think that as a political organ within the movement, at regional level right up to central level, though it can't enforce things they do get fed into the channels that affect decision making.

The political position of the movement is that the emancipation of women is a task for all of us but, as it has been put, the oppressed have the greater duty to take up the initiative and strive for liberation so there is that orientation. But in terms of practical issues . . .

I feel it necessary that there is a women-only debate on, for example, wife-battering. In Nicaragua, the women's organisation has demanded and achieved from the government that wife-batterers get expelled from the organisation or imprisoned. They stress that women's liberation is the responsibility of everyone, that the men have a role to play but there is a need for women to claim their own autonomy and space to debate and decide on things such as that to be implemented by the central body.

The difference in the Nicaraguan situation is that their government is in power and is building and progressing rapidly. These are all the things that we will look forward to.

It's not just a question of the Sandinistas being in power. Cuba went through nearly 25 years without any acknowledgement that women are a valid force. Suddenly they are awakening to the horrendous status of women, which is the same as that of most women in Latin America who find themselves without socialism. That's why it is important to question, challenge and pose those things now so that they are not left aside.

I think the concept that you can postpone these questions until after liberation is a very self-defeating one. We have been enriched particularly by the experience of the Organisation of Angolan Women, which we have a lot of contact with. So many of their issues are exactly what is going to be facing us, for example, an incredibly high rate of illiteracy among women. This is one of the major things they took up during the struggle, let alone after they achieved power.

What is women's involvement in Umkhonto we Sizwe (the ANC army)? What sort of support is provided for women at the front line?

I wouldn't be in a position to talk about specific arrangements. What I know is that women who become combatants in our people's army get the same training as men. I think it is true that they are still in a minority but they are not given a different type of role.

The army's journal, *Dawn*, and also the internal propaganda that goes into the country, has descriptions from young women explaining why they joined Umkhonto and how they find their experience in the army. I remember a phrase that one of them used, about the struggle in Lamontville (which started with an anti-rent increase protest). She discovered that the bullets of the Boers did not discriminate between men and women and that very much determined her to join our people's army.

What about your work within South Africa – links with the UDF (United Democratic Front), and the level of organisation or non-organisation in rural areas (particularly isolated areas of white-owned farms which employ a large number of black workers)?

Without any doubt, the level of organisation and mobilisation in urban areas is much stronger than in rural areas but because of the government's policy of forced removals, influx control and so on, you find people from the urban areas are dumped in some of the rural areas.

Often there might be resistance in the rural areas that never reaches the light of day. Because it's isolated, it's more difficult for those people to link up with the national movement.

People in rural areas – and increasingly they are using female labour – are notoriously difficult to organise. The difficulty is to get a place where one can meet them. It would be easier if there was a little town or a shopping area. These are the strategic problems in mobilisation . . . I think I can say, after the consultative conference, that it is one of our priorities that women in the bantustans and the white-owned farming areas are organised into trade unions and so, therefore, into the ANC (not the ANC as such, but into mobilisation and organised resistance). For a lot of women who are dumped in the bantustans and so on, their resistance is to leave those areas and come and squat in the squatter camps around the cities. They fight and they keep on coming back no matter how many times they are moved.

It seems that the emphasis of the ANC is on dismantling apartheid as an aberration of human rights. Is it a strategy to concentrate on the issue of apartheid rather than the class issue?

No, I don't think that's quite a correct interpretation of our policies. First of all, one of the clauses of the Freedom Charter is that people shall share in the country's wealth and then it specifies that banks and monopoly industries must be nationalised.

It isn't a socialist programme – saying that the working class will take control of the means of production – but it envisages a kind of people's democracy in which the state ensures that the welfare of the people is catered for in the economic structure of the country. Our strategy and tactics document goes a bit further because it looks at the experiences of countries that have attained liberation but where this hasn't really changed people's conditions of life very much – although obviously independence was a very important gain and the ANC would never dismiss this lightly.

We are very conscious that we want a much more far-going transformation of our society. We have said that we feel the best way to guarantee that is for the working class to play a leading role in the liberation alliance. The ANC has of course had a very long alliance with SACTU (the South African Congress of Trade Unions) and the South African Communist Party.

The call for general rebellion in recent months hasn't been accompanied by the provision of arms for people to defend themselves. Why is that? Does the ANC ideologically want to destabilise the regime by organising "spontaneous uprisings", not necessarily launch an all-out armed struggle?

I think there has been a definite shift towards a call for a people's war and I don't think it's a question of not wanting to arm the people but the amazing difficulty of arming the people. There are cases – many of which are not reported properly – in which the people are armed, which indicates that arms are going into SA but very slowly.

There was a funeral in Guguletu, which is a Cape Town township, where they threw a grenade from among the crowd which exploded and injured several police. The ANC is calling on people to form cells and get weapons and use guerrilla tactics to do hit and run operations. We want industrial sabotage as another aspect of the people's war.

Our tactic is to make the country unworkable, ungovernable for the regime. We've called on people not just to destroy the puppet councils in their communities but to set up people's committees, street committees etc., to start the embryos of people's power. There are various possibilities of how things could develop. There could come a stage where the tactic of a national general strike might be a possibility but that depends on the conditions that have come about.

Our main challenge at the moment is to strengthen our underground organisation. There is massive popular support for the ANC but we have to have those people organised so that they can act cohesively to start shifting the balance – where casualties are not so largely on our side and too few on the side of the enemy . . .

Do you have any contact with, or do you work with, the South African Women's Federation?

That is one of the legal, democratic organisations in SA but there is a whole historical link. When the ANC was legal, the ANC Women's League was the backbone of the SA Women's Federation. There are still personalities there who were in the Women's League.

Today the Federation isn't really a national organisation, it's active mainly in the Transvaal. The ANC would like to see a national organisation developing, but up to now this hasn't been achieved.

What kind of solidarity work would you like women to do in Britain?

The main campaign that we are involved in at the moment is for women to give material aid for the women and children in our school in Tanzania. We also need financial support in the sense that people should understand (and particularly we would hope to reach the women's movement here) the specific kind of oppression that women in SA experience and the nature of their incredibly brave struggle under conditions like the so-called population control programme. There is more or less enforced sterilisation or enforced use of Depo Provera as the only contraceptive offered.

You get stamped in your pass book if you've been sterilised or if you're on Depo Provera and you stand more of a chance of getting a job.

The regime must have contradictions in fulfilling its economic needs on the one hand (i.e., it needs a large, black workforce) and its racist ideology on the other . . .

There are these contradictions. Although essentially the white establishment has common interests, big business might want a whole lot of women as cheap labour, but apartheid, the ruling clique, says no, if women come to the towns they'll get permanent and established and then we can't have proper apartheid any more.

We would also like women in this country to campaign around and demand the unconditional release of women political prisoners and detainees, who are often sexually assaulted. Political prisoners aren't allowed any study material, regular visits or letters.

We would like British women to add their voice to the call for sanctions. Also, if you are in a women's section of a trade union you can push through motions that your union will encourage and support people who boycott SA goods or refuse to handle them.

The women at Dunnes Stores in Dublin, for example, were absolutely magnificent. They were prepared to put their jobs on the line . . . they were very, very brave women.

10 Kanak Women: Out of the Kitchen into the Struggle

Susanna Ounei

Susanna Ounei is a representative of the Kanak Socialist National Liberation Front and founder of the Group of Kanak and Exploited Women in Struggle, based in New Caledonia in the South Pacific. While studying in New Zealand in 1984, she spoke to the newspaper of CORSO, the relief agency which sponsored her trip, about the role of women in her country's struggle for independence.

Since the beginning, the women were always the grassroots of the struggle. It was the women who raised the children and hid them while the men went to war against the French. The French understood that, and when they killed they killed not only the men but also the women.

The women worked quite hard during the occupation of land. When we go to occupy land, we don't go by car, we go by foot and it's not flat land but like a mountain.

We build a symbolic Kanak house on the land to tell the whites this is our land and they don't have to come back to it. We start at 3 or 4 am because the men have to go to the forest and cut the trees and the women get herbs and thick bark to use for a roof.

Some of the men stand guard because the fascists come with guns ready to shoot our people. When they come – the white settlers or the army – we both, men and women, face them.

So after each occupation of land each movement or each group says what we think about the occupation – if it was positive or if there was something wrong or if there is any suggestion. We raise the problem of women, the exploitation of women in the tribe, in the house, everywhere.

For us Kanak women, we have to politicise everything to get a just society. Their [Kanak men] attitude to the women is just exactly that of the army. Other political movements created their own women's section to cook for the men when they had general assemblies. We wanted a group to fight against that.

The Kanak women's struggle doesn't date from today or last year, but for 131 years. In 1853 when the country was first colonised, the men were fighting against the French army. It was the old women who hid the children from the French army and that's one of the reasons we survived.

The enemy upfront – racism

Our generation knew racism very well. It was blatant and we watched our parents bowing and scraping to the bosses because they had seen how these bosses had treated their parents.

We knew racism in our classrooms from our teachers. I was brought up in the white town of Noumea, not with my tribe in Ouvea. Our teachers used to call us 'dirty Kanaks' and other abusive words. These same people who treated us so badly are now in positions of authority in the church of New Caledonia.

The hidden enemy – sexism

In 1969 the reputation of Kanak women was to sleep in the beds of the white bosses. They were only good enough to be chatted up by the whites. When the French soldiers came from France to do their military service in New Caledonia, they made a lot of our women pregnant.

About this time the first Kanak student to return from France, Nidoish Naisseline, had formed a group called 'Les Foulards Rouges' – the Red Scarves. This group was formed to reclaim the Kanak identity for women as well as men. Also at this time I met Dewe Gorodey and we fought together to give back value to the words used by the whites to abuse us. We formed three groups of Red Scarves, one for each of the Loyalty Islands. The group formed on the main island was called '1878' after the year of the first major revolt of the Kanak people against colonisation.

These groups came together to protest and work on the mainland. At this time we worked in mixed groups, but had none specially for women.

In 1974 we protested on 24 September, the date of French colonisation. This time 12 of us were imprisoned, nine men and three women – me, Dewe and another woman. We were badly beaten up. We spent a whole day being questioned while they tried to pin responsibility for the action on one of us. The next day we were all sentenced to six months prison, and at this point the Kanak people woke up and started asking themselves why we were in prison. They campaigned right through New Caledonia to collect money so that they could bring two lawyers from France. The lawyers arrived one month later for the appeal, and managed to reduce the sentences to two months.

While I was in prison with Dewe, we began to look more deeply into the problem of women. We were both very active as women in the struggle against the colonists and the army. Talking to each other in prison we found that we had both been beaten up several times and had both ended up in the courts.

Not just racism

Both of us felt it was important to look more deeply into the problems of women. We began to realise that we weren't just fighting for independence – the struggle was on several levels. It was a question of racism but it wasn't just that, because while we were fighting racism, women were still being beaten up, being made to stay at home with no opportunities whatsoever.

We also asked why there were only two of us struggling, why weren't more women with us? We realised that while the men talked about politics, they didn't like it when the women talked about politics.

When Dewe and I came out of prison we planned to pose these problems to the Red Scarves.

We decided that tradition had something to do with this, so we said we wanted nothing more to do with tradition caused by the culture of colonialism. So they began to treat us as theoreticians. It was okay to fight against colonisation but not against sexism. We said we were conscious of sexism because at meetings it was always the women in the kitchen and the men sitting around the table.

So we toured the whole island and had many meetings but each time the woman would be in the kitchen, we would meet with the men but the women couldn't come. At each meeting we asked why the women couldn't come and meet us.

Assembling the women

After the creation of Palika, the Kanak Liberation Party, we called a big meeting, a General Assembly for women. Many women came from a region called Koindomé but their spokesperson was a man. When I saw that I asked why on earth a man was speaking for women, why didn't the women speak for themselves? I spoke up because none of the women had dared to tell the man to leave because of tradition and custom, and because the women had always been brought up in this society to be very timid. We had a vote and all the women voted that the male spokesperson from Koindomé should leave. The man then said he thought the decision was sexist!

At this stage of the struggle for the rights of women, we were having many problems. In many ways it wasn't the women who were selling out, it was the men.

In 1979 there was a hotel in Ouvea which kept on being burnt. Our young people were accused of being responsible. We brought all the women together and had a big demonstration and brought out pamphlets to denounce the system. The demonstration lasted all morning and we blocked all the cars and the roads. The men were also involved but this time it was organised by the feminist section of Palika.

Political divisions

About this time there were divisions emerging within Palika, with disagreements on strategy. Eventually Naisseline and I left with others and founded the Libération du Kanak Socialiste (LKS), the Kanak Socialist Liberation Party. Dewe stayed in Palika, and I continued to pose the problem of women in LKS. A women's committee was formed in LKS. There was a women's section in all the New Caledonia independence parties, but they didn't change anything.

Even in LKS it was the husbands who formed the women's sections, and their activities were limited to sewing and making cakes for the Party. When I tried to bring up the problems of teenage mothers or battered wives, they said it was just theory.

A new women's group

In 1983 I gave up trying to influence the women's sections within the party and formed a Kanak women's group, the Groupe des Femmes Kanaks Exploitées en Lutte (GFKEL).

We still have to take some very strong stands to get the men to take our ideas seriously and it's very difficult. We take part in political action at all levels. We decided to take action to demand the release of Kanaks arrested after the Koinde tribe had protested against a sawmill owner whose milling operations had polluted the river on which the tribe depended for survival. Six of us chained ourselves to the railings of the French Governor's residence for 20 hours until the cops came and removed us. They didn't press charges, so that night we went to the local television station, at the time the news was being broadcast live, to publicise the reasons for our action. We threw a statement in front of the newsreader and chanted 'Release the Koinde prisoners. Kanak independence now'.

After all these actions, we (the GFKEL) posed the problem of battered women because we were always seeing women with black eyes and teenage mothers who have suffered because of ignorance about contraception. We also asked about the status of women in the struggle and after independence. This question was rather embarrassing for some men. They understand the problems of colonialism, but they don't understand the women's struggle. We have realised that only we women can do anything about it.

The only group which is helping us is the Kanak Trade Union Movement. They are the only men who have finally recognised that more than lip-service must be paid to the role and status of women.

11   Kurdish Women: Their Lives and Struggles

Iranian Women Students' Federation (USA)

This brief article is taken from the quarterly magazine *Women and Struggle in Iran* (No. 3, Summer 1984), published by the Women's Commission of the Iranian Student Association based in Chicago, USA.

In September 1979, less than seven months after the February uprising, the Islamic Republic's regime waged a major military attack against Kurdish towns. The fighting that had been going on since the declaration of *de facto* autonomy by Kurdish nationalist and leftist forces in March 1979, had reached new dimensions. The indiscriminate bombing of towns, coupled with the advance of tanks on Kurdish cities in September 1979, was the first of many attempts by the government to 'wipe out Kurdish resistance'. Far from bringing about the quick victory sought by the regime, however, it marked the beginning of four years of struggle by Kurdish men and women. Four years of civil war during which the government imposed economic sanctions on the liberated areas, executed thousands of revolutionaries, massacred hundreds of Kurdish peasants and bombarded civilian areas. During this period Kurdish men and women have shown exceptional courage and determination to stop a far better-equipped and stronger army. In this underdeveloped region of Iran, women suffer countless forms of exploitation and deprivation, yet they have played a unique role in defending the Kurdish revolution. In paying tribute to their courage in the present article, we shall try to describe some of the aspects of their lives and their struggles.

In Kurdistan, like all other areas of Iran, the division between the town and countryside is very wide. In the urban areas women participate in social production. Sections of petit bourgeois women are employed in service industries or by the bureaucracy, while the poorer women find work in small manufacturing firms. Inevitably the participation of women in politics started in the cities. Kurdish women who had participated in the demonstrations prior to the overthrow of the Shah, took an active role in opposition to the Islamic Republican regime when it refused to grant autonomy to Kurdistan. In the first major attack against the city of Sanandaj (southern capital of the Kurdish region), as the army advanced on the main road to town, Kurdish women and children lay down on it, physically blocking the entrance to the city. The retreat of the Iranian army tanks, in the face of such a resolute resistance, was a major victory for the Kurdish people. It proved to the world that, contrary to the claims of the Islamic regime, it was not small 'groups of bandits' who had taken over Kurdish cities; it proved that the Kurdish nation, men and women, young and old, were united and determined to fight for the right to self-determination.

In the first year of the civil war, in many Kurdish cities, women took up guard duty. In the city of Morivan, women shared guard duty in most of the posts set up around the city. In later battles for the control of the cities, most eyewitness reports mention especially the role of and the courage of women: nurses who stayed in the hospitals throughout the fighting, while hospitals were shelled by army tanks and planes; women who, with little military training, went to the trenches built throughout the city.

Soon after the first war, most of the guerrillas were forced to leave the cities in order to stop further destruction of life and property. The women who stayed behind took over the political organisations. Their immediate task concentrated on collecting financial and material support for the *pishmargehs* (Kurdish guerrillas) in the mountains. Their role in maintaining the link between the guerrillas in the liberated areas and the Kurdish people in the towns and villages under government control has been a crucial factor in keeping the revolution alive. Women regularly cross the government road blocks, defeating the economic sanctions imposed on the liberated areas. They supply the guerrillas with everything from food and medicine to books and gunpowder.

Women have been instrumental in maintaining the level of political activity in Kurdish towns, in both the publication and distribution of revolutionary newspapers, leaflets and pamphlets.

In the Kurdish countryside, the remnants of feudal and tribal customs still govern day to day life. In many villages the custom of 'Zan be Zan' (exchange of women) prevails. A family will allow the marriage of their daughter only if they can gain a woman from the groom's family (i.e., if their son can marry a daughter from the groom's family, usually a sister). This tradition shows clearly most peasant families' dependence on the chores taken up by women. Housework itself is a difficult task in the harsh weather conditions of this mountainous region; women have to carry water from distant fountains, break wood for heating and cooking, and wash dishes and clothes in freezing water. But in addition to their housework, Kurdish peasant women have to work in the fields, look after the cattle or weave carpets day and night. In many areas, polygamy is common. Because of the patriarchal family relations, men often beat up their wives and daughters.

During the last four years, the living conditions of Kurdish peasants have deteriorated considerably. It is the women who bear the burden of the difficult conditions as they have to feed the family despite the severe food shortages caused by the government sanctions and the destruction of agriculture. In recent years many peasants have become homeless (forced to flee their homes after the capture of their village by the army and the revolutionary guards). Most villages in the liberated areas face new problems because of overpopulation. For the refugees it is difficult to adapt to their new conditions, they are left landless and penniless in a region of Iran where basic food prices are enormous. But the sense of solidarity is very high; most families in the village share their meagre food rations with the refugees and the guerrillas who are staying in or passing from the village. There can be no doubt about the solid support expressed by Kurdish men and women for the nationalist cause. In the fierce battles of 1983, waged to recapture villages, Kurdish peasants fought alongside the guerrillas. In many villages, middle-aged Kurdish women stayed on during the fighting, helping the guerrillas by bringing ammunition, looking after the injured, preparing and distributing food amongst the fighters.

Since the February uprising and the initial formation of the liberated areas, many women have joined the ranks of the guerrillas. Most of the women guerrillas work in areas traditionally associated with women: welfare (both in the field hospitals, the village clinics, etc.) or in the publication of revolutionary newspapers in the liberated areas. All women *pishmargehs* take part in military training but only a small number participate in military operations.

The success of women *pishmargehs* has been in raising the consciousness of peasants, especially peasant women. Initially their arrival in the liberated areas caused an uproar amongst the peasants. Many villagers did not respect women guerrillas, nor did they take them seriously. Peasant women were even more hostile as they found the idea of 'women in men's clothes, armed with rifles' distasteful and alien to their culture and traditions. Yet, after the initial difficulties, with patience and perseverance, the women guerrillas proved in practice their seriousness in revolutionary struggle. Today they play a very important role in the social welfare of villages in the liberated areas, working as teachers, nurses and political activists, as well as taking up guard duty in defence of the village. Because of strict Islamic traditions, Kurdish women, especially in the countryside, rarely speak to male strangers. But women guerrillas usually find a receptive audience amongst women and the youths in the villages they visit for political propaganda, thus transforming the general support for the nationalist cause into active participation of peasant women in the people's war against the Islamic Republic's regime.

On the military front, the government, despite using heavy artillery and tens of thousands of soldiers and *pasdars*, has been unable to recapture a considerable section of the liberated areas, especially away from the main roads. But even in the areas where the regime has gained control, the special relations between the guerrillas and the peasants stemming from the experience of the last four years, have insured the continuation of the support of the population for the guerrillas. The Iranian army and the Pasdaran are treated as an occupying army, and the government is, indeed, a very long way from 'wiping out' Kurdish resistance.

12　Women Behind Bars

Palestinian Women's Work Committee[1]

In keeping with a long, though little recorded, history of women's participation in Palestinian resistance against foreign domination, a new grass-roots women's movement has been built up in the occupied territories in recent years. Most of its work is carried out by four women's committees, each representing different political tendencies within the Palestine Liberation Organisation (PLO). The women's committees, though autonomous, have formed a coordination committee within which to work together. In the words of one of the committees in the occupied West Bank and Gaza Strip, the Women's Work Committee:

> All women's movements in the occupied territories are an integral part of the Palestinian national movement. Palestinian women have participated in the ongoing struggle for social progress and national independence. The occupied territories have witnessed a continual increase in the number of women taking part, not only in social and charitable women's institutions, but also in the ranks of the national movement . . .
> To strengthen these positive developments a well-rooted approach was needed in order to build a united, mass women's movement that would contribute to the efforts of all women and women's institutions in the occupied territories. This new approach was necessary for strengthening the public's support for women's issues and for attracting large numbers of women from rural and urban areas, as well as refugee camps, and from all different sectors of society.
> The Women's Work Committee [WWC] in the occupied West Bank and Gaza Strip is a mass-based social, educational, cultural and national organisation composed of Palestinian women from all social classes. It works towards improving women's economic, social and cultural positions and defending women's basic right to work, to education and self-development. The WWC also gives equal importance to uniting women in defence of the Palestinian people's national rights, including the right to return, to self-determination and to the establishment of an independent national state.

[1] The Women's Work Committee (WWC) is one of four women's committees in the Occupied Territories, and has been quoted from here because it is the oldest (established 1978) and largest of the four. The main Palestinian women's union, representing also those in exile, is the General Union of Palestinian Women (GUPW) (see Vol. 1), which is an official section of the PLO.

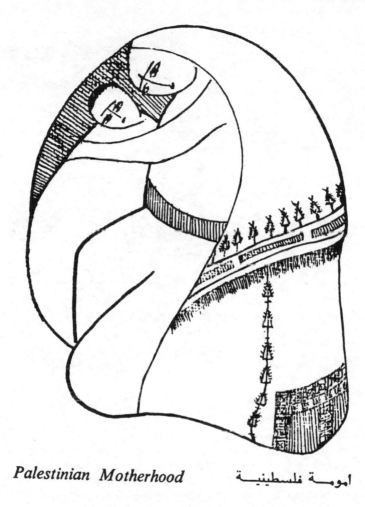

Palestinian Motherhood   امومـــة فلسطينيـــة

The Committee's goals include equal pay for equal work, union membership for women, and paid maternity leave; the establishment of literacy centres, especially in the rural areas; provision of health guidance, and mother and child-care centres; and support for prisoners and their families.

This article and interview describing protest action by Palestinian women in Israeli prisons is taken from the newsletter of the Women's Work Committee (No 3, April 1985) which was formed in 1978.

All these resources have been kindly provided by Sara Gowen who has visited the occupied territories on several occasions to carry out research and to work as an editor on a local Palestinian magazine in the English language. She has just completed a book on Palestinian women's organisations in the occupied West Bank, to be published in late 1987.

طريق المرأة

International Women's Day, 8 March 1984, marked a particularly important achievement for Palestinian women under occupation, and in particular for Palestinian women in Israeli prisons. On that day, prison authorities in Neve Tirza prison near Ramle finally agreed to Palestinian women prisoners' demands that they not be forced to cook and serve prison guards, thus ending a 15-month strike by women prisoners there.

The strike had been not only exceptionally long, but extremely harsh. Prison guards had tear-gassed women inside their cells in a widely-reported incident; authorities had also tried to break the strike by locking women in their cells for 23 hours a day, and forbidding them family visits and access to books and newspapers. Women in Neve Tirza had launched several hunger strikes in the 15-month period; the last finally led to their victory.

As we celebrate International Women's Day 1985, however, women in Neve Tirza have once again been forced to go on strike to protest against inhuman prison conditions. After women prisoners marked a Palestinian anniversary in December 1984, prison authorities retaliated by removing all books and newspapers from the women, and placed 14 women in solitary confinement. Prisoners were on strike for much of January and support sit-ins were held at the International Red Cross

offices in Jerusalem. On 12 February, women began a hunger strike to protest against the new restrictions and to demand an end to work in defence-related industries and an increase in visits and educational activities among prisoners.

Prison conditions, however, are only one aspect of the problem of Palestinian women prisoners. Even more basic is the issue of *why* these women are imprisoned in the first place. Siham Barghouti, a WWC Executive Committee member, was released in August 1984 from Neve Tirza prison after serving a two-and-a-half year prison sentence. What was her 'crime'? Siham was stopped by soldiers when she was outside the city of Bireh, at a time when she was restricted to that city by a town arrest order.

Town arrest orders are imposed without any judicial proceedings on individuals in the occupied territories for six-month periods and can be renewed indefinitely. No reason other than the general rubric of 'security' is given for the order and the individual has no chance to defend him or herself in court. These orders are thus a convenient way to restrict individuals who have not broken any military regulation, but whose activities or ideas are disapproved of by the military authorities. Over 100 individuals in the West Bank and Gaza are currently under such restrictions.

Now entering her fifth year of town arrest is Zahera Kamal, another member of the WWC Executive Committee. Her last order slightly eased the terms of her restriction, thanks, it can be assumed, to growing international concern over her case. Amnesty International adopted Zahera as 'Prisoner of the Month' in 1984, and a number of women and human rights organisations around the world have been active in combating Zahera's town arrest, the longest town arrest to date of a woman in the occupied territories.

International and local protest also played a part in lifting the town arrest of Amal Wahdan, on 12 February 1984. Amal, also on the WWC Executive Committee, is the first case of a town arrest order being lifted before it was fully served. Amal attributes this success to publicity and protest, and especially noted the activity of the Israeli organisation, Women Against Occupation.

The widespread detention and imprisonment of males in the West Bank and Gaza inevitably both affects and propels women to act. Women's sit-ins at the International Red Cross in Jerusalem to protest against conditions at such infamous prisons as Nafha and Jneid have become familiar sights. In addition, the WWC and other women's organisations in the occupied territories have active programmes to support prisoners' families whose economic and social situation is often extremely difficult while the main breadwinner is in prison.

The series of travel restrictions and bans imposed by the military authorities also seriously affect women in the occupied territories. These range from collective bans where all inhabitants of a targeted village or town are banned from travel for a certain period of time, as a collective punishment, to individual bans on travel for persons the military government opposes. Many activists in the WWC, for example, have been refused permission to travel abroad. Other active women are also targeted: Samiha Khalil, the head of the Ramallah-based charitable society Inash El Usra, has, on a number of occasions, been denied permission to attend conferences abroad that were important for the development of the society.

The woman prisoner is perhaps the most dramatic example of the denial of freedom to Palestinian women under occupation. In addition, however, a web of restrictions and regulations constantly remind Palestinian women that they live, not under their own government and representatives, but at the mercy of a foreign military occupation.

Interview: Siham Barghouti

Early in 1982, Israeli soldiers stopped Siham Barghouti on the road between the towns of Bireh and Nablus on the occupied West Bank. By being there, she was committing a 'crime' for, since June 1980, she had been under town arrest in Bireh. For being outside this town, Siham served two-and-a-half years in prison, from February 1982 to August 1984. She was a part of the historic nine-month strike at Neve Tirza, Israel's only women's prison. Here, Siham speaks about the conditions Palestinian prisoners face and about the changing position of Palestinian women under occupation.

Some people have asked me what I'd done to be under town arrest. What I'd done was to speak of our national rights as Palestinians and that we want an independent government. Every Palestinian wants that – it's not a crime. And I was active in the Women's Work Committees. As for breaking the town arrest, it's my right to go anywhere in my country.

When I was arrested, I shared the experience of thousands of our people. First you're interrogated – often in the Moscobiye prison in Jerusalem. It's cold there, you're not allowed a change of clothes, the food is disgusting. They pour hot or cold water over you, maybe keep a bag over your head for days at a time. They put you alone in a cell, won't let you see your lawyer or the Red Cross until they finish with you . . . and that can take weeks.

After the interrogation, they put you in prison. Neve Tirza is a tough place, but the West Bank prisons make it look like a showplace. [*Editor's note*: Neve Tirza is near Ramle, inside the Israeli state]. There at least we got milk every two weeks – on the West Bank never. West Bank prisons are in bad condition, and in winter they're very cold. There are 25 men in a room. They get stomach problems, back problems: after a few years, their health is permanently damaged just from the living conditions – especially the teenagers, who need good food to grow.

But I found that to be arrested and live in prison is a very rich experience, because you get to know your enemy face to face, and you get to know how Palestinian women can struggle. You learn that women can take an important part in the whole resistance to the occupation. Because of the things they have learned, women who have been prisoners can take the whole Palestinian women's movement forward.

The strike at Neve Tirza was a good example. In June 1983, the warden ordered us to cook for the guards. We refused – the guards always tried to humiliate us – but we offered to cook for all the prisoners instead. The warden rejected this. We stopped doing our regular prison work, and the warden took away our so-called privileges: clothing and books our families and the Red Cross had brought. Radios and newspapers were removed as well.

They were trying to isolate us. We were locked four or six in a cell 23 hours a day. We had visits only every two months. But we smuggled the books back from the library; newspapers out of the wastebaskets. We'd lie on our beds with our back to the door and read. We'd read in the bathroom. We'd turn our faces to a corner and read. It was our right to read.

The warden must have thought, 'If they don't have their books, they can't keep up the strike.' He said that if we insisted on reading the books, he'd take them away altogether.

That's exactly what happened. On 21 October 1983, when we were locked in our cells after supper, the guards came to the library in our section and we could see them putting our books in bags. Those books were like our children or our food. We couldn't bear to see them taken away. We began to chant slogans and beat on our cell doors.

A special squad of soldiers came then and sprayed us with gas until we could no longer shout. Two weeks later, some of us still couldn't speak. But we only became stronger. 'Even if they want to kill us,' we said, 'we will continue.' We began a hunger strike.

By that time, the prison administration was getting a lot of questions: In a democratic country in the 20th century, is that how you treat people for wanting to read? They asked us to negotiate, and on 9 March 1984, they agreed that no political prisoner would cook for the guards.

So we achieved the aim of our strike: to let them know we were political prisoners. We said, 'We are not instruments but human beings. We will not obey orders that are against our principles, no matter what they do to us. Inside these walls, behind these doors, you can see how Palestinian women can struggle.' Like Palestinians in the Israeli men's prisons, we taught the authorities that political prisoners are strong.

But we have a special position as women. We live in a Third World society. People start telling us as small girls that we must only get married and keep house. But we're half the nation – the occupation has taught us that. The occupation has forced many of us to go out and work: a first step towards being active politically. And whenever our relatives are put in prison, when we see soldiers beating shopkeepers or students in the street, there's a revolution in our souls.

So Palestinian women are breaking out of old restrictions to play our part in the national cause. We must take that part, not as helpers, but as equals. Without our work and our strength, our people can never win our self-determination.

Part 3:
Education: A Woman's Right to Learn

13 The Myth of Equal Opportunity in Nigeria

Ayesha Imam

Ayesha Imam is National Co-ordinating Secretary for Women in Nigeria, an organisation of women and men based on the belief that, while both sexes are exploited and oppressed by Nigeria's socio-economic system, women suffer most. Here she outlines some of the demands and conclusions expressed during the Third Annual Conference of Women in Nigeria, held in Port Harcourt at the end of April 1984, which took as its theme 'Women and Education'.

The theme of this conference reflects the profound importance education plays in providing the individual with the basic, necessary tools for informed interaction and participation in Nigeria today. Women make up more than half the Nigerian population, and have always contributed fully and unstintingly to the development and betterment of society. Their continued contribution and full participation require that they have access to the benefits of formal and informal education, to the same level and of the same quality as that given to men. Only in this way can women provide their full input to the socio-economic development of Nigeria.

The Conference was attended by people from all over Nigeria and included teachers, students, journalists, administrators, lecturers and research specialists. Over 30 papers were presented. After three days of analysis and discussion the conference participants reached the following conclusions.

A Federal Ministry of Labour report of 1971, which states that 'A Nigerian girl has equal opportunity for education as a boy', is wishful thinking. In every state of the Federation there are more boys receiving formal education than there are girls. For example, in Borno State only two girls are in school for every five boys.[1] While generally at primary school level the percentage of girls is 30–40 per cent, at secondary it drops to 20–30 per cent and at tertiary level it is only 10–15 per cent.[2]

Not only are there more boys than girls in schools but also there are more schools (and school places) for boys than there are for girls. In Kaduna State there are three times as many boys-only as girls-only schools.[3]

Women in Nigeria therefore calls on State and Federal Governments to create more school places for girls, since at present, though there are more girls than boys in the population, girls are competing for far fewer school places.

Another factor which reduces women's participation in education is social prejudice against girls' education. Thus for example, 76 per cent of families in one study would educate their sons but not their daughters, if finances were limited.[4] Another study showed that sons are more likely to be educated but that girls' chances of education increase if their parents are in a high socio-economic group.[5]

Women in Nigeria wishes the government to engage in a strong and positive drive to enrol more girls in schools. There should be no school fees at any level as this discriminates against all children of parents in the lower socio-economic groups, but particularly against girls.

Not only are there fewer girls receiving education, but even those who do receive a different type of education from boys. Girls are always encouraged to follow subjects related to the home, the family, arts and social sciences, in order to be qualified to take up jobs as secretaries, nurses, teachers, caterers, and so on – the acceptable 'feminine' occupations. Very few girls are encouraged to study science subjects with the aim of following technological and scientific careers; in fact, many girls are actively discouraged from doing so.

Credit: World University Service

Women employed in technical and mid-level occupations constitute only 8.4% of the total employment figure. This is hardly surprising since at college level the figure for women enrolled on these courses is very low.[6]

It is for the above reasons that Women in Nigeria strongly supports the National Association of Nigerian Students (NANS) in their protest against the reintroduction of school fees. The organisation urges the government to enter into dialogue with the students in an effort to find a solution to the funding of education.

In addition, Women in Nigeria calls on the government and the media to introduce a campaign actively encouraging females to study science and technology subjects. More emphasis and importance should also be placed on science subjects in girls' schools.

When people have had little or no chance of formal education in their youth, adult education becomes essential. Women form the majority in this group.[7] But not only are there fewer adult classes for women, but the types of subjects taught do not enhance the positions of women economically. Studies indicate that while men's adult education includes training in trades such as carpentry, welding, etc., the women are instructed only in what are considered to be 'feminine' fields: cooking, sewing, home economics, etc. This perpetuates the situation where women work only at home and earn hardly anything from their labours.[8]

The disparity in access to adult education classes is not simply between men and women, but also between women of different socio-economic groups. For example most women's adult classes are attended partially, and in many cases wholly, by the wives of men highly placed in society.[10]

Similarly the rigid hours fixed for these classes contribute by limiting the number of women who enrol. The nature of women's responsibility within the home makes it imperative that there is more than one option for women to attend these classes.

Women in Nigeria asks all agencies dealing with adult education (governmental and non-governmental) to open up more adult education classes for women in both rural and urban areas. The organisation also recommends equal access to all categories of women and a review of the curricula so that women can also be trained in the higher income earning trades. Flexible hours must be incorporated into the programme as a way of encouraging enrolment.

For women already working, on-the-job training should be made part of their training programme since women with families find it difficult to go for further training. Trade unions are asked to particularly note this factor.

The well-meaning attempts of the present government to solve the present economic chaos are, however, likely to reduce educational opportunities for the majority of people, and especially for women, and generally result in a further erosion of the living standards and progress of Nigerians.

The reintroduction of hospital fees; the increased retrenchment of workers; the reintroduction of polls and taxes; the ever-increasing shortage and high prices of consumer essentials, and the non-payment of workers' salaries, will all contribute to a further deterioration of living standards for the vast majority of Nigerians. After having lost their jobs and spent all their money on essentials such as food and soap, it will be a miracle if most parents are able to pay school fees, etc. Once again it will be women who are hardest hit.

At present it is the woman who has to make the meagre salary stretch so that the whole family can manage to survive on it. She spends hours in the market searching for the cheapest goods or a cheap alternative. In the rural areas it is also the woman who has to work harder and longer coaxing the land to produce more to feed her family – including, in some cases, the workers and teachers who have not been paid for months. Without this unpaid, and unrecognised, labour of love by women, many people would have been in an even worse position than they are now.

But instead of being applauded for their role in keeping the economy going it seems that women are being seen as the ultimate cause of the present social and economic situation. The focus of the 'War Against Indiscipline' (government-led campaign against prostitution, absenteeism from work, alcoholism, disorderly behaviour and other 'social problems') traces the lack of social discipline to children's indiscipline which is seen as solely the responsibility of women, as mothers. Women in Nigeria protests strongly against this trend. Men, as fathers, are equally responsible for children's discipline. More importantly, the government focus sidesteps the central issue, namely why should it be that people can work all their lives and still be unable to educate their children or be assured of a decent old age?

Similarly, Women in Nigeria condemns the Kano State Government's pronouncement that 'single women' should get married within three months or be 'dealt with'. We question the moral basis on the part of the men making the pronouncement; the material basis of forcing women into marriage for economic sustenance, instead of encouraging them to engage in productive work; and the discriminatory basis in not saying that single men should also get married or be similarly dealt with.

The conclusion of the Conference reaffirmed the fact that no nation can realise full social and economic development unless its citizens are educated to their fullest potential, and that includes women. The education of women must not be considered as secondary because, not only do they make up over half of the population, but they are also the mothers of future generations.

References

The papers referred to below were amongst those presented at the Third Annual Conference of 'Women in Nigeria', held at the University of Port Harcourt, 26–28 April 1984.

1. S. Ogbuagu, 'Statistics on Women in Education'.
2. Federal Republic of Nigeria Social Statistics, 1979: 27, quoted in C. C. Ntamere, 'The Perverse Effect of the New Educational System in Maintaining the Employment Differences Between Men and Women'.
3. A. Imam, H. Mahdi and H. Omole, 'Women's Access to Education: Issues of Development and Equality'.
4. G. B. Roberts, 'Parental Attitude Towards the Education of Female Children: A Survey of Gokana in Bori Local Government Area'.
5. A. Carter and A. Mere, 'Child Rearing in Nsukka: The Impact of Mothers' Education on the Socialisation of their Children'.
6. D. S. Enahoro, 'Constraints to Women Entering Mid-Level Technical Occupations in Nigeria'. (See also 3 above.)

7. H. Seymour, 'Obstacles to Women's Participation in the Development Process: The Need for a New Self-Awareness'.

8. T. Myadze, 'Women's Training Centres from a Broader Perspective'.

9. Ibid.

14 Literacy for Women, Why and How! Some Thoughts in the Indian Context

Kamla Bhasin

Kamla Bhasin has long been dedicated to the mobilisation of India's rural poor, both through her work as an independent feminist activist and as a Programme Officer for the UN Food and Agriculture Organisation in Delhi.

Towards the end of 1984 some women and women's organisations in India called for the start of a nationwide movement for the eradication of female illiteracy by the year 2000. This paper, reprinted from the Indian feminist magazine *Manushi* (No. 26, January–February 1985), was written as a response to this call.

Before launching a nationwide movement to eradicate illiteracy among women there are certain points which need to be thoroughly discussed. First, why such a campaign? What is the analysis on which the launching of such a campaign is based? It is necessary to ask and answer this question because often such campaigns, like the national campaign for family planning, are based on false premises and assumptions and use slogans and arguments which are offensive and insulting to illiterate people.

Often, campaigners for literacy start with statements like 'illiteracy is an offence to mankind'. They ask: 'What is the difference between animals and illiterates?' Some of them assume, or at least their arguments give the impression they assume, that illiteracy is the same as ignorance and lack of intelligence. Such statements are false and offensive to the millions of illiterates in whose name such campaigns are started. These statements also smack of a patronising attitude.

Because illiteracy is widely prevalent among the poor, it is often taken to be a cause of poverty, exploitation and the inhuman conditions of the poor. Conversely, literacy is expected to be the remedy for the removal of poverty, the magic word which will open all doors for the poor. These assumptions need to be challenged because, like the family planning propaganda, they divert attention from the real issues, they catch the wrong end of the stick and, worst of all, they make the poor responsible for their own poverty and misery. The messages which come through are: 'The poor are poor because they bear too many children. They are poor because they are illiterate.'

A campaign for literacy which is not based on a scientific analysis of socio-economic and political realities and which does not explicitly talk about the actual causes of poverty and how becoming literate can and will help the poor, can end only perpetuating false assumptions and confusing the real issue.

It needs to be stated unequivocally that there is no causal relationship between illiteracy and poverty nor is there any evidence that literacy precedes development or that just by becoming literate people have overcome poverty and exploitation.

In the developed countries, universal primary education and literacy came after the process of development was well on its way. In such countries as the People's Republic of China, Vietnam and Cuba, where millions of people were made literate in a short span of time, the literacy campaign was part of a process of revolutionary change and not a separate campaign. The relevance and usefulness of literacy is also not the same for all societies. It is related to how literate the way of life or environment of people is.

Literacy, or for that matter even higher education, does in no way ensure more rational, scientific and human behaviour. Literacy and education alone also do not ensure socially responsible behaviour. In fact, the major problems threatening our world today (nuclear holocaust, over-exploitation of natural resources, environmental pollution, the increasing gap between haves and have-nots, vulgar consumerism) are those which have been created by societies and people who are not only literate but 'educated', and scientifically advanced.

At the level of an Indian village, it is the literate and the educated, such as middlemen, moneylenders, petty bureaucrats, local politicians, who exploit the poor masses. In fact I can never forget what a tribal once told me: 'We are not as afraid of wild animals as we are of "educated" people. We run for our lives when we see someone with white and clean clothes.' By people with white clothes, he meant all those who do not earn their living by physical labour. They can keep clean because they live off the labour of others. They use their literacy and education to dupe and exploit others.

In the context of the proposed movement, what I am pleading for is a clear and scientific analysis of the structure of poverty and exploitation in our society which prevents 75 per cent of women not only from being literate but also from being treated as equals, which prevents them from leading a hunger and disease-free life.

I am of the opinion that literacy alone is no solution to poverty and exploitation and I am also convinced that illiteracy cannot be wiped out without a wider movement and struggle to wipe out poverty, exploitation, maldistribution of resources. Those who are saying eradicate illiteracy, are they also saying eradicate hunger, poverty, exploitation? What is their strategy for that? The strategy for eradication of illiteracy has to be part of and related to the strategy of removal of inequalities and exploitation.

With regard to women, we have to ask some additional questions like – are we also talking of eradication of inequalities between men and women, removal of male domination and patriarchy? How will our literacy campaign ensure this?

Target totally unrealistic

Regarding the 'slogan' eradication of female illiteracy by the year 1990 or even by 2000, in my opinion such a target is totally unrealistic, given the present state of our country and the kind of leadership which exists. Realisation of such a slogan requires a high level of political commitment and political will to eradicate poverty, to reduce the widening gap between haves and have-nots, to stop the further marginalisation of the poor and of women. It also requires a nationwide network of committed workers of all kinds, at different levels, and relevant literacy material in different languages. Unfortunately, none of this is available.

Moreover, literacy is neither a felt need of the poor nor is it a skill which they perceive as the most important one to help them improve their lives. Because of this, such a campaign is not likely to spread like wildfire. My experience of the national adult education programme, which had the government machinery, a very large number of voluntary organisations and vast amounts of money behind it, also does not provide much hope. In view of all this, why give a slogan which we know is unrealistic, why play another trick on the illiterates, why make them even more sceptical of national campaigns? Let us set targets which are attainable.

Literacy: another tool to domesticate the poor?

Related to the question of *why* such a campaign is the *what* or the content and method of literacy campaigns. All literacy classes, primers and campaigns have an underlying ideology, a set of implicit and explicit values – and a purpose. In the past, in India, most efforts made to make people literate have not been related to attempts to liberate people or to empower them. Literacy and even education programmes have led to the domestication of people rather than to their liberation. The content of literacy programmes has not, except in a very few cases, questioned the unjust and exploitative structure of our society. They have in fact been doing the opposite, strengthening and justifying the status quo and the dominant ideology.

The content of most literacy primers has not even been related to the real issues and lives of the poor, their deprivation and exploitation. The village community is shown as harmonious, where every one lives lovingly and peacefully. The conflicts which exist, the perpetual exploitation by one class of another, are never even mentioned. When realities are not discussed, when they are purposely ignored or beautified, how can the process of meaningful change even start?

The primers, in most cases, have been written by urban, middle-class males for middle level, male farmers and they propagate middle-class values. At best, these primers provide some information but they fail to provide a questioning attitude, a sense of confidence and self-respect to the working masses.

To substantiate this point, I would like to quote from a paper by Krishna Kumar entitled 'Politics of literacy' (from *Adult Education and Development*, Bonn, Number 19, September 1982) which gives an overview of literacy programmes carried out in various Third World countries.

The happy village life symbolised through illustration and text in literacy primers is, of course, a figment of imagination. Real villagers are more often characterised by rivalries and strife than harmony and community spirit.

No one who has lived in an Indian village can overlook the dichotomy between the dominant and the oppressed. Yet, the village literacy instructor is supposed to talk about a harmonious community. The primer he [sic] is obliged to use hides all the conflicts and fears that his [sic] illiterate pupils permanently face.

In the attempt to conceal real life conflicts and modes of oppression, the literacy programmes follow a political and economic goal that is seldom stated in an explicit manner. This ideology consists of a plan to 'modernise' the illiterate sections of rural society by incorporating them in the prevailing patterns of consumption and control. The plan operates under the banner of 'social change', but its real intent is to make all strategies of change ineffective. At the same time, it strengthens the existent pattern of authority and distribution of power in the name of evolutionary change and reform.

A typical literacy primer tells the learners how one poor peasant gradually became prosperous by making certain rational decisions, such as the decision to plan his family and to start a new method of cultivation. The gist of such narratives is that a man changed his economic condition by dropping a set of backward and disabling characteristics, and by adopting an alternative set of characteristics that were modern and healthy. The underlying moral of this theme is succintly given in a Turkish literacy lesson: 'Poverty and prosperity depend on the person's own ability'.

According to this economic theory, some people are rich because they are well informed, hard working, and have the motivation to accept innovative ideas. Others are poor because they lack information, and because they are lazy and tradition bound. Following this analysis, literacy primers exhort the illiterate learner to change his [sic] attitudes and behaviour along the lines offered in different lessons.

The areas covered by a typical literary curriculum follow a certain mythology that is now a part of any development project sponsored by government or international aid agencies. A planned nuclear family, mothercraft, sanitation, balanced diet, improvement of technology, a positive attitude towards bureaucratic services, and increased production in agriculture and industry are some of the recurring themes of this mythology.

What is said here is true of most literacy programmes carried out in India so far. I agree with Krishna Kumar when he says:

A realistic curriculum for adult literacy cannot be developed without acknowledging the presence of deep rooted injustice and conflicts in rural society. How can a programme that hides so significant an aspect of the life of poor peasants and the landless capture their imagination? Literacy classes have a poor turnout rate because the curriculum taught in these classes does not relate to the life of the learners as it is. What it reflects is an artificial fantasy world which proclaims the success of the prevailing order.

Perpetuating stereotypes

In order to see what messages, information and values are given through the existing primers for women, we analysed seven such primers used in North India. These primers have been produced by the major government and non-government organisations which are pioneers of literacy work.

The main content of all these primers is housework, childcare, family planning. Although all these primers are mainly for rural women, the only roles in which women are shown are those of housewife and mother. In fact, one of the primers is called *Grah Laxmi* or the House Goddess. Out of seven primers, three talk about marriage in the very first chapter. All these primers completely ignore the fact that 50 to 60 per cent of rural women, all of whom are illiterate and therefore are the main 'targets' for literacy programmes, are also involved in agricultural production, they are farmers and labourers just as the men are. The reality of the primers is the reality not of the poor women but of the middle-class women who sit at home and perform the role of *Grah Laxmi*, they are shown as model women, who live within the four walls and are only mothers and housewives. The cultural norms of a small minority, the upper classes, are imposed on all women. The contribution of millions of women to agricultural production is negated. In one primer, women are told about earning money through sewing. Of what relevance and help can such primers be to women who labour outside the house, who produce food, store it, look after the animals, bring fodder and fuel?

Besides dowry, frequent pregnancies and other social evils, these primers question nothing. The widespread male domination, the double burden of work on women, different kinds of discrimination practised against women are not even mentioned, let alone challenged. In fact, in an Urdu primer, women are shown in *burkha* (meaning the veil) without a comment, as if being in *burkha* is the most natural thing.

The qualities prescribed for women are the age-old ones of sacrifice, self-abnegation, living for others, docility, love, softness. There are stories of Sita, Savitri and Draupadi; there is talk of places of pilgrimage. All these are considered more important and necessary than information on the legal rights of women, and social legislation, like minimum wages, dowry and inheritance legislation, marriage and divorce laws, equal wage laws.

No attempt is made in any of the primers to initiate discussion on any issue. Information and messages are delivered as pre-packaged truths. The learners are not encouraged to ask questions or to challenge existing notions about women's position and role and to form their own opinions.

Defective methodology

Like the content, the methodology of adult literacy has generally been wrong and in effect anti-people. Most adult literacy classes are run like classes for children. In most of these classes, the flow of information and knowledge is one sided – from the urban to the rural areas, from literacy teacher to the learners. The village adult who knows so much about so many things, who knows how to survive in the most adverse living conditions, is suddenly reduced to and treated as someone who knows nothing. The message which often comes through the literacy campaigns is that those who are illiterate are also ignorant, unwise, unintelligent. This is perhaps yet another way for the literate élite to show their own superiority over the illiterates. Such attitudes and behaviour towards illiterate people, instead of building their self-confidence and self-respect, further erode it. This becomes another form of cultural domination. Because most literacy classes are in the main languages and not in local languages, people are given another complex, that 'not only can you not read and write but you cannot even speak properly. The language you speak is no good.'

Such literacy classes end up being another farce, and an insult to the illiterates. Neither are such literacy campaigns meant to, nor can they, equip the poor to master their environment or to deal with the oppressors more effectively.

In the context of all this, it becomes not only legitimate but necessary to ask *why* a campaign to eradicate illiteracy? Why not a campaign to eradicate malnutrition or hunger? Why so much stress on providing literacy skills to women who live in an environment which is by and large not a literate environment? Why not a campaign to provide skills to analyse, or articulate or organise; skills which are more urgently required? Is literacy the first thing rural women want? Have we asked them what they want? My own experience with rural and urban poor, both men and women, shows that becoming literate is not their first need or aspiration. Their urgent and basic needs in most cases are: more income, clean water, fuel, or access to health services. Unless literacy is related to the satisfaction of their basic needs, women are not and will not be interested in acquiring literacy. Imposing literacy from above can only frustrate the campaigners and alienate the illiterates.

Empower the oppressed

I appreciate and share the feeling of those who are proposing a campaign to eradicate female illiteracy, that something needs to be done immediately to change the inhuman living conditions of millions of poor women who also happen to be illiterate. All concerned people need to join hands immediately to take on the challenge; but the challenge, I feel, is not simply eradication of illiteracy. This is only a part of the challenge. In my opinion, the real challenge is to help the poor, oppressed, illiterate women not so much to read and understand the word but to read, understand and control their world. They have to be helped to learn to master not just the three Rs but their entire lives. They have to be helped to acquire the necessary analytical skills to understand the fast changing realities. They must feel that they do not have to continue to accept and adjust to conditions of inhumanity and indignity. They must develop the desire and power to change their own lives, to write their own destiny.

Literacy by itself is no solution for the poor, it is not an adequate skill to bring about any real changes in their life. Illiteracy is not a disease which needs immediate eradication. It is merely one of the symptoms of a very dangerous disease which is inequality, exploitation, poverty. Without attacking the disease we cannot remove the symptoms. Let us start with a correct diagnosis because wrong diagnosis and wrong treatment can only delay things and make the disease worse.

I believe that what we need are consciousness-raising campaigns, campaigns to eradicate superstition. We also need campaigns to remove hunger, malnutrition, exploitation, male domination. Literacy work can be part of these campaigns. It can be a vehicle to carry these campaigns forward.

In the context of any such integrated literacy campaign for women we need to ask the following questions:

1. For which class of women is our campaign primarily going to be? If it is for poor women, then the content of all literacy materials should be related to their lives and roles.
2. What values do we want to propagate?
3. What kind of role do we want women to have in the family and in the society?
4. What are the qualities we would like women to have?

The answers to these questions should determine the content of literacy material. Literacy primers should become vehicles to bring about the desired changes in the knowledge, attitudes and behaviour of women. Folk media like theatre, puppetry, songs, can also be effectively used to provide information and initiate discussion.

A lot of attention needs to be given to the teaching methodology. The methodology used should be participatory and democratic; it should increase the self-confidence, self-respect, articulation and analytical skills of the participants. It should encourage questioning, fearlessness, honesty. There should be a two-way relationship between teachers and students. In fact, they should all be students.

The most crucial part of any meaningful adult education is orientation and training of all the people who conduct adult education centres. This training needs to be properly planned and executed and must be ongoing. A meaningful campaign must be based on a scientific analysis of the situation. It has to be extremely well-planned and well-prepared in terms of teaching material and cadre. Such a campaign should start from below upwards, it should grow from small to big. It should be decentralised and flexible. It should not impose targets and plans from above. It should allow for ample flexibility, innovation and experimentation at local levels.

15 Education: A Tool for Liberation in Tigray

Besserat Asfaw

Tigray is a northern province of Ethiopia whose five million people rely mainly on subsistence farming. After nearly a century of Amhara rule, since 1975 this isolated nation has been engaged in an armed struggle, led by the Tigray People's Liberation Front (TPLF), for self-determination against the central Ethiopian government.

Until the advent of the TPLF life in Tigray had many features of a typical feudal society, also characterised by intense economic and cultural prejudice against women. Deprived of land ownership and bound by tradition, usually in the name of religion, women remained dependent first on their fathers and then on their husbands and/or male children throughout their lives. Today, however, the active participation of women in the liberation struggle, including a high profile on the People's Councils, and the introduction of numerous legal reforms to protect their rights have led to a significant improvement in their status.

Central to this process has been an overwhelming emphasis on education, both in terms of consciousness-raising and the need for women to acquire new skills towards their fuller participation in social production. In January 1986 Besserat Asfaw, longstanding member of the TPLF, spoke to the editor about the changing situation of women in Tigray and, in particular, the role played by the nation's two (shortly to be three) women's schools.

In traditional Tigrayan society women were second-class citizens in every way, both on the cultural and economic level. They were not allowed to own land which is very important since it isolated them from the national source of income. As 'unproductive' beings their main role was to maintain the household. Parents dreaded having daughters as they had to pay a dowry to marry them off – something which often happened to girls as young as seven or eight years old since they were chiefly a burden, another mouth to feed. A rich peasant who had, for instance, three daughters would certainly be poor by the time the last one had found a husband. This economic condition meant that many women had to live either as landed peasants, working as farmhands in the villages, or as prostitutes in the towns. In Sudan there are still about 150,000 Tigrayan nationals working as prostitutes. On top of all this women received no education, had no right to divorce and suffered numerous injustices based on their inferior and 'unholy' status in society.

The TPLF was started by ten people – students and intellectuals – who were committed early on to the equal participation of women in the overall political struggle. Yes, we were influenced to some extent by developments in Vietnam, China and the Soviet Union, but it doesn't take much to realise that one half of society should not just be sitting and watching. For us, as a people cornered by poverty and deprivation, it was a real eye-opener when we began to see how the condition of women indicates where you are and the direction you should be going in if you are to change society. Our political programme has always been very consistent on this issue . . .

Before 1975 there were four schools and only four hospitals for five million people. You can imagine the deprivation. Owing to their inferior status, educational facilities for women weren't even considered. Today, as well as more hospitals and many public health clinics, we have at least 58 schools, two of them specifically for women . . . and that's on top of all the hundreds of literacy schools throughout Tigray.

Our two women's schools are basically for adult women. The first, called March 8th after International Women's Day, when I last heard had 1,300 women. We have no crèche facilities outside so they come with their children. Over four months these peasant women learn how to read and write; do woodwork and participate in agricultural pilot projects on plots of land provided by the school; they learn about the basics in science and nutrition based on the products of Tigray and about their bodies. Religious concepts of women being low and dirty, all have to be defeated.

The second school, Marta, named after the first woman to join the armed struggle, is for fighters. Here, the course lasts for two years, similar to the other but more intensive. Afterwards these women, together with others trained in hospitals, for instance as midwives, are taken in groups around all the villages in order to disseminate their knowledge, and influence people to change. Take for example the problem of land distribution: now women own land, but people's minds don't change straight away and there is still some prejudice amongst the peasantry. Before, women weren't even allowed to use a plough since it was considered to be holy. Skills and laws are useless if attitudes remain unchanged. In this way we see education as first and foremost about consciousness-raising.

We have tried to understand movements in the West, like the suffragette movement and women's struggles in the textile industry earlier this century, and what's happened in countries like Algeria where women played a heroic role in the fight for independence, only to be later forced back into a position of subservience. For Tigrayans the fact that women make up half the world isn't merely some romantic slogan. We are convinced that we, as women, are just as important as are men to any kind of human development. We see education and projects like the women's schools as central in our progress towards justice and equality. But we need help. We want women in the West to understand our struggle and realise that these women in Tigray – 30 per cent of them active fighters – really believe in themselves. We are willing to go as far as we can in the struggle, but we need supplies, more schools, equipment, books, money . . . We ask other women to stretch out their hands, not out of charity but out of the responsibility of all us, as human beings, to help each other.

16 Travel and Training for Rural Women in Papua New Guinea

East Sepik Women's Project

The following two accounts, together with a slightly shortened introduction, are taken from a series of three prepared by the East Sepik Women's Development, Documentation and Communication Project, Papua New Guinea. They are faithful transcriptions of cassette recordings, in Melanesian pidgin, made with these women in their homes in 1985. Thanks to Elizabeth Cox for making them available for this book.

Introduction

During the colonial period and throughout the Island states of the South Pacific region there has developed a certain tradition in the education of women to train other women. Whether this training of trainers has a general orientation or is more directed towards village-based extension and community development work, the means and ends in the process of establishing women leaders tend to be basically the same.

The subjects taught are typically, and often exclusively, home economics and the underlying rationale is the making (moulding) of good wives and mothers. That most Pacific Island women (in fact most women everywhere) might be wives and/or mothers at one stage in their life is not denied. But this does not seem adequate reason to predestine women, through education, to that role and to effectively cut off all other options.

In Papua New Guinea's Non-formal Education programmes today it is usual to find separate training programmes for each sex; young men and women are, in fact, usually taught in different/separate institutions. The same division extends to most village-based extension work. Examination of the content of these sex-differentiated education programmes reveals that despite national programmes and policies to reorient non-formal training back to the village and so-called 'grass-roots' programmes, the training of young men goes on sometimes rather tongue-in-cheek with its rhetoric and routine of extension work. The reality is that all kinds of options are being kept open to young men – should they wish to seek urban employment, set up their own small businesses or simply play around with what are considered appropriate tools and technology for the village.

Women do not have the same options. The 'new-style' appropriate technology

Detail from the newsletter of Ofis Blong Meri, Fiji.

and village-oriented approach in non-formal education has tended only to reinforce domestication, to justify baking, sewing, hygiene and mothercraft, rationalised on the basis of nutritional and self-reliance concerns. If a drum oven or solar drier is to be built, our non-formal educators are calling in young men to build them for young women. There is no real equality in this education as few, if any, of these women could seek employment even if they wanted to. Yet too often, the educators of young men will openly admit that urban employment aspirations are a primary motivation for young male trainees and that 'morally' they cannot deny them this aspiration/determination and therefore they should equip at least some of them with the knowledge and skills that they might need.

The work of organised women all over Papua New Guinea (PNG) and through the National Council of Women, the churches, and some autonomous groups has gained considerable momentum in the last decade. Some of these groups have undertaken creative, innovative and consciousness-raising education, giving women new visions, new horizons and hope for a more equitable role in society. In other words they have done much more than any government programmes in education or community development to implement the national government's decade-old principles for a rapid increase in 'women's participation in all forms of social and economic life' and 'the right of every citizen to pursue his/her own potential for full integral human development'.

It is time for these groups to share their experiences and time for the education and welfare services of government to adopt these new and much broader parameters for women's education. We have a long way to go and many institutional and individual/personal barriers to break down. Publishing these accounts of East Sepik women's experiences in travel and training possibilities is a start.

Mai, at 25 a 'veteran' women's leader, remembers her experiences of taking part in the First Appropriate Technology Workshop in Papua New Guinea in 1977.

I am Mai. For the past eight years I have been coordinating the work of the Gavien Women's Development Group. I never went to school. All I know I learnt from my mother, from my big sister and in an agricultural training centre where I lived and worked with a community of young men and women for five years.

I also had one chance tò go out to a special training programme in Goroka – in the Highlands of PNG. This was the first National Appropriate Technology Workshop, where people came to learn all kinds of work we could do with our hands or with simple tools. That was at Ukarumpa which is not nearby. It is not so close to Goroka, and it is very far away from the Sepik, where I live and work with women.

The organisers selected me and paid for my plane ticket. I flew from Angoram to Wewak in a small plane, and then in another one to Goroka. It was my very first time to travel in a plane and I was very nervous. I went alone – no wait – there was another man from this province who went with me, but I didn't know him and he didn't talk to me or help me by telling me how it goes in the plane and where I must change planes etc.

Things did not go straight. It was a hard time for me because when my ticket was sent from the capital to our province, there was no proper arrangement about where I could collect that ticket. So I spent almost a week waiting round our small town, and trying to find that ticket.

They had organised the workshop for two weeks but I wasted one whole week to find that plane ticket. The man who was to go with me had this ticket, but the welfare officer told him to wait for me.

Eventually they found my ticket but I could not go straight away so they took me to a hotel to sleep. The welfare officer told me that because the government was paying I should leave my relatives' house and stay in the hotel at the organisers' expense.

Well, I wasn't too happy about all this because I'd never slept on my own in a strange place like that. It wasn't my wish to go – but I was told I should 'use the money'. I stayed in the hotel for some days.

On the first night I didn't even sleep. I didn't feel good at all. Those beds in the hotel had wheels, and if you turned over the whole thing moved. It made me feel afraid. I ate and slept there. It was silly because it cost a lot of money and I didn't like it at all.

Anyway, after four days I went to the workshop. I was already one week late. The organisers were not cross. They were only very sorry that I had already missed a lot.

It was a good course. There were plenty of things to learn. Some things I knew already but some I was learning for the first time. For example how to make peanut butter; how to make flour from different beans and sago; how to sun-dry or salt or smoke fish. I also learnt basic weaving.

Many of these things that I learnt, I came back and taught many people again in my home area. For example with peanut butter it was the first time that they saw how to make it. I have since taught so many people – because no one else in this area knew. Now many people know – mothers, school teachers, nurses, youth leaders. I taught them all. Whether they continue to make it or not is not so important. The point is that they know how to make it and why it beats what we buy in the store.

Inside this workshop there were a few people who worked like me. There were also many government officers, with 'high education'. But still, I found I could talk with many people. This appropriate technology was not at all hard for me and I was really happy to meet all those different people. I was given a certificate for appropriate technology training. The workshop organisers told me to go home and try hard to do these new things among my own people.

One other good thing was that I met some people who came to visit me later to see if I did continue with this work. When they saw what I was doing for the women's group in our area they were very happy. One special woman arranged for me to get a small village development allowance for two years to try to give me some small support for my work. That was back in 1977 and 1978.

But there is more to tell you about that first trip. When the workshop was over, again things did not go straight. The organisers had actually booked a ticket for me to fly first to the capital city [Port Moresby] before returning home (which happened to be in the other direction).

I don't know what kind of idea they had, but they told us that we should take this chance to go and see the big town for a few days and then return home. They did this to all of us. Even though I did all I could to convince the organisers that I did not want to go to the big town, they took little notice of me. They insisted that because the government had already bought this ticket I must make the most of this chance. I think they thought that I was mad because I did not want to go to the capital city. So I had to go for a whole week, or more. I was crying as I stepped on that plane.

When I arrived in the capital I had a very hard time. I had nothing to do. The organisers dropped me at the house of a white man who had married a Sepik woman. I slept there for a whole week. I had no way to organise my own way back. The organiser never showed his face again, and the people I stayed with had no time to show me around. In the second week I was really starting to feel very bad. Finally the woman who had first trained me in Wewak, and who had helped me to take part in this workshop, rang me on the telephone. She had been very worried trying to locate me because I had not come back.

At this time I was still very young – about sixteen-years-old. I had no way to find relatives who could help me or do something for me. So fortunately my friend who rang from the Sepik was able to contact friends who came to 'rescue' me. They got me on a plane within two days – and also managed to show me around a little, so that I felt safe again and could actually see and learn something about that big town. This all happened a long time ago. Once I got back home I was immediately happy again. Looking back I am very, very glad that I had this chance to travel and to learn some things. At least I can say I had a big experience and that I managed. When I came home everything returned again to normal. It was with this training that I first began to work with our women's group. I learnt more about development, gardening and food-processing, and I came back to teach many people – men and women in our community. I also taught many school teachers and I even taught some new things to the woman who had first trained me.

One other really good thing for me about this workshop was that a film was made about our programme, and the things we did together. I am shown in this film and now many of the people I work with have seen it over and over again. It makes people realise I was one of the first to do this training, and that I am still doing it today. I look so young in that film. It's funny for me when I watch it these days.

This was all eight years ago. In that time I have only had one other opportunity to go to the capital to a seminar on women's work at the university. When I went I met again some of my friends from that first workshop. They were very pleased to hear that I continued to work in this field. I had one special friend in that woman who met me at Ukarumpa, and who later had helped me to get a village development fellowship for two years. She was very surprised to see that I have two children now and she was glad to hear me tell the story of my work and show slides to that big group of people. Yes, that travel and training was a big thing in my life.

Ani looks back on her participation in a study-tour of organised women's work in the South Pacific Islands.

I am Ani. I work as a women's leader in my local area, and as a coordinator of other women's groups in my own district. I went to community (primary) school, until grade six. Then my parents sent me to a girls' vocational centre in town where I did two years religious and home economics training.

Some people asked me to come and work in their big trade store but my parents did not want me to work in the town. Around that time my whole family resettled in a rural area.

In this new place I went again to a training centre. This was an agricultural training where both young girls and boys learn together with a young woman volunteer worker.

I stayed for four years with my 'brothers' and 'sisters' in this centre. When I first came there I learnt many new things which were quite different to the basic cooking, baking, sewing and bible study work of the first centre I went to. Here I did lots of outdoor practical work and we were all busy learning from each other in gardening and other activities. We were a very close community. We grew up together while training together.

Even now, many years later, long after we left that centre, there are still about eight of us who continue to do local development work and who continue to cooperate with each other in different community activities, and in the work around our own homes. For example, myself and one other woman, we often work together now to run training programmes for local women. When we do things we can ask five of our 'brothers' who trained with us and many of our sisters whom we later trained ourselves, to help us run these courses.

I had even more training opportunities than this. I have had a chance to go to other provinces of PNG and to some other countries – other South Pacific Islands. In 1980 I went on a short study tour in the islands and then came back again to my own work. I went to the Solomon Islands, Vanuatu, Fiji, Tonga and Western Samoa. Quite a few islands.

During this study tour I was able to visit and work with a number of different women's groups, church groups, kindergartens and pre-schools. It was a good chance to go out and see something new and to get some more ideas for my own work back home, and to compare what I was already doing. This chance came about by accident. The woman who helped to train me at the agriculture centre was once stuck at an airport in PNG; this was in 1979. While waiting around she noticed another woman who carried a bag with the women's decade logo printed on it. When she saw this she decided to start talking with this woman while waiting for her plane.

It was then that she found out that this woman was the South Pacific Area Secretary for the world YWCA. She showed her some slides of our work and discovered that she had met the woman I work with at an appropriate technology workshop. She showed a lot of interest and asked what she could do to help us. At this time I was training to assist the leader of our local women's group but I did not have any clear idea about the kind of women's work that was going on in other parts of PNG or in other South Pacific countries. So my friend suggested that this woman help to arrange a study tour for me and another young woman.

The planning was not simple. We wanted to visit many islands. The Fiji woman from the YWCA gave us a list of women's groups to contact. She wrote to them and we wrote too. The Australian Professional and Business Women's Association was interested in helping PNG women have more opportunities for education. They offered to pay our fares. But our travels would take us from place to place and we had to organise dates and accommodation everywhere. This meant we had to write many letters to contact women and organisations all over the Pacific to be sure things would go smoothly, and that we would be safe in these foreign places. Everything was organised so that women and families would meet us and look after us. I went with another young woman, who had worked with me at the training centre and then with our women's group. Now she is working as a rural librarian, still within our community. While travelling we were looking more at women's activities, especially in appropriate technology although we did see a few libraries for children at pre-schools.

This trip was my first and only chance to travel out of PNG. It was the first time for both of us and naturally we were quite nervous about who would meet us at the different airports. The plane travel was all right because we always managed to find and make friends with people who were prepared to look after us even when things did not work out as planned at some airports.

There were bigger problems at the beginning because just as everything was arranged, the priest who managed the agriculture training centre became very angry about our trip and it seems he was prepared to do anything to stop us. He intercepted our mail, withheld my friend's wristwatch and wrote to the organisers in Fiji to say that we would be spoilt and urbanised if this trip took place. He even went as far as destroying my passport photos just a few days before departure. It was a very difficult time for us. You can't imagine that a priest would behave like this and why he would not want us to have this good chance. But it was clear that if he had his way we would never have gone. At this time we were still trainees, in 'his' centre so he thought he had the 'right' to threaten us in order to try to stop us. But it was too late. Everything was organised and we really wanted to go. We had to leave this training centre. We were 'banned' from it by the priest because we took this trip and refused to be frightened by him.

Beyond this there were no other real problems. At every place, people met us. Only at Honiara we had no one to meet us, but luckily there was a young girl our age

119

who took us back to her home for one night.

We also had a bit of a problem in Vanuatu because our trip took place at exactly that time they were fighting for independence. We were almost convinced that we could not go into this country. Our contact there was Hilda Lini who is now head of the South Pacific Women's Bureau and whose brother is now the Prime Minister of that country.

There was some talk at first that planes could not go in, but this trouble seemed to clear up just as we took off. But two days after we left PNG Hilda Lini sent a telegram to tell us not to come because of the flare-up in conflict. But it was too late. We were already on our way and knew nothing about this message.

It seems we were very lucky; there was a lull in the fighting and on the one day that we flew, planes were allowed in, and Hilda was there to greet us. It seems strange to think we did this – but at the time it was very easy. We went around and left again right in the middle of those 'fighting days'. A few weeks later Vanuatu was independent.

We met some special friends on this trip. We got to know a lot of people who play very important roles in women's work throughout the South Pacific including Hilda, Dianne and Ruth and other women whose names we often hear in stories or news of women's work in this part of the world. We feel we are part of that. Also now, many years later, we have had the chance to play host to some women from the South Pacific in our own home area. For example, in 1983 we had women from Vanuatu, Samoa and Tonga join us in an Appropriate Technology Workshop. We found it very easy to work and communicate with them; and we enjoyed telling them about our trip.

I have never had a chance to go out of PNG again. But I still remember very clearly who we met and what we saw on that trip – women who worked like us; women who did more difficult practical work than we did (like building cement water tanks) and women who were happy to hear stories of our work and achievements. I did have a chance to go to a short leadership and basic book-keeping course in Madang, and another handicrafts course on Manus Island, later in 1982. These trips were actually very easy for me because I had made a much longer and more difficult visit in the beginning.

This trip had a big meaning for me in my life. I was very pleased to see women doing so many things. Even now, five years later, I look back at my photo album and remember those friends and the things they did and how they did them. For example those women of Tonga made showers, toilets and water tanks and sinks. I am still trying to organise myself to do this kind of work with our women. We are starting this year.

At the moment I am too busy training other women to even do these small things for myself. However I have not forgotten anything from that trip and I still have big plans for my own programmes. I am still busy encouraging very basic organisation and nutrition education among our women.

17 Nicaraguan Prostitutes: Protagonists of Their Own Transformation

Interview with Jacqueline Cuevas

Jacqueline Cuevas coordinates a project to re-educate prostitutes in her country, Nicaragua. In the following interview, translated by Linda Wine, she spoke to the Women's International Resource Exchange (WIRE) based in New York, about her work. The interview is reprinted from a WIRE publication, *Nicaraguan Women: Unlearning the Alphabet of Submission* (November 1985).

WIRE: *Jacqueline, tell us about your work.*

JC: I coordinate a project to re-educate prostitutes. It's jointly sponsored by the Antonio Valdivieso Center* and the Nicaraguan Social Security and Social Welfare Institute (INSSBI).

Was yours the first such program in Nicaragua?
No. Ours is the newest; three others predate ours. The first one was organised in Corinto, a port town, in late 1979. I worked with the mass organisations and especially with the Christian community in Corinto during the first stages of our project. The León project began a year later, followed in six months by the Julio Buitrago neighbourhood project in Managua. The Corinto program is run by a parish and is state-supported; the one in León is directed by AMNLAE (Luisa Amanda Espinosa Association of Nicaraguan Women); and Julio Buitrago is run by the John XXIII Department of Research at the University of Central America. Research and outreach for our operation began late in 1983.

Would you explain how the program operates?
We try to link the re-education process to the character of the Revolution itself. We think that a revolutionary social project which has its deepest root and ideological basis in people's power – in other words, in the organised expression of the people

---

* The Center has been described in Thomas Walker's *Nicaragua in Revolution* as "A . . . major vehicle for linking the churches and the Revolution . . . This center for Christian reflection was established within a month after victory 'to keep the revolutionary spirit alive among Christians, to help Church leaders understand the Revolution, and to counteract the pressure of rightist businessmen on Church leaders'." (WIRE note)

themselves, as agents of their own development – requires a society which is struggling toward autonomy, toward the personal and collective development of the human being. And since we believe this so deeply, we see the re-education process of a prostitute *compañera* as one in which she, as a woman, is the protagonist of her own transformation. As she develops, she is more and more able to express herself through revolutionary organisations: through the block committees in her neighbourhood; through AMNLAE, if she's fundamentally interested in women's problems; and through her union, when she begins to work at a new job.

We deeply respect these *compañeras* as people, and we of the staff see ourselves as merely a support system for their self-development process; they take from us, gradually, those elements needed to deal with society and to interact with those organisations involved in the building of a new society.

The entire re-education process is developed through the methodology of popular education. This methodology entails three stages. In the first, the *compañera* looks at her own life and tries to figure out what made her a prostitute. Many dynamics are at work in this period. She becomes involved in many activities and begins to observe herself, to try to uncover what makes her tick, what is the nature of her relationship with men, with her children, her neighborhood, with society. For the first time she becomes aware of how strange her life has been, strange from the point of view of building a just, egalitarian society.

The second stage consists of helping the *compañeras* to explore the origins of prostitution itself – how it emerges from unjust social structures, how this injustice is part and parcel of certain types of societies. From the moment she is able to see the relationship between her own problems and the existing social structures, she sheds the personal blame she has assumed for her own situation. The prostitute is a woman filled with guilt, who feels like a sinner.

And that's the way society treats her.

Exactly. When she realises this, she quickly begins to change. And then comes the third methodological stage: her transformation as a woman when she gets a productive job. At this point, most of the women leave prostitution.

Does the project undertake to find such jobs?

Yes, of course. All these stages are essential parts of the project's operation.

What is your approach to education?

We work within the system of popular education. The women are organised according to their levels of formal education, the introductory level being literacy, with the next level building on the first; then come the levels we call intermediate and advanced. We use the guidelines on reading, writing, and arithmetic prepared by VIMEDA, the Vice-Ministry of Adult Education. The very content of the lessons grows out of our discussions with the *compañeras* and is concerned with their own perspectives as prostitutes.

And the materials you use were developed by the project staff?

All of them. We're currently working on materials dealing with women and violence, and obviously we have had to put everything together here, since nothing appropriate had yet been written.

We approach the work from various angles: in other words, although the thematic axis is prostitution, we examine it in terms of the specific conditions and characteristics of each group. With some women the point of departure is sexuality and the discussion begins there; with others it's the general problems of women, what it means to grow up in a dependent capitalist society, such as Nicaragua was. We try to adjust the techniques of popular education and the materials we use to the conditions of the women, so that they can identify easily.

As they begin to question the issue of prostitution, they find that they need to learn to read and write. For example, if we are teaching the use of the syllable *cha*, we place it in the context of a word with various shades of meaning, such as *chavalo* (kid). This generates ideas and associations. We examine this word from several angles: *chavalo* as it refers to their children, who are one of their strongest sources of motivation; *chavalo* as it refers to the youth of Nicaragua and its commitment to the social process; and then, *chavalo*, the word they use for their clients. In this way they delve deeper and deeper into the problematic of prostitution and *chavalo* takes on great meaning in their lives at the same time as it serves as a learning tool.

This approach suggests an indebtedness to Paolo Freire.

Right. It's the pedagogical method which he practiced and promoted; and Freire's concept of education is, of course, a profoundly liberating one.

How long are the courses?

That depends on the level the woman reaches. We now have two work groups. We began with a group of 15 women working in a plant nursery. They've been working for four months. Everything went quite well in the beginning; the work atmosphere was good, and the women were well received by the other workers. That was very important because they are used to rejection. Everything was going quite well but problems arose when the nursery was classified as not being part of the strategic sector of the economy; wage cuts followed and this caused a sense of let-down among the nursery workers which adversely affected our *compañeras*. We urgently need to transfer them to a productive industry where there's more consistency and where the industry's economic development is consonant with the country's strategic needs.

In any case, the most advanced group of our *compañeras* is doing fine. There are five women who left prostitution right away; they have incredibly high aspirations – to study, to acquire technical training, to continue developing as human beings.

One group of 15 *compañeras* is about to begin work at a cannery whose construction has been temporarily delayed. Thanks to funding and equipment donated by Bread for the World, all positions will be held by our *compañeras*. They're in special training courses on Mondays, Wednesdays, and Fridays, where they're learning mathematics and how to weigh fruit, sugar, and vegetables, how to calculate percentages, how to operate the machines. In addition, they learn about human relations, trade unionism, cooperativism. Meanwhile we continue to discuss the issue of prostitution – combined with the teaching of literacy.

Does the project have contact with the Sandinista police?

Yes, we've been working closely with them since its inception. At first the women identified the Revolution with the police – who had been very repressive – and even mistrusted us. So we began an intensive training course for those police who patrol neighborhoods where prostitution goes on. And we give refresher courses from time to time. Thanks to our courses, the police are now able to analyse prostitution as a social problem, and they see themselves as partners in the re-education of these *compañeras*. We go out on patrol with them at least twice a week, visiting the houses of prostitution that still exist and inviting women to join our classes.

We also collaborate with the Ministry of Health in its anti-venereal disease programs. And, because of the risk of US aggression, we've taken intensive courses in first aid. We've also been working with a number of Christian communities and block committees which support our work.

Are there laws prohibiting prostitution and if so are they recent or are they the legacy of somocismo?

During the Somoza period, one of the biggest businesses – along with drugs and alcohol – was prostitution. There were prominent families with wealth and social status that owned houses of prostitution. The National Guard divided the country into sectors for the purpose of getting the houses to pay protection money. A sliding scale was in effect: houses in the more elegant sections paid the National Guard Commander directly; the more modest and sordid houses paid off lower ranking officers of the Guard. The Guard also charged a sales tax on prostitutes who were sold by one sector to another.

A form of slavery . . .

Yes, the women were virtual slaves. The older prostitutes who were no longer in much demand would be sold and a percentage of the purchase money went back to the National Guard. And there was another form of control over the women. The bordello owner would sell shoes, stockings, dresses, cigarettes, and liquor to the women. If the day came when the prostitute wanted to leave the profession, the owner would demand an exorbitant amount for the items the women had bought; and if the woman tried to run away, the owner would call the Guard, who knew how to stop her.

One of the first laws passed after the Revolution was against prostitution. In the beginning the penalty was incarceration, but it became apparent that the Revolution couldn't provide for the thousands of women who, from one day to the next, would have to learn new work skills, customs, another life-style.

So, by default, prostitution is not outlawed. We and the police are its *de facto* regulators. According to the police, since we began working in Managua the incidence of disorderly conduct in the neighborhoods where prostitution exists has dropped. In the beginning we would arrive with the police at a street corner where prostitutes congregated and the group would disband like a flash . . . everyone running in different directions. Now when we arrive they greet us affectionately and give us big hugs. Some who have skipped class tell us why and we have a good talk.

So today's prostitute knows that the Revolution is extending its hand to her and it's up to her if she wants to take it. Those who reject help are becoming more isolated even from their own sister prostitutes.

How do you recruit for the courses?

The women who are attending bring others along; sometimes the block committees bring people to us, and the police, of course, are constantly publicising our project, but without the repressive attitudes they held earlier.

How old are the compañeras *who attend?*

Between sixteen and fifty.

Do they continue to live where they have always lived?

Yes. Housing is a serious problem. Rents are high and of course the social environment is not a healthy one. We're trying to get funding from an international organisation to finance pre-fabricated houses for the women. We contacted the Ministry of Housing which offered us building lots in several neighborhoods at a nominal cost.

We urgently need to build 100 homes in two years. So far we have financing for a women's center in the Larreynaga neighborhood; it's an area with wonderful organisations and an excellent Christian community. We need the house both for ongoing activities and for crisis-intervention on a 24-hour basis. We'll have two bedrooms there for women with serious immediate problems who need temporary shelter while they resolve their housing situation. We will also have recreational facilities, alternatives for leisure-time activities. You see, we've realised that the women who now have jobs go back to their old hang-outs because they don't yet know how to amuse themselves in other ways. Amusement means *guaro*, rum, and hard drinking. Recently we've been organising other activities, such as excursions, family gatherings with dancing and so on. That's why we need a house.

I imagine that many of the compañeras have children.

Yes, the majority, and they are generally good mothers. The women don't operate in their own neighborhoods; therefore their children and their neighbors are usually unaware of how they earn a living. We arrange social services when necessary and we usually have the children in daycare while their mothers are in class. But there's no need for orphanages or other special arrangements for them.

Are there statistics on prostitution?

Of course none were gathered before the Revolution. We know that many women left prostitution at the time of the Revolution, but we also know that when some factories closed down, prostitution grew as many women were left alone with children to support, and few job possibilities.

Although my question has no direct bearing on the project, can you tell us about battered women and the resources available to them

This is a male chauvinist society, especially because of religious influence and the other ideological elements which make up capitalist society. The more macho the male is, the less formal education he has had, the more brutally he treats his wife. He considers her, along with their children, to be his property. Let's say things go badly at work or in the street; he comes home feeling violent and beats his wife. Since she can't hit him back, she hits the kids. But women have been thinking a lot about this form of behavior and they very quickly begin to understand the underlying mechanism. Unfortunately this awareness exists only in certain women, and women in general still don't have it. I think that in societies like this one, with a revolutionary program, what's at issue isn't only battering; what has to be dealt with is the attitude of men toward women. And since this is a society which encourages discussion of all kinds of problems, it's easier to advance, both ideologically and on a practical level, toward new lifestyles and goals.

The Office for the Protection of the Family is responsible for aiding women with these problems. The Nicaraguan Social Security Institute and the Office for the Protection of Working Women, a branch of the Ministry of Labor, are expressions of the Revolution's specific interest in women. The mere fact that there are four projects working with prostitutes, in the midst of the disastrous economic situation that imperialist aggression is causing, reveals the sensitivity and tenderness of this Revolution toward the more deprived sectors of the population.

Do some women, out of embarrassment about revealing details of their private lives, not avail themselves of the services these organisations offer? And are there many women who are unaware of these governmental resources?

Battered middle-class women are often embarrassed and don't go to these organisations for assistance. Some of them turn to AMNLAE for help. I personally know many women in government posts who, through the support of women in AMNLAE, have gained a deeper awareness of their problems and have confronted their husbands, proposing separation in some cases, or fighting for custody of their children – and sometimes meeting violence with violence. But women from the popular sectors are not at all embarrassed and frequently call in their neighborhoods or the police for support.

Is any effort being made to educate, to change the ideology of, those men who beat their wives?

The Office of the Protection of the Family is making a great effort in that direction, first by demanding that fathers be responsible for their children, and then by giving women the financial support they need to develop themselves, to educate themselves, while providing the best possible care for their children. Here, the job of the social worker is fundamental in supporting the couple's efforts and establishing a fruitful dialogue on these problems. Union women, in the countryside as well as in the urban industrial unions, have begun a real struggle alongside their other worker sisters to oblige men to understand that equal treatment is called for.

18 Vietnam Women's Union: On the Way to Equality

Interview with Dong Thi Duen by *Connexions*

This interview with Dong Thi Duen, member of the 17-member Presidium for the Vietnam Women's Union, was conducted at the NGO Forum in Nairobi, Kenya, in July 1985. The Women's Union is a non-governmental organisation with eight million members (out of a population of 58 million). Dong Thi Duen's work is in the area of education and international relations. The interview is reprinted from the magazine *Connexions* (No 21, Autumn 1986).

Connexions: *Could you first give us some background on the Women's Union?*

Dong Thi Duen: It was founded in 1930, when our country was under French colonialist rule. The women who founded it wanted the emancipation of women, but they realised that first you must have national liberation. That is why the Vietnam Women's Union, since its inception, has mobilised women all over the country to participate actively in the struggle to gain independence. Our women's union is a very broad organisation. We unite all kinds of women-workers, peasants, mathematicians, buddhists, catholics.

In 1945, our first revolution under the leadership of President Ho Chi Minh succeeded, and this has meant a great change in the lives of our women. Before the revolution, women had no rights, they could not go to school. Only the boys could go to school. So, almost all women were illiterate. Immediately after the revolution in 1946, the first constitution for independent Vietnam was created. This constitution granted equal rights to men and women in all areas. Since then, the women's organisation has sought to educate women so that they understand their equal rights. The Women's Union participates in the drafting of laws that concern women, and works to see that they are put into practice.

How does the education of girls differ from that of boys today?

Within the schools, the education of boys and girls is completely integrated. They work together. But for the girls, the Women's Union has an educational programme to add to what they learn in schools, because they will have not only the task of being a citizen, but also of being a mother. In the women's clubs we present many issues they can discuss, such as issues of family planning, educating children, and even issues of love and marriage.

In the primary schools, 50 per cent are girls and in the universities, 38 per cent. These statistics are good, but we are still pushing for more women in the universities. There are also many vocational schools, because many cannot pass the exams to get into the universities.

We are trying now to heighten the knowledge of the women in our country because, although they now have equality with men, there is a gap between men and women's average knowledge because of the long feudal and colonial history when only men were allowed access to schooling. We still have a long way to go. That is why our women's organisation proposed that women be given priority in certain areas.

For example, there are training programmes at the factories for which men must complete ten years of school to attend, while women need only seven years. Also, there are age limits placed on those attending the training programme. For men this limit is 30-years-old, whereas for women it is 35. With this professional training it is hoped that the women will earn higher wages.

What work do you do in the area of health education?

We have organised many conferences for health education in the villages. We invite doctors and health workers to speak about and discuss various concerns with the women. There are many old conceptions about health. For example, in the home gardens in the villages, women grow all sorts of fruits, but they often do not feed these to their children. Instead they take them to the market where they sell them to buy medicines and vitamins to give to their children. In the conferences we explain that it is better to keep the fruit to feed their children instead. Or when a child has diarrhoea, the mother often thinks that the child shouldn't eat or drink. But this is very dangerous. We hold classes to explain how to deal with basic health problems. We have reached five million mothers in our programmes on health care.

We also hold many classes in the area of family planning. [Sex education is provided for all young people over the age of 18 by the Youth and Women's Unions.] We receive help in this from UNFPA (UN Fund for Population Activities). First, we explain the necessity of family planning. We cannot oblige people to use family planning practices, but we educate them so that they can choose. We promote the idea that each family has no more than one or two children. Second, we teach about the various methods. After that people can go to the hospitals or clinics to get contraception. But if we do not begin this task of education, then they will not go to the clinics.

Abortion in Vietnam is free and legal. Any woman who doesn't want a child can go to the hospital to get an abortion, but our organisation tries to emphasise family planning because many abortions are not good for the health of the women.

You mentioned to me that teaching peace is one of your educational programmes. Could you talk more about this?

We are trying to teach a feeling of humanitarianism and not one of revenge. This is a very difficult task because you know we have suffered so much because of the US war in Vietnam. So many women have lost their husbands, their children, their fathers, their mothers. There is a natural feeling of bitterness and a desire for revenge. The women cadres spend a great deal of time explaining our country's policy of not seeking revenge. We want to rebuild our country. We want peace with all our neighbours in South-East Asia and with the rest of the world. The possibility of nuclear war threatens to end our world, and so we must participate in the global movement against war and for peace. We try to teach this in conferences, classes and other gatherings.

With such a large rural population, are you involved in educating women in the area of agriculture?

Yes, because many of our members work in agriculture. For example, the work of transplanting rice is done almost entirely by women. We teach new techniques for transplanting to get higher yields. The Women's Union in cooperation with the Ministry of Agriculture holds classes to show women how to transplant rice in a new way. The research and recommendations of the Ministry of Agriculture are implemented through the education work of the Women's Union. We hold classes, and then the women return to their cooperatives to teach the new methods to the other women. This is how new knowledge and techniques are spread in all areas whether it is how to raise pigs or transplant rice. Without the Women's Union these new developments remain only on paper.

What obstacles or difficulties do you face in trying to educate women or in implementing your programmes?

Our aim is the total emancipation of women. First, if we want this, we must have it in the laws. Second, we need it in actuality. We do have equal rights with men in many areas, but you understand that the thinking of people, men and women, must be changed. Because of the many, many years of feudalism, even the women believe themselves to be incapable. Now we need to work to change people's thinking, and this is the problem of education. And this takes time. We must be patient. So, these attitudes are the greatest obstacle we face.

For example, currently, if there is a position open for a factory director or cooperative leader and there are two people, a man and a woman who are both capable, the policy is to choose the woman. But the old way of thinking causes people to be resentful when the woman is chosen. Of course, if the man were chosen this resentment would not exist, even among the women.

In our women's union, we try to create favourable conditions for women to heighten their knowledge. And we try to help the women who have reached leadership positions to prove that they are in fact capable. We don't want to have women in high positions if they are not capable. We do not ask that women be given priority in being promoted; we ask for priorities for women in education.

Part 4:
Media: Channels for Change

19 Women, Development and Media

Kamla Bhasin

This article originally formed the introduction to the journal *Women and Media: Analysis, Alternatives and Action* (1984), produced jointly by Isis International and the Pacific and Asian Women's Forum (PAWF), both of which feature in the final chapter of this book.

> In 1972, the United Nations Commission on the Status of Women noted that in all its efforts to promote the advancement of women, it had encountered a serious obstacle in the deep-rooted attitudes of men and women which tended to perpetuate the status quo. The Commission also observed that those attitudes were due to cultural patterns which, to a great extent, determined thoughts and feelings about women and men. These in turn were being disseminated on a vast scale as a result of technical advances in mass communication media.
>
> *UN Expert Group Meeting on Women and the Media, Vienna, 1981*

> Expenditure on girls' training is like giving a dowry. There is no point in training girls as they get married and go to other places after acquiring the skill so the investment in them is lost.
> *A Block level official in Uttar Pradesh, India*
>
> Quoted in *Women in Focus* by Kumud Sharma, Sahiba Hussain & Archana Saharaya, 1984

Two years ago when some of us in Delhi initiated a group on Women and Media, many women – both individuals and from organisations – joined enthusiastically. But there were others who did not, partly because they felt media was not an important issue (as compared with, say, work, basic needs etc.) – it affected only urban, middle-class women and had little relevance for rural women.

This response made us realise that although media is all-pervasive, its functioning is very subtle. It is highly insidious but also equally invisible. It is similar to, say, environmental pollution in a fast-growing urban centre in that it is everywhere and yet invisible. What is worse is that we seem to get used to this slow poisoning without realising its cumulative effect on us. There is very little protest and the poison gradually settles in our bodies. Similarly, the poison of media settles in our minds and slowly affects everything else.

From *Women in Media: Analysis, Alternatives and Action* (Isis International, 1984).

In the last two years we have looked at different media consciously and critically, particularly with regard to the position of women. At the end of our research we are more than ever convinced that media as an issue is related to all women's issues and it affects not only urban women but all women and all men. Modern technology has vastly increased the outreach of media and made its centralised control possible. I was both fascinated and shocked recently to hear that within months of telecasting the US television series *Lucy*, there are little girls in the villages of Haryana called Lucy. From Radha, Sita or Kamla, straight to Lucy! For people who have perhaps never visited a big town in India suddenly to be exposed to chunks of US and British life must indeed be mind-boggling.

More frightening than the direct reach of media, however, is its indirect influence. By gradually shaping public opinion, personal beliefs and even people's self-perceptions, media influences the process of socialisation and shapes ideology and thinking. Added to this, there is a general uncritical acceptance of the views and facts presented by the media – very often the only proof and argument people give in favour of something is 'But I saw it on television' or 'I read it in the papers'. The 'objectivity' of this truth is questionable. Few people realise that most major newspapers and magazines are owned by a handful of business houses and that television and radio are under the total control of the party in power. Because of the increasing commercialisation, television and radio time is also controlled by a few rich business houses. In this way, the views, prejudices and interpretations of a few people come to be accepted by the majority. Such views become 'respectable' and 'objective', they become facts and prescriptions, the prevalent ideology. The minority which control media uses this technique to strengthen its own position. Therefore, media often acts as a conservative force in society – one which wants to maintain the status quo and avoid major changes, whether in relation to class or sex.

There have been several studies of media with regard to women (in various countries) that have found it guilty of sexism, distortion of the image of women and propagation of sex stereotypes: mothers, housewives, dependent, passive, etc. The other side of such misrepresentation is that in most popular media women are seldom shown as working women – capable professionals, labourers, farmers. Rather, the predominant image is that of the self-sacrificing housewife.

It is often held in the media's defence that it reflects current social reality. But this is only partially true. Media has a two-way relationship with social reality. On the one hand it reflects what exists but, on the other, it affects social reality. By being selective in what it shows, and how it shows it, it interprets and creates its own reality. A part of this is the selective reinforcement of values, attitudes, behaviour. Thus, by always perpetuating the view that the male is in every way superior to the female, media misrepresents the roles women play.

A recent publication of the Food and Agriculture Organisation of the UN entitled *Women in Agriculture* states:

> Of all the hours worked throughout the world, women contribute about two-thirds . . . Women in rural areas grow at least 50 per cent of the world's food. They work in all aspects of cultivation, including planting, thinning, weeding, applying fertiliser and harvesting . . . In some regions they also market what they grow. Many of them provide the main or only support for the family – in some developing regions *a quarter to half of the rural households are permanently or de facto headed by women* [emphasis mine].

From *Women and the Mass Media in Africa* (African Training and Research Centre for Women, Addis Ababa, Ethiopia).

135

Illustration by Porise Lo.

One does not need more than a quick glance at our media to realise that this kind of social reality finds no reflection there. All farmers and most workers depicted in the media are male. Most media reports are about male farmers and workers. These biases are found not only in the popular media, but also in educational and development communication media, i.e. media focused on development issues, as elaborated below. Analysis done of the so-called educational media such as children's books, text books, adult literacy primers and even literacy primers for women, shows that they are sexist, they perpetuate sex stereotypes and almost completely negate women's economic contribution.

Women as seen in development communication media

Development communication media remains silent about the role of women as workers and professionals. It does, however, show them as mothers and housewives. Because such media sounds serious, authoritative and concerned about development, the stereotypes it perpetuates are likely to be more effective. Further, because it is the brainchild of development and communication experts, its inaccuracies are more harmful and alarming.

Some years ago a Delhi-based English daily set a new trend in development journalism by introducing a weekly column on a village it had 'adopted'. On going through several reports on this village a woman journalist found that her male colleagues had not even alluded to the existence of women in the village. When she visited the village, however, she saw women all over – carrying water, fuel, fodder, working in the fields, looking after animals. The eyes of the male journalist had somehow succeeded in missing them – thereby consigning them to further invisibility. Recently, a male journalist defended this by saying: how could they write about women when they could not speak to them? The inability and handicap of a journalist becomes an excuse for distortion! The thought had not occurred to the journalist that his colleagues could not speak to the cattle and poultry either (perhaps they could?) but that did not deter him from writing about them.

Similarly, radio and television programmes on agriculture are almost entirely male-dominated and oriented. Statistics may tell us that half the world's food is produced by women but television presenters still begin their programmes with: 'Greetings to our farmer brothers'. All experts, interviewers, model farmers are men (even though women produce more than half of India's food) and after they have discussed business, rural women appear in their 'picturesque' costumes, to provide song and dance and a little entertainment. To add insult to injury, every now and again a programme deals with 'women's issues' such as nutrition, home management, etc. Because most programmes are by, about and for men, women do not feel addressed so they do not watch or listen to them. When they are interested in watching (as was found by a Delhi-based research organisation), their men often discourage them from doing so with the excuse that the programme contains nothing for women.

In recent years a number of attempts have been made to use media and communication techniques to support ongoing development projects. Films, videotapes, radio programmes, slide-tape shows, charts, etc., have been made for use as development support communication. Because the main objective of development projects has been to increase production (and ignore questions of equity and distributive justice) this support communication has concentrated on the big, viable farmers who, because of their size, access to resources and services, have come to be known as 'progressive' farmers. Women, marginal farmers and the landless do not feature in these programmes. The entire machinery of such rural development projects is 'manned' by men, right from the decision-making to the implementation levels. For example, the 13 massive and expensive training and visit projects for agriculture extension in India, planned and funded by the World Bank, totally ignore and by-pass women. Similarly, a report on media support for a big reforestation programme in Nepal does not mention women, even once. Thus women have not been involved even in projects related to reforestation, water supply, grain storage and other such areas which are primarily managed by women and are of concern to them.

Because most rural development programmes, training, credit and other resources are for (upper-class) men and they completely ignore women, development support communication, which is a tool to promote such projects, obviously does the same. The vicious circle is complete. Because women are not seen as agricultural producers and decision-makers (among other reasons) all projects are by and for men. And because of this, the media talks only of men, reinforcing the view that only men matter, and only for them do plans have to be formulated.

Typically, the communication programmes in which women have been given prominence are those on family planning. National and international resources have been made available to make multi-media programmes on this subject. Even traditional media has not been spared the ignominy of delivering family planning messages. As can be expected, in these programmes women are wooed not as individuals or subjects but as 'targets' (at which all contraceptives have to be shot) and objects of family planning messages and programmes planned by men. The sexist bias of these programmes is quite blatant. As a Bangladeshi woman put it: 'Earlier our bodies were controlled by our men. Now they are controlled both by our men and our government.'

The content of the family planning communication programmes also perpetuates sex stereotypes. A woman editor of a feminist journal, reviewing two family planning films made by the Indian Films Division, writes: 'What strikes one about this documentary (*For the Love of Munna*) is the cult of glorious motherhood through which the women are appealed to.' She further asks: 'Why is it that, in this documentary, the love of a child becomes synonymous with the love of a male child, as the very title of the documentary suggests? Why is it that the male child Krishna is always used as the archetype of a precious child and never any female mythological figure?'[1]

Hundreds of religious and other films deepen people's faith in miracles, in fatalism; they encourage unscientific thinking and irrational behaviour. Their messages are anti-development and basically reactionary. They prescribe personal salvation through (falsely) religious deeds. This successfully diverts attention from the real issues our societies face.

The widespread impact of distorted portrayals

What impact does this kind of distortion have on the position of women in society and their development? The impact of the media is different at different levels.

The perpetuation of inequalities in the home
Statistics tell us that women and girls are more undernourished, underfed, uncared for than men and boys. Our media provides the necessary ideology to the society (women the eternal sufferers; women the rejoicers in self-sacrifice and self-denial; woman the mother-earth) to calmly accept this blatant discrimination against half its people.

By reinforcing sex stereotypes and constantly glorifying motherhood and subservient wifehood the media makes it difficult for women to break out of these prescribed roles, norms and behaviour patterns. Such conservative depictions reduce the few statements in the Constitution about sex equality and equal participation of women to mere window dressing. The resultant conservative thinking justifies the decisions of parents who do not educate their daughters, or give them freedom, or let them take jobs, and who discriminate between daughters

[1] Madhu Kishwar: 'Family Planning or Birth Control?' *Manushi*, No. 1, 1979.

and sons. Are not these real hurdles in the way of women's development? Are not these attitudes partly responsible for the lagging behind of women in literacy, education, vocational training as also for the neglect and consequent higher mortality rates of girls and of the declining sex-ratio in India?

Creating a distorted self-image

Media not only influences the social image of women but also their *self-image*. Most women are themselves uncritical consumers of anti-women media. Media affects their socialisation process, it influences their choices regarding what they consume and wear, how they behave, what they learn, dream, aspire to and what they ultimately become.

Media has, therefore, not only not helped women and society to redefine their own and men's roles; it has also ignored, even trivialised, whatever attempts women have made to redefine their roles, to create alternative behaviour patterns and life-styles. By so doing media has clearly discouraged the emergence of a new woman, a new man and a new relationship between them.

Such treatment of women by the media, instead of reducing their isolation, increases it further. Instead of empowering women, it weakens them. Women remain unheard, unrepresented and more *'uncommunicable'* than before. They continue to blame either their fate or themselves for their plight, often they turn to religion for their salvation. Media succeeds in depoliticising women's miseries and issues. Women's oppression remains a personal and a family matter and the misery and marginalisation continue.

Reinforcing biases in development plans

As has been already stated, media reinforces the conservative view of women and ignores their economic participation and contribution, especially that of rural women, over 50 per cent of whom are directly involved in economic activities, in addition to housework and child-care. All this means that media, instead of challenging the view that women are inferior, subservient, unimportant, reinforces it and establishes man as the active force, the doer, the one who matters. It also means that a curtain is drawn over the real lives of women. Their needs and concerns, the problems they face are not articulated publicly, no public thinking and debates are initiated on their real concerns. Because their concerns and interests remain unarticulated, women also remain neglected.

The near total silence in the media about the productive and economic role of women makes their absence in decision-making and implementing bodies seem quite natural. Planning is left entirely in the hands of male, upper-class, urban planners who, in addition to their own misconceptions and conservative views on women, have the omnipresent media to (mis)inform and (mis)educate them. They have little or no commitment to women's development. Most of them see women as part of the family and believe their interests are identical with those of others in the family. According to them, it is not only unnecessary but also blasphemous to separate the interests of women because such a 'separatist view' destroys the 'harmony' and 'peace' of the family. Needless to say, media strengthens such views.

Not surprisingly, this results on the one hand in biases in national data collection and on the other in inappropriate plans and programmes for women. It has been pointed out by a woman economist for example that, 'In most Third World countries, the accuracy of national level statistics which usually serve as the principal data input in the framing of development policies, is impaired by gender biases which lead to an undercounting of women in the labour force.' Using examples from several countries in her paper, she spells out the nature and sources of these biases (specially in Census data), such as those stemming from the definition of 'worker', the respondents and enumerators being male, cultural perceptions regarding women's appropriate roles and the type of work that women usually do, especially its unpaid character.[2]

Obviously, such biases in data collection lead to inappropriate planning for women. Such miscalculations and misconceptions on the part of our planners and policy-makers take the shape of policies and plans which determine women's lives. These misconceptions, among others, are responsible for the fact that in the mainstream plans for industry, agriculture, commerce etc., women do not figure; they figure only as a separate, small section.

In planning for rural development, it is the poor and women who have been neglected and further marginalised. Most training, information and resources for the development of agriculture, horticulture, animal husbandry, are given to (better off) male farmers, in spite of the major contribution of women to these activities. All extension programmes are almost exclusively by and for men. For women the reserved areas have been the 'feminine' ones, such as home science, nutrition-education, mother and child-care. *Mahila mandals* (women's groups), *charca mandals* (discussion groups) and *bhajan mandals* (hymn-singing groups) are 'women's' preserves; not credit unions, trade unions or cooperatives. In the name of income-generating activities women are given schemes like sewing, embroidery, *papad* making, which have generated little income but many myths about what is feminine and what masculine.

After three or four generations of such planning, we now discover that women have been thrown out of jobs they were traditionally doing; and have been handed jobs which are more tedious, repetitive and back-breaking; that commercialisation of agriculture has led to increasing control of cash and family resources by men. A review of 11 major rural development projects in Nepal shows that because of distorted concepts of 'housewife' and 'head of household', 'economic activity' etc., the productive roles of women have been completely ignored. In most of these projects:

women have either been left out of all the major national development projects, or included only in peripheral activities. This by-passing of women in activities which have traditionally been theirs, both as workers and as decision-makers, has led to situations where their traditional responsibilities, authority and status have been weakened or lost. In other words it has diminished their role and contribution rather than enhancing them. The corollary to this is that the

[2] Bina Agarwal: 'Work participation of Rural Women in the Third World: Some Data and Conceptual Biases', mimeo, Institute of Development Studies, Sussex, 1979.

development projects themselves have failed to make use of potential resources, in this case the traditional skills and expertise of women.[3]

Biases in international development aid

In the relatively limited areas where foreign aid has been directed at women it has mainly encouraged housewife-related activities, as noted in the context of Nepal. Also as a recent FAO (Food and Agriculture Organisation of the United Nations) document, *Women in Agriculture* (based on research in a number of countries) states: 'In the past, development assistance has often failed to reach women in rural areas, both in absolute terms and relative to that of men. Such failures stem from two principal causes: agricultural development programmes which focus primarily on the man as producer; and *lack of knowledge or false assumptions about the role of women in agriculture*'. [emphasis mine].

Similarly, a study conducted by the International Research and Training Institute for the Advancement of Women shows: 'A multitude of studies demonstrate that women, as producers and providers, have often been hindered rather than helped by development programmes. Although more assistance has been directed towards women, it is predominantly of a type inappropriate to their real needs and circumstances, based as it is on a prevailing *misconception* that a woman's only role is that of mother and housewife and not of producer.[4] One well known writer looking at development programmes in several countries shows that there is a deep-seated sexism in the workings of development agencies, especially several of the United Nations bodies. According to her: 'One of the most important blocks to a development process that really helps women, is the blindness and rigidity of the planners to the needed changes, from headquarters staff to those in the field, almost all of whom are men. Because they never deal professionally with women, they have little comprehension of women's real contribution in development, or even that women may have needs that differ from those of the men'.[5] Thus, under the guise of development aid new methods and machinery have been made available only to men; often they apply only to traditionally male tasks, such as ploughing. Or, if mechanisation is introduced for a female task, it becomes men's work – as has happened with the introduction of mechanised milling for high-yield rice varieties in Indonesia and Bangladesh.

The FAO document also points out that:

Emphasis on reaching the men may change the mix of crops grown. In Bangladesh, for example, women grow vegetables, fruits and spices for home use, while the men grow rice and wheat. Training and credit directed only at men have caused a shift in emphasis to their crops – with a potentially adverse effect on the diversity of food and nutrition of the family. New agricultural methods and machinery may lighten the work of the men, but it can mean more work for women. One irrigation/settlement project in Kenya was directed at men even

[3] Bina Pradhan and Indira Shreshtha 'Foreign Aid and Women in Nepal'. mimeo. Institute of Development Studies, Kathmandu, 1983.
[4] New monitor for Women's progress, Development Forum, Nov–Dec 1983.
[5] Barbara Rogers, *The Domestication of Women*, quoted in 'Integration of Women into Development: What Does it Really Mean?', ISIS, *Ideas and Action*, 137, FAO, Rome.

though women do most of the work in rainfed agriculture. The mechanisation of land preparation relieved men of much hard labour but introduction of irrigation increased the workload of the women. Previously, decisions on disposal of the crops and proceeds from the sale of crops went to the household head, and the women, other than those recognised as household heads, lost control over their earnings.

This multi-sided neglect of women has, over time, further reinforced the image of the patriarch and his power vis-à-vis his wife and other women. The knowledge, information and power disparities between men and women have increased tremendously over the last few decades as a result of 'development' and 'modernisation' aided by male-dominated and male-oriented media.

The (media reinforced) thinking that men are the heads of household and they need jobs more than do women and that the natural vocation of women is that of mother and housewife leads to the prevalent discrimination against women in matters of recruitment and their displacement especially in times of widespread unemployment. This happens in spite of the fact that what women earn goes almost entirely for the upkeep of the family and there are a significant number of woman-headed households in many countries.

Conclusion

I strongly believe that as a shaper of ideology and public opinion, media is a major influence on society and women. As has been shown, it affects all aspects of women's lives including their self-image. It influences most decisions regarding women's development. Thus it would be nothing short of tragic if women and men activists concentrated only on economic and political issues and neglected to grapple with such a powerful and insidious force as the media.

It is important that we recognise the manipulative role and the class and gender bias of media and that we challenge it. Instead of remaining a tool in the hands of men and the élite, media should be increasingly controlled by those who want to challenge and change the present system.

We women must create alternatives in different media and use them to inform and empower women, to get women out of their isolation. We must make ourselves more visible and audible so that our concerns do not remain unarticulated and unattended. Not only must we create alternative messages but also evolve alternative methods of working together; methods which are more democratic and participatory and which break the divide between 'media makers' and 'media takers'.

It is heartening to see many women making feminist films, publishing magazines, writing plays, songs, children's poems, to express themselves and to initiate a dialogue with other women, to challenge stereotypes and myths. The fight is long and hard because the adversary is very strong. But is there an alternative to fighting?

20 Group Action for Change in India

Bina Agarwal and Kamla Bhasin

Like the previous article, the following piece is reprinted from the journal *Women in Media*, produced by Isis International and the Pacific and Asian Women's Forum, and published in Delhi by India's first feminist press, Kali for Women. Kali also played a key role in the editing and production of the journal.

> We have suffered enough, we'll suffer no more;
> We will fight for our rights, struggle to the fore
>
> *Feminist slogan chanted during a Delhi street demonstration*

Given that the nature and form of media growth is structurally linked with big capital and commercial interests, and given the subtle ways in which media images permeate our consciousness, attempts to effect change in the way women are portrayed are neither easy to specify nor undertake. Yet it is imperative both to campaign against the existing negative portrayals and to create alternatives which do not misrepresent. It is the emergence of such attempts in India in recent years that provide the few havens of sanity in a nightmare of distortions.

One such attempt is the campaign of a Delhi-based group – the Committee on the Portrayal of Women in the Media. Constituted in January 1983, the Committee aims at: monitoring and analysing the way women are depicted in films, advertisements, newspapers, magazines, theatre and children's literature; mobilising public opinion and launching a wide-ranging campaign of protest against sexist, negative and distorted portrayals; and, in some small measure, to create alternatives.

The Committee is composed of concerned individuals as well as members of 13 women's and other Delhi-based organisations working towards social change. Among the 60 women and some men who constitute the Committee and who have come together on a voluntary basis, are journalists, college and university teachers and students, community-level workers and activists, researchers, actors and directors, and housewives. For the initial year a smaller, core group of women met regularly to plan and carry out the work of the Committee, to undertake in-depth analyses of each aspect of the media in order both to improve their own understanding of issues concerning the media, women and society, and to evolve a strategy for action. Now the group is more loosely structured, and meetings are directed specifically to forms of action to be taken.

The attempts by the Committee to effect changes in the media depiction of women have been of three kinds: protest action, that is action *against* objectionable portrayal; public consciousness-raising action; and positive action, that is action *for* creating alternatives.

Protest action

Writing letters to the editors of national dailies against offending advertisements, newspaper or magazine articles, TV programmes, and films; writing letters of protest to advertising agencies which promote offensive advertisements; holding street demonstrations against pornographic films and offensive film hoardings; and initiating legal action against pornographic magazines, are some of the strategies adopted. On the whole, there has been a perceptible degree of success in these campaigns. For example, the Committee analysing radio advertisements found that they were not only sexist but were also promoting dowry: '*Apko shaadi mein jolly bibi hi nahlin, Jolly TV bhi mila hai – yani double entertainment*' (You have received not only a jolly wife at your wedding but also a Jolly TV – that is, double entertainment!). A letter to the editor of an English-language daily and one to the Director-General of All India Radio led to the withdrawal of this and other advertisements propagating dowry.

Sometimes, when the Committee finds certain hoardings, films and magazines blatantly anti-women, more direct forms of action, such as street demonstrations, have been taken. The first such demonstration was held in early 1983 to blacken a set of objectionable hoardings of Hindi feature films. Following the publicity it received, the municipal authorities publicly denounced the display of obscene posters around the city, and had several of the more offensive ones removed.

The second major street demonstration by the Committee was in September 1983, against Indian pornographic films, 14 of which from South India were running as morning shows in Delhi cinema halls. They were advertised in the newspapers with titles such as *Crazy Lady, Sexy Boy, Sex Hungry, Evils of Rape*, etc., with graphic visuals. These films were found to be presenting extreme violence and sadism towards women as entertainment for men. (One Committee member rightly described them as 'horror films'.) Yet they were extremely popular amongst a primarily male audience. Many such films are now being made for export (especially through video cassettes) to the Gulf countries. In most cases, having received censor certificates, the clips censored out are reinserted and the titles changed from those originally used.

In this particular instance, about 150 women and some male supporters demonstrated outside a centrally-located cinema in Delhi, where one of the films was showing. Carrying placards with slogans protesting against the screening, advertising and viewing of such films, the demonstrators blocked the entrance to the cinema. A leaflet (in Hindi and English) highlighting the Committee's objections to the films, and to pornography in general, was distributed to those who had come to see the film. Some members also confronted the cinema manager, forcing him to cancel the show. Within a few days of the demonstration all such films being screened in cinemas in Delhi were withdrawn, and newspaper advertisements ceased.

A significant contribution to the success of this campaign was the widespread and sympathetic coverage from the press and TV, which brought the issue to wider public notice and brought adverse publicity to the cinemas in question. As a follow-up, members of the Committee met the Minister of Information and Broadcasting and some members of the Censor Board. This demonstration did bring an offensive and angry rebuttal from the Malayali Film Society which tried to turn it into a North India–South India confrontation, but for almost nine months after the September demonstration, not a single such film was shown or advertised in Delhi.

Consciousness-raising action

Street demonstrations essentially constitute short-term actions aimed at calling public attention to the issue. The struggle for effective betterment is, however, a long-term one, requiring wide-ranging changes both in public consciousness and in government policies. The initiation of a dialogue with as wide a cross-section of people as possible is thus an essential aspect of the Committee's efforts. To this end, the Committee, in collaboration with the Centre for Women's Development Studies (New Delhi) organised a seminar on 'The Portrayal of Women on Indian Television' in which women and women's action groups from all over India, involved with media in different ways, participated. The views and recommendations of this seminar were outlined in a paper and publicised through the press as well as presented at a half-day seminar to the Working Group on Software for Doordarshan (the State controlled Indian television) appointed by the Government of India. They adopted many of the recommendations made in the paper.

An integral part of the Committee's campaign to raise public consciousness is to present the analyses of different sub-committees and of individual members through articles in newspapers and magazines, including special numbers of selected journals. Several discussions have also been held with journalists and journalist trainees, with students and teachers in schools and colleges, and with communities, to create a critical awareness on the subject. To make these discussions more interesting, three slide-tape shows (on women as portrayed in advertisements, magazines and films) prepared by Committee members are used, along with a half-hour video film on women in Hindi films (containing excerpts from feature films with a background commentary) made for this purpose by the Centre for the Development of Instructional Technology (CENDIT). Interactions and discussions with students and other groups based on these audio-visual aids have been extremely lively.

Positive action

Several members of the Committee have also been directly involved in producing alternatives. One attempt was the production by the drama sub-committee of a play in 1983 entitled *Aks Paheli* (The Image Riddle). It sought to reinterpret the characterisation of well-known female figures (such as Sita, Kaikeyi and Laila) in Indian mythology and literature. A noteworthy feature of this play was that it evolved through participative group interaction. Also important is the play's explicit recognition of the relationship between myth and media, and its attempt to 'demystify' mythological female characters who have long served as models for media depictions of women, historically and in the present. Another member of the Committee has written a book of children's rhymes which move away from male-female stereotypes and role specifications.

But all this is only a beginning. To make a dent in the existing media, much more needs to be done by concerned individuals and groups to create alternatives which incorporate the complexities of human experience, emphasise equality and respect between the sexes, and challenge the existing media thrust towards male glorification and female degradation. Further, control over media represents a special kind of power. In this context, it becomes important both that women have greater access to and control over media technology, and that 'conscious' women are more widely represented as 'media-makers' and not simply as consumers of anti-women media.

Building the chain

Ultimately, the work of this media Committee is only a small link in the chain. The Committee recognises the need for and has sought to establish links with groups in other cities which, too, have been monitoring the media, so that protests carried out in Delhi can be taken up on a geographically wider basis to create a greater impact and become part of a *movement*. It is also critical to link up with the women's movement and with the efforts of other progressive groups working towards fundamental changes in the structure of our societies. It has also tried to link the media issue with other issues being taken up within the women's movement, and to collaborate with other progressive groups that are working towards fundamental changes in the structure of our society.

21 Organising Women through Drama in Rural Jamaica

Joan French

Joan French is a member of the women's theatre collective, *Sistren*, based in Jamaica and rapidly gaining recognition all over the world. Concentrating on drama as an effective means towards self-discovery and change, *Sistren* has also developed into a women's cultural organisation, initiating workshops, producing silk-screen designs and a quarterly magazine.

This article is reprinted from the bi-monthly bulletin, *Ideas and Action* (No 163, 1985) with kind permission from the Food and Agricultural Organisation of the United Nations (FAO).

Sistren is a women's theatre collective established eight years ago to 'perform drama about how women suffer and how men treat them bad'. With the help of professionals and other resourceful persons, the Collective has produced a series of plays on the conditions of women, drawing material from the personal experiences of its members and of other women, and analysing these in relation to the social fabric within which they take place. The group has gained international recognition because of its appealing combination of humour, social analysis and unique theatrical experimentation.

Besides these major productions, *Sistren* also performs sketches, skits, and other creative devices for popular education with smaller groups at community level. For more than six years, the Collective travelled across the country, organising consciousness-raising workshops for women's groups, and bringing a women's perspective on social issues when performing in front of other sectors of the community – men and youth.

Arriving in Sugartown, *Sistren* realised that the time had perhaps come to concentrate on fewer groups and start building longer-term organisational structures. The experience we recount here relates how the Collective used drama to motivate and organise a group of women to act around their own concerns.

Sugartown was built for sugar workers in the 1970s, when the dominant philosophy of workers' participation brought workers material and other benefits, previously not available to them.

Most of the women in the community are connected to men who used to be employed on the sugar estate before the massive lay-offs in the sugar industry at the beginning of the 1980s. Most of them stay at home to look after their children or grandchildren; a few do odd jobs outside the community to get a little money of their own. Three women teach at the elementary school and one takes care of the children of those who work during the day. A few are ex-sugar workers but today none of the younger women work on the estate.

Sistren's decision to operate in the area arose from an interest in exploring the conditions of rural women and in particular female sugar workers, sugar being the oldest and most important agro-industry on the island.

At the first session, the team introduced themselves, and explained that they had come to learn from rural women about their problems and concerns, so that these could be shared with their urban sisters. They used a scene from their play, 'Domestic', to provoke the discussion and collect data and information about the lives of the women themselves. The scene was about rural-urban migration:

> A woman goes to the city to work as a domestic, leaving her two children with their grandmother (her own mother). In the play, the domestic returns to the country on one of her rare days off and finds that her mother's health is failing. She is no longer the strong, healthy, hearty person she used to be, and finds it difficult to manage the task of bringing up the children. Discipline is breaking down because she is physically unable to force the kids to obey. These take advantage of the situation and carry out all kinds of pranks – beating the neighbour's donkey, tying up some other neighbour's goat, or just going down to the river for hours while there are things to be done at home. On top of all, money is short – both for looking after the children and after her own health. As there are no health services in the district, how can the grandmother find the money to travel miles to the nearest town and buy very expensive medicines? So, in spite of her failing health, she has to keep on working to try and make ends meet. The only job available in the area is stone-breaking, using a hammer to break rocks into smaller pieces used in road repair and road building. This strenuous activity, a traditional occupation for poor women in Jamaica and elsewhere in Third World countries, is certainly much too hard for a person of her age and health condition, but it is all she can get. When her daughter arrives from the town, she has not even the time to sit and talk as she would like to; she has to go to work, while the daughter has to rush to catch the evening bus and get back to town before her time off is up. The play ends with the grandmother collapsing on her way to work. It is her daughter who finds her, and calls out to the children for help, but in vain – they are nowhere around!

Before showing the play, we had told the three women present that we had come to learn from them. One of them had reacted immediately, saying: 'Me? Learn from me? Me, no know nutten, ma! A wha me a go teach anybody?' (I know nothing. What can I teach anyone?) After the presentation, the same woman was the first to speak: 'Lord Jesus, a how conu know all dem-deh tings, ma? A how conu know me fe put me inna de play?' (How do you know all that? How did you know about me so that you could put me into the play?).

Recognising a familiar situation, the women started recounting their own life experiences and concerns, with regard to the issues of migration, child-care, and women's work as raised in the play. *Sistren* assisted this process by asking questions

aimed at clarifying details of the women's experiences and attitudes. The women were visibly enthused, and said that it was the first time they had been involved in anything that seemed to apply specifically to them. Thereafter, five other women joined the group. *Sistren* worked with them steadily over a few months during which the information gleaned from them was used to build a dramatic presentation on women's lives in the sugar belt.

This was a very important moment in the process of mobilising and organising a women's group in Sugartown. How did it happen?

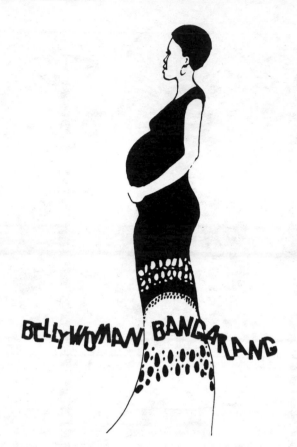

The stories of the first women we met were examined by the Collective and a decision was made as to which one of them had the greatest potential for exploring all the themes raised. *Sistren* chose the one of a woman who had to work on the sugar estate because her husband was not supporting the family properly, squandering what little money he ever got. She worked on female traditional tasks (we discovered that there was a sexist division of labour on the estate, and that there were many ways through which women were discriminated against, in terms of wages, lack of job security, exclusion from the union structure, etc.). Eventually she was appointed supervisor but had to struggle to get equal pay with her male colleagues, despite the existing equal pay law. In the end, she lost the battle owing to lack of female power on the estate and collusion between the trade union leadership and management. This story was chosen as holding the best potential for incorporating the majority of the themes discussed during the talks with the five women.

To ascertain whether these themes reflected the experiences of the broad spectrum of women in the area, another exploratory session was held at the community level. The five women were thus becoming the nucleus of a larger group. At this workshop the participants came to the conclusion that their number one need was 'organisation'. An informal group, including the original nucleus, was formed, becoming the reference point for the rest of the work. Other women workers were contacted; interviews were also held with the estate management, trade union leaders, etc. Out of all this the educative drama entitled 'The Case of Iris Armstrong' was composed.

In the process of drafting this play, the research material was periodically brought back to the reference group in a dramatic form, not so much to describe a situation familiar to many of the participants, as to encourage analysis and reflection and get participants to decide what exactly had to be changed, and how.

Apart from composing the drama, *Sistren* also started the process of transferring it on to film. Once finalised, the two products were brought back into the hands of the community. For a number of reasons, the film was shown first.

It was on this occasion that the Sugartown Women's Organisation was formally launched. The impact of having their concerns dealt with in a medium as 'alien' as a film was tremendous. It must be remembered that the majority of films shown in Jamaica come from the US, the United Kingdom and Japan and that it is rather unusual for ordinary Jamaicans to see people like themselves in a film. After the show, some 30 women expressed interest in participating in the organisation and their names were taken down. Some men also expressed interest in supporting the women's efforts, and their names were also taken.

At the next meeting the group reviewed the community issues raised the previous weeks. These were listed, and participants were asked to isolate an issue which they felt could be acted upon with a good chance of success. The one chosen need not be the most important one, but it had to be an important community concern, specifically relevant to women. Community issues that had arisen in the course of the work included: unemployment; price increases and rising cost-of-living; housing; water; child-care.

Of these issues, the first two were felt to be the most crucial. But the participants did not think that they had enough power to do anything effective about them. They chose instead to act around the water problem.

The community water supply depends on a pump which serves the various sections. This pump was in need of repair, and at the time when the action was proposed, large sections of the community had been entirely without water for three weeks.

Thus, the following two sessions were used as a process to underscore, through drama, the importance of the water problem, especially for women; find out the information necessary to act on (for example, who was responsible for the pump; why it was taking so long to be fixed; who controlled turning it on and off and what were their instructions; why it had not been turned on for three weeks; who were the authorities in the area to whom they could appeal to, etc.), decide on a form of action, and prepare for it; set criteria for evaluation and follow-up.

The first session began with a warm-up activity which involved using bodies to simulate a machine. The aim of the exercise was to stress cooperation – how different actions and motions (skills and tasks) should be coordinated in order to produce meaningful results, and how this depends on the proper functioning of each part. At the end of the exercise one piece 'collapses', and this leads to the collapse of the entire machine. The *Sistren* team first demonstrated by making sewing machines with their bodies (participants were not told what machine it was – they had to guess); then it was the participants' turn – they were at a loss to decide what machine to simulate. *Sistren* suggested that they imitate the water pump. The idea was enthusiastically received, but the problem was that none of the women really knew how a pump worked. Luckily, there was one lone man in the workshop (the husband of one of the participants) who knew all about a pump and assisted the women to learn about it and imitate its functioning. This exercise led to a brief discussion on the different modes of integration of men and women in society, how they confined each group to specific areas of training, work experience, etc. It was decided to return to this theme in more detail later.

This warm-up took participants to the main activity: to underscore the importance of the water problem and its crucial effects on women's life. Participants composed skits based on their everyday life experiences to show the kinds of situations that developed in their homes when water was not available. Apart from setting participants afire with a zeal for a solution, the skits provided a lot of humour and entertainment, while allowing for a discussion on the sexist division of labour in the home, its causes and implications.

After these skits the participants identified the information they needed in order to act, and what form of action they thought appropriate. They chose to send a delegation to the local Councillor who was rarely seen in the community ('except during election time'), but who nonetheless was responsible for seeking solutions to local problems through the Parish Council. In case the meeting with the Councillor proved unsuccessful, they would demonstrate before the office of the Parish Council in the main town. A delegation of four was chosen.

The next session was used to prepare the delegation for the meeting with the Councillor. This was done through role-playing. Participants took turns in playing the part of the Councillor (whom they knew well). They imitated her mannerism, predicted her attitude to the delegation, and the arguments she was likely to use in response to their representations. One participant volunteered to play this particular role; the others had to pretend they were part of the delegation. They had to present their case and seek to get a commitment from the Councillor to do something about the situation. The person role-playing the Councillor had to respond in character. Wherever her responses or actions were judged out of character, any participant could replace her and 'do it right'. All participants collaborated in assessing what were the Councillor's 'true' and 'false' characteristics. At the end, delegation members were asked to summarise key points and review counter-arguments.

The visit to the Councillor resulted in the decision to send a water-truck to the area, on definite days and at definite hours, twice per week. By the time an assessment meeting was held, the truck had made four visits on schedule. Participants were enthused; group attendance rose from 18 to 28; and new members signed up.

The delegation gave its report in drama form, acting out the details of the visit to the Councillor. Participants then commented on the skit, evaluating the delegation's performance and reflecting on the Councillor's attitudes and behaviour.

These comments launched a discussion on the system of people's representation in the country, on real democracy as against sham democracy, on the power of people's action, on male chauvinism preventing women to be effectively represented in the system.

It is relevant to point out that even if the action had not been successful, the educational value of the exercise would have been retained. As it happened, participants felt so encouraged by this success that they were anxious to get on to the next stage of having the pump fixed, an objective in fact eventually achieved.

To return to the question of organisation-building, however, *Sistren* felt that now that the participants had tested their power of action, and had come to know each other's capabilities, strengths and weaknesses over the weeks of dealing with the water problem, the time had come for a more formal structure. A natural leadership had emerged, both around the water action and out of the organisational tasks associated with preparation of the educative drama. The matter was raised with participants who supported the suggestion enthusiastically, anxious to prove themselves even further. Alternative organisational structures were discussed. They rejected the idea of an 'Executive' with a 'President', etc., in favour of a Planning Committee with specific tasks assigned to each of its members. Their experience had made them aware of their exact organisational needs, and of who among them would carry out the tasks best. They chose a name for their Committee; decided on confining membership to women, though inviting men to participate in special events; established a set of rules, a system of dues, etc. (all of this on their own, without any prompting from *Sistren*).

Then, on *Sistren's* suggestion, the Planning Committee took on the preparation of the following session. The idea was to lead it to gradually replace *Sistren's* organisational role. This was not immediately successful. The first Committee meeting ended with little achieved because no one was clear on how to tackle the task before them. At the next meeting, this was analysed, and measures introduced to help solve the problem; for example, a Convenor was appointed; it was decided to elect a Chairperson; a format was developed for drawing up an agenda, for defining tasks and monitoring implementation. In spite of all this the following meeting did not take place – owing to lack of punctuality. In the course of it all, *Sistren* maintained a strong supportive role, filling the gap whenever the Planning Committee fell short. During this period of trial-and-error, the Planning Committee members gradually came to appreciate what elements were necessary for good organisation and programme implementation. They realised the difficulties of planning, the need to establish priorities, not to take on more than they could manage, to list and assign tasks, to monitor implementation.

The problems were gradually overcome, with the Planning Committee moving more and more towards an organising role. By the end of the year, a 'Concert and Social' event was entirely prepared and implemented by the group.

This is the stage the work is at now. Enthusiasim is high, and *Sistren* hopes to build the group even further in the coming year.

22　Evolution of a Slideshow

Amauta Association, Peru

More and more women involved in grass-roots' organising, from housewives' committees in the shanty towns of Peru to peasant women in Bangladesh, are discovering the value of audio-visuals as a tool for popular education and organisation. Especially in areas where there is a high rate of illiteracy, videos, films and tape-slides have the potential for reaching a far wider audience than do printed media. This brief article, taken from the Isis International resource guide *Powerful Images: A Women's Guide to Audiovisual Resources* (1986), describes the experience of one group in Cuzco, Peru.

In 1982, the Amauta Association of Cuzco promoted the organisation and training of women from three poor areas of the city: Pueblo Joven Barrio de Dios, Pueblo Joven Primero de Enero and Asociación Pro Vivienda Manawanonga. In a publication produced by themselves, the women from these communities describe their living conditions:

There are 200,000 of us living in Cuzco and half of us are women. Cuzco is an archaeological zone with a lot of tourism but the tourists cannot imagine how we live on the sides of the hills where the majority of the people live. We do not have water, electricity or drainage. We do not have health-care, markets or schools. Our only means of transport is our feet and when it rains there is a lot of mud. We women are the first to get up in the morning and the last to go to bed at night after a hard day's work. Yet most of the time our work is not valued. Even though we participate in meetings and assemblies and always do our part of the heavy work in our neighborhood, such as carrying mud and stones, the men do not respect what we do. When one of us wants to speak up in the assemblies, for instance, they say 'It's better if your husband comes because we have to discuss these things among men.' This makes women afraid to speak up during meetings.

These are only a few of women's problems. Most of us are illiterate. It is hard for us to meet together: we do not have time; we have no place to leave the children; our husbands don't want us to go out of the house . . . But in spite of all this, we decided that we must organise ourselves to find solutions to our problems. Encouraging each other, we began to meet and talk about what is happening to us. Women need to meet. In talking together new ideas come up and we find out what women are doing in their organisations in other places.

155

During their meetings, the group had the opportunity to learn about the situations of other women through pamphlets and audio-visuals. Stimulated by this, they too began to feel the need to let others know about their own opinions and to promote a dialogue about their own problems within their communities. To put this into practice, they first made a series of charts which they took around to the different neighbourhoods. Then they produced a magazine and finally they decided to make an audio-visual. Through these means, they tried to give not only an analysis of their situation, but to relate the evolution of their experiences.

There already was a magazine talking about women's situation in our communities. But this publication has many words and most of us do not know how to read very well. Fortunately, we received a magazine from Ecuador called *Warmicuna Riman*. We looked at this magazine during a literacy course and discovered that the problems in Ecuador are very similar to ours. We liked this publication because it has a lot of photos and not many words. As soon as we saw it we said: We should have a magazine like this. So, in spite of the fact that none of us had ever done this before, we began taking photographs. At first, almost all of them came out badly, but we began to learn with time. We took photographs in the market, in our neighbourhoods, and in our houses to show the work women do. Afterwards, we stuck these photos on cardboard and under each one we wrote something about our problems: about work, taking care of our children, misunderstandings with our husbands. Later we took these to other neighbourhoods to talk about the problems with other women. Then we made a magazine using the same material.

Finally we decided to make an audio-visual because we thought that this was the only way we could communicate and share our experiences with many women who, like so many of us, do not know how to read. With the support of the Amauta Association, we took other photographs, wrote the texts and made the recordings. We did not conceive of this audio-visual as a final product but as a working tool to contribute to our process of development. And so, little by little, we have changed it, trying to perfect it, on the basis of suggestions and criticism which we ask for from the audience after each showing. We still do not have an evaluation of the final version. Perhaps we will keep on changing it.

We feel that this has been an interesting and useful experience not only for ourselves but for our communities as well. We have shown our audio-visual many times in our communities and this has enabled us to discuss our situation with the whole community, men and women, young and old. But, most of all, it has given many women, including those who cannot read, the opportunity to listen to what they have to say, learn about our experiences and to become interested in changing their own situations, just as we are trying to do.

Part 5:
Women at Work

23 Organising Women Workers in the Free Trade Zone, Sri Lanka

Kumudhini Rosa

Kumudhini Rosa works closely with women workers in Sri Lanka. She has also worked with the Committee for Asian Women (CAW) who co-produced the issue of the Isis International Women's Journal on *Industrial Women Workers in Asia* (No. 4, September 1985) in which the following article first appeared.

From as early as 1977, when the Asian Women's Forum in Malaysia stressed the importance of responding to their needs, through to the first organising committee meeting of CAW in Thailand at the end of 1982, women from different countries and religious denominations have been publicising the plight of women working in the electronics and garment industries, to name just two. In the words of Teresa Dagdag, an Executive Committee Member of CAW:

> The struggle of the Asian women worker is three-pronged: Firstly she is a worker, which puts her at a disadvantage as someone who sells her labor for a price, hence her efforts become a commodity. She is usually overworked, underpaid and barely protected by labor laws. Secondly she is a woman, which puts her at a secondary position because she is hired for her dexterous hands and nimble fingers, her submissiveness and her docility which prove her an asset on the factory assembly lines. She is also highly prone to sexploitation in exchange for jobs or promotion. Thirdly, she is Asian, and as an Asian, she belongs to the Third World, a region usually exploited for cheap labor.
>
> As the response to the needs of the women workers in Asia formally started within Church circles, specifically taken up by women in the Church, there is a need to highlight these concerns of the women workers so that more women, Church women, other concerned women may give more attention to their struggles. The work is vast and we are just beginning. There is need not only to be *concerned* but also to be *connected*. This means that women responding to the plight of these Asian women workers need to link up in solidarity in order to address this issue which is closely related to the flight of transnational capital. The third challenge is to be *committed* to their cause. To the women who are aware and able to respond to these needs of the Asian women workers, we put out this challenge: to be *concerned*, to be *connected* and to be *committed*.
>
> The women workers' issues have their roots in the international flight of capital; hence this problem needs international solutions and approaches. International linkages among concerned women all over the world need to be established and strengthened in order to support effectively the struggles of our sisters in the industrial sector in Asia, in this part of the Third World.

Trade unions and women workers

In a country like Sri Lanka, trade unions have been the traditional form of organising the workers, irrespective of whether the workers in question are men or women. Since independence (1948) the trade union movement in this country enjoyed a rich heritage of a very high degree of organisation. Trade unions in Sri Lanka have almost always been organised by and controlled by political parties. Every party would have its own trade union which would function independently of other trade unions. Workers are organised along lines of industry or trade. Workers in a particular factory can belong to several different trade unions – each worker choosing the trade union she/he prefers. As a result each factory can have several trade unions functioning within it.

The structure of the trade union has always been male. The key positions of president, secretary and treasurer have always been held by men while one or two women might sit on the executive body of the union. There have been ironic instances where the membership of a trade union is dominated by women (ranging up to 85%–90%) but men continue to dominate, control and structure it according to their particular demands.

The control exercised by the political party responsible for setting up the trade union is subtle but has been seen as the main reason, or one of the main reasons, for the situation that exists in the trade union movement today. Often, decisions taken at the level of the central committee of the particular political party in question seek to be implemented in the trade union. The political parties, too, have almost always been male-dominated. Thus the total reflection on the trade unions has been male oriented. It is not surprising, therefore, that the trade union movement in this country has rarely, if ever, taken up demands specific to women workers. In the trade union movement, women have always been regarded as labour only and not as a specific section of the labour force, oppressed because of their sex.

Thus workers, irrespective of their sex, have been mobilised only around general working-class demands, for example, wage increases, production targets, etc. Questions such as equal wages, maternity leave, child-care facilities, have hardly ever been discussed in trade union circles.

After nearly 50 years of working long hours and carrying the triple burden of being a woman, worker and Indian Tamil, a plantation female labourer earns less than her male companion who works fewer hours in less arduous forms of work. Only in 1984 were equal wages introduced and then only after a considerable period of strikes and struggle.

Another example in this context is the introduction of the law permitting night shift work for women. The International Labour Organisation clause 98 was rescinded by the present government (which came into office in 1977) with little or no resistance from the trade union movement. With the exception of one or two trade unions, this was not considered as an important issue and the cabinet approved the law with little opposition from the trade unions in March 1984.

It is evident from this course of events that women have not only been denied representation in the leadership levels of the trade unions, but also that their specific problems have rarely been taken up within the movement.

This in no way implies that women have not fought, struggled and won their demands. Women workers have always fought around demands pertaining to their working conditions or general working-class issues. Given their particularly oppressive conditions, women are found to be stronger in the face of state repression, join their strength and move fast to achieve their demands. There have been examples of women who were beaten up by the police, tear-gassed, arrested but stood firm together on their demands, not moving until they were met.

Women's organisation

The independent organisation of women is a more recent phenomenon. This does not deny the existence of women in history who have fought and struggled, especially during the struggle for independence prior to 1948. In 1975 when the United Nations declared the Decade for Women, the issues relating to women's oppression were raised and discussed in Sri Lanka. Although no significant advances have been made in actually combating specific oppressive conditions to which women are subjected, it at least helped to raise the issue, considered to be unimportant and secondary; an issue which was also considered to be dividing the working-class movement.

The present United National Party government introduced the Free Trade Zone (FTZ) in 1977 in which local and foreign investors are invited to set up their industries, utilising the labour of Sri Lanka, producing goods for the foreign market. Women's organisations more intent on organising women workers were encouraged to further strengthen their mode of operation. The Free Trade Zone employs a labour force of 27,000 workers, of which 85 per cent are women.

Many bodies which organise and contact women workers in and around the FTZ sprang up. It has been estimated that in the Greater Colombo Economic Commission (GCEC) area alone (within which the FTZ is also set up) there are around 50,000 women workers, living either in boarding houses, in their homes, or with relatives. The forms of organisation that can be observed in the country as a whole cannot continue to be the blueprint for organising women employed in the GCEC factories, because the employers (mostly foreigners) do not encourage trade unions or any sort of organisation. They even take disciplinary steps against women workers who identify themselves with any organisation.

As a result, various strategies are utilised to reach these workers. For instance there are women's centres, workers' centres, religious centres that have been set up to meet the needs of these women workers. The centres provide facilities for reading, leisure activities, group dynamics, and discussions among the women workers. These organisations are run by women workers themselves while at other times, activists in the women movement or religious persons (mainly Catholic nuns) are the initiators. The aims of these organisations differ. For instance some organisations would emphasise a purely social service orientation while others may be more political. For the latter, independent mobilisation of women around their own issues may be only a transitional demand.

There are also women's sections in trade unions; these are not independent but subject to decisions taken at the level of the executive body of the 'Mother' unions, which are almost always male-dominated. Political parties, too, have their own women's wing, but do not seek to organise women workers alone but women in general. Women who belong to these organisations are either members of the Party in question or sympathisers.

Alternative organising: an interview

I talked with a Catholic nun who is at present working with women workers employed in the Free Trade Zone in Sri Lanka.

I have been working with women employed in the Free Trade Zone for over a year now and have been able to come to terms with their situation in a very . personal way. As soon as I came here, I carried out a survey to find out for myself the problems these women face and also to identify their needs. The women themselves helped me a great deal to carry out this survey – taking the questionnaire from house to house – putting me in touch with women from different factories.

This survey assisted me not only to get an insight into the situation but put me in touch with around 1,000 women. Initially we just talked, got to know each other, sometimes assisting in personal questions. Gradually we became more organised, meeting once every week. We decided to set up a library and reading room. A place where the women could come and meet other women – a place always open to them. After a while I realised that we were going around in circles – the same women came week after week.

I'd like to tell you of some of the difficulties we face in organising these women.

First, these women are very young, aged between 18 and 25, and doing their first job. They lack experience and have no idea of the methods utilised by the managements to extract their labour. They tend to take things for granted. The intense discipline which they are subject to at home is used by the managements to extract maximum profit from them. As the experience of being controlled is not new to them, they accept this without any questions.

The second difficulty is the fear they have even to talk of organising. The constant threat which looms over them is that they will lose their jobs if they organise themselves. It is therefore extremely difficult even to approach these women. Although we promise them that we do not intend to organise a trade union, they are still afraid and it is a justifiable fear. There is a background to this. Women are normally recruited through Members of Parliament – those representing the particular area they come from. It is through their parents or some other member of their family who works as a member of the United National Party that they are able to obtain this job. So the control is already on them when they come to the city. They come from the rural areas, several hundred miles from the village and live here in boarding houses. In addition, to have a job in the city is to realise a dream and these women come with all types of expectations. They are forced to endure the oppressive tactics used by managements, to earn money to meet at least some of their expectations.

Thirdly, these women do not visualise themselves as workers, let alone as women. Most of them come from lower middle-class rural families but with middle-class values. They have a high degree of education compared with women workers in the rest of the country. I have come across women who have a degree, or specialised in a particular skill; they have at least 10-12 years of education.

Linked to this third difficulty is that the women see themselves as temporary workers. The expectation of the society is that they should marry and have a home; children play a very significant part in the lives of these women. I often feel that they are all the time planning their lives this way, with the ultimate goal of marriage in view. They do not consider the possibility of continuing a job after marriage. If you ask any woman how long she would continue with her present job, she would reply maybe another year or two, not more.

Considering herself as a temporary worker only presents numerous problems, such as the idea that she should not do anything that might jeopardise her job, and thinks of herself alone.

There are other difficulties too. One is the repression that we often have to confront. Despite the fact that we are not a trade union nor are we trying to form any kind of organisation inside the Zone, we have to constantly face harassment from the police, questioning, false rumours and intimidation. All kinds of actions are taken to instil fear in the women, threatening that they may lose their jobs if they continue to work with us. They also try to create a hostile ring around the area we work, even to the extent of making the villagers suspicious of us. We work openly; our publications are openly distributed. But still they fear that we have the potential to identify the needs of women workers and take concrete steps to change their situation.

The other difficulty we face is in trying to enter the boarding houses. The landlords discourage the women, and often put obstacles in our way when we try to get through. We have to try to meet them outside, but it is not easy. The women are more at ease when we talk to them in their own surroundings.

We have to realise that within this situation traditional forms of organising won't succeed. For instance we cannot work like a trade union, especially the way trade unions function in this country, along party lines. We cannot build memberships around organisations. We need to build open-ended organisations which do not make any woman worker feel she has to be committed on a lifelong basis. We must let the women make the decisions which they think they can handle and to which they feel they can win over other women as well. This is very important because the traditional way of operation of the trade unions, where decisions are taken at the top and are implemented by the women workers, has no future in these areas; we have to develop new forms of organisation, new ways of working, of reaching women workers.

For instance, one of the main problems that the women workers in the FTZ face is security . . . sexual harassment, usually when they leave factories and on their way to their boarding houses. We discussed this problem. The decision was to get the entire village involved in the process of eliminating this menace. The women workers went from house to house to get support for a campaign to change this situation. Finally a meeting was summoned of all village councils, youth groups, church groups and religious organisations to discuss this matter. The women themselves took the initiative and led the discussion. As a result, a consensus was reached whereby the villagers pledged to see that such forms of harassment did not take place in the future. Churches, temples, public platforms were used to put this message across and, to a very large extent, the menace has been lessened. We could never have reached this situation by ourselves. The women workers residing in this area are from the rural areas, not from the village . . . we have to be very conscious of this when we agitate for any demand affecting them.

The future prospects are not bleak. We realise there are women who are willing to take risks – even at the expense of their jobs. And this gives us courage to go on. The number of women participating in different ways increases daily and this is very positive. For instance, when there were queries about a publication we release bi-monthly, the women were questioned in their factories by the managements and by the authority of the GCEC – but they were not to be put off. Even with the threat of a letter of dismissal they were willing to continue the publication. You must understand that this is not the normal situation – or that all the women working in the FTZ take these risks, but the number is increasing. In our work we realise that it is imperative that we have the support of the village. I think this is important for any organisation that functions for women workers in this country.

The other point I want to make is that we have never worked as a 'women workers' organisation'. It would be an unnecessary risk to do so. Our work is directed at the women workers, organised and controlled by them, but we do not want to wave a flag saying that we are a women workers' organisation. We call ourselves by another name. We also work in close collaboration with other organisations working towards assisting women workers. We must be careful not to duplicate the work or to form many organisations serving the same purpose. We must not compete with each other because the women will get confused. We have to work in a completely different manner to achieve the maximum results. Our organisations should not be rigid and take up positions which could lead to varying kinds of corruption. We should be effective with minimum forms of rigid structures.

We have to work slowly but with deliberation. We should not take any steps without the women workers being completely aware of and part of the decision. Our demands must always be consistent with the demands of the majority of the women workers. But they should also be transitional demands which would lead to more long term demands. For instance the demand to the Authority of the GCEC to make the women workers aware of the implications of the night shift for women is a common one which should also give way to asking the Government to implement the promises of security, transportation, choice, when/if the women agree to work on the night shift. This also raises questions relating to sexual harassments, rape and also basic demand for security.

It is only if we continue to work in a non-sectarian manner, to raise the issue of women workers in a deliberate and systematic way and work with them in their interest, that we can change their situation. This is my experience and the way we work for the best results.

24 A Question of Tactics: Interview with South African Trade Union Organiser, Lydia Kompe

Outwrite

Lydia Kompe is Transvaal Regional Organiser of the Transport and General Workers' Union (TGWU), which represents workers in the transport, municipal and cleaning sectors. She came to Britain at the end of 1985 for the launch of the book, *Vukani Makhosikazi* – South African Women Speak, based on testimonies reflecting her life and the lives of other African working-class women under apartheid (see Suggested Further Reading). While in London she spoke to the feminist newspaper, *Outwrite*, about the South African trade union movement, its role in the fight against apartheid and organising women within trade unions.

Shortly before the interview, reprinted below, trade unions in South Africa formed the Congress of South African Trade Unions (COSATU). After the banning of the ANC, although the South African Congress of Trade Unions (SACTU) itself was not an illegal organisation, its leadership was broken. It took a long time to revive the trade union movement – unions were legally allowed to register only in 1979.

Since then, although half the workforce is still unorganised, membership of unions has grown in numbers and strength, but they have been split between the Federation of South African Trade Unions (FOSATU) and the United Democratic Front (UDF). The forming of the new Congress aimed to bring together the existing federations into a new mass movement.

What has it been like for you as a woman trade union organiser?

When I started I was working with the Metal and Allied Workers' Union. I was the only woman organiser and the metal industry is mainly men. At first I accepted that I would be exploited by male colleagues – being asked to make their lunch, do the shopping etc., but then I decided not to take it and organised a rota to do those jobs. I also had problems getting male workers organised. They would say, 'you being a woman can't help us with our problems', or 'where is your boss, why don't you send him along?' Some of them say they will get their men to join if you agree to sleep with them. You have to decide whether you are going to be tame, tactical or hostile. I decided to be tactical. Of course, I wouldn't go along with any of their 'love abuse', but you have to keep them hanging on the wall. After you have got the membership, then you can take your stand and tell them to fuck off.

Do you work mainly with women in the TGWU?

Most of the TGWU membership is men, but we've got a lot of women cleaners in the union and we are still struggling to achieve recognition in most of the companies in the cleaning sector. We only have an agreement with one company – Anglo-American Property Services – we didn't get 100% of our demands, but workers think it is a step forward. We are still trying to get recognition in other companies like Supervision and Prestige, which are the companies which contract out to the big enterprises – they sell these women's labour. They don't own the buildings so it makes it hell of a difficulty for us to organise properly because you don't have any place to meet. The owners never want us to come and interrupt the workers because their purpose is to clean and then leave. They have no other relation to the building except cleaning.

Where do most of the women working in the cleaning industry live?

Most of them come from the Vaal triangle, very far from Johannesburg. They travel about two hours to Johannesburg station and then split up to go to the areas where they are allocated. They spend three to four hours on the road. They catch the 3pm train but they start work at 6.30-7pm. The whole afternoon they are just on the road, eating in the street, waiting for transport and then packed in a truck.

What time do they get home?

They finish working at about 3.00-3.30am. They always carry blankets with them and until the buses start to run they have to wait on the street. Maybe they catch the 6 am train home.

And do they get home in time to give their children breakfast?

They won't find their children because school starts at 7.30-8am. The children don't see their mothers until Saturday morning.

Has the union taken up specific demands around women?

We have taken up things like maternity benefits, which in SA don't exist. We're negotiating house agreements with managements to cover each company – but very few women will benefit from these agreements because we haven't managed to organise everyone.

By law, it is completely at the bosses' discretion as to whether to give you your job back, it doesn't matter how long you have been working for him. If you have a child, they say it's your own choice, they've got a business to run and they are not going to be delayed by women coming in and out having children. So having children in SA is not 'natural', it's a 'choice'. Management say, 'I have called the family planning clinic to come into the company with pills that you can use if you want to protect your jobs.'

Do the employers have clinics in the workplace, or do they just hand out the pills?

They have first aid stations for emergency injuries but they also bring in family planning once or twice a month to issue the pills. Each and every woman is given time to visit the clinic during working hours. Where I was working it was in fact compulsory to have pills as long as you were still menstruating.

Unless the union is there to pressurise to secure the jobs there is nothing you can do. We see it as important that women have children when *they* like to have them.

Has it been difficult to get the trade union movement to recognise and take up women's demands?

Yes, we do have to fight. The men there see that it is important for women to have the same rights in the work-place but we still have problems at home. Management has been replacing men's jobs with women and paying them less, so the men have realised that it is time to take joint stands in all these issues. Some of the unions have achieved good maternity agreements which have been negotiated mainly by men because you find only one or two women organisers. Although they have done very well, we still feel the majority should be women because they are directly affected by these issues.

What about organising separately as women?

A women's group exists within FOSATU bringing together women in all eight of the affiliated unions. We have had a few seminars with shop stewards and organisers and have drawn up a list of demands to present when the new federation (COSATU) is formed next week. Sexual harassment is the main problem, also contraceptives, abortion, maternity rights and men being replaced by women at a lower rate of pay. Our resolutions propose that within the structure of the new federation there will be women officers there as representatives of women, not a particular union.

As you probably know, during the British miners' strike, the miners' wives set up an organisation called Women Against Pit Closures. The attack on miners was seen not just as an attack on men's jobs, but also on the women in those communities. Because there was such a strong community feeling, the women were the backbone of that strike.

It is very interesting because in our country there is a completely different set up. The miners are mainly migrants. The urban African group aren't actually working in the mines at all because they have Section 10 rights which give them the privileges to get better jobs. The people who have no choice are those who come from different so-called independent places, the 'homelands' – the wives and children have no rights to enter the RSA.

Women like ourselves, who stay in the urban areas, need to give moral support and approach the wives of these men and mobilise them. They are out of touch and don't know what's happening. Like their husbands, who have no choice but to work underground, they are not educated.

That's why I wanted to meet those women [against pit closures] because to us it is very interesting but we really don't know how we will be able to have those kind of structures to support our husbands.

Do the unions organise within the community to get support for strikes?

Sure. We feel the time has come to give that moral support because when you talk about fighting the regime, it's to the workers' benefit to see that the regime is actually destroyed and completely swept away. We do plan with the political organisations what strategies we can use. We are not completely isolated even though we are not day-to-day involved. The workers see the first priority being to fight capitalism, which we know is the backbone of apartheid.

One of the issues we are taking up is the scrapping of the hostel system because it is a weapon that divides workers completely. It's difficult to mobilise the hostel dwellers because they are totally isolated. They have terrible living conditions and they see themselves as a separate group from the community – the 'urban blacks' as they call us. It was proved in this present unrest.

The division isolates the migrants in the hostels from the activities in the townships. They will say my children are in the homelands so I am not party to that, which in principle is not true – we must take joint action to fight the hostel system. Parents in the township have actually selected a committee to meet the hostel dwellers to discuss and expose this division which has been created deliberately to divide us and break our solidarity and strength. Things are improving – there was a lot of tension at the beginning of the unrest, but we shouldn't see each other as enemies.

Is one of the problems in sustaining strike action that replacement labour is readily available?

When workers go on strike and management sacks them all, the next morning there is a pool of workers because of the unemployment. People are starving because they can't get jobs. Because of influx control, people have no choice in getting jobs where they want them or to live where they want to.

Have the trade unions seen part of their work as raising the general level of consciousness about not replacing sacked workers?

Workers have found that it was the wrong strategy to attack workers who replace them. Instead when they go on strike these days they occupy the factory. Two weeks ago, workers at a company called Polyfoil went on strike, and occupied the factory for four days. The police came and the workers said, 'you can shoot if you like but we are not going to move an inch until our colleagues are reinstated'. Management was too scared to take action because they didn't know what would happen to their factory if they threw the workers out. This is the third company that has taken this action successfully but we really don't know how far it will take us because the police may take drastic steps.

Are there political differences between the unions and the different federations?

Yes, the reason why we have got duplication within the same sectors is mainly because of political differences. This duplication loses us strength and we are looking forward to bringing all the individual trade unions together when we disband the existing federation and form a country-wide federation.

In 1984 we had a huge two day stay-away. The Chemical Industrial Workers'

Union, which is affiliated to FOSATU, had organised in SEKUNA (a sort of mine). About 7-8,000 workers were dismissed. All the political organisations and unions protested and warned management that if they didn't talk to the bosses we are going to take a national action. All the workers were reinstated, the union was recognised and they have got an agreement now. The more we come together, the more pressure we can maintain.

25 Notes on a Study of Women Workers in the Dominican Republic

Centro de Investigación Para la Acción Femenina

Founded in the late 1970s, the Research Centre for Feminine Action (CIPAF) is dedicated to action-oriented research aimed at improving the conditions of women in the Dominican Republic. All research findings are put at the disposal of the women's movement and various grass-roots organisations through papers, pamphlets, cartoons, poster campaigns and the co-ordination of workshops, seminars and courses, in response to requests from outside groups. Besides work, themes have included rape, domestic violence, prostitution and health. The campaign inspired by the study on women workers, discussed below in a translation from CIPAF's bi-monthly paper *Quehaceres* (May – June 1984), became renowned for its impact on the country's trade union movement.

Before the rise of CIPAF – and we say this without false or subjective pretensions – the field of research about women in our country was sterile ground. Hardly any studies were carried out from women's own viewpoint and those that were tended to be determined by other priorities in which women merely figured as objects.

CIPAF is rooted in the understanding of this situation and the need to overcome it – an understanding complemented by the conviction that research makes sense only when accompanied by the will to convert its findings into a weapon for organisation and action.

Embarking on a study of the 'Female Workforce in the Dominican Republic' was to be our centre's first great challenge. Short of resources and lacking the kind of experience that comes only with practice, the women of CIPAF decided, with a strength born out of their commitment to militancy, to tackle a task which many deemed impossible. Three years later the seed has begun to germinate.

One of the first things to come to light in the survey, which we started in 1981, was the high percentage of women workers who were unaware of the existence of the Labour Code and, consequently, the laws it contained which applied to them as working women. From this knowledge we prepared a monograph entitled 'Capitalism and Patriarchy – Women in the Labour Code', which was widely distributed among grass-roots trade unions and even used by several union head offices in their training programmes.

Title heading from CIPAF's regular paper, *Quehaceres*.

Similarly, in 1982 CIPAF organised three series of workshops under the heading 'Women and Work', with the participation of women workers from the free zones of Santiago and San Pedro de Macorís, and the industrial sector of Herrera. Each one of these workshops was a revelation for the CIPAF research team. Where we imagined there would be a latent awareness there was a consciousness about exploitation and oppression which far exceeded the realms of intuition. The evidence of women workers, their extraordinary capacity to know and control the realities of their everyday life, though they couldn't always put this into words, proved to be one of the greatest incentives behind a study that was forever coming up against pitfalls.

This steady work developed alongside the processing of different study data until finally, when we had all the information together, it was published and CIPAF began its campaign of broad distribution.

To be honest, when we decided to carry out our first campaign to publicise the results of our study we were not at all confident of its complete success. Socially alienated, women have never (or very rarely) been a group registered as a political priority in this country, a situation that includes the progressive sectors. The weight of patriarchal ideology permeates the class system and provokes, as in the particular case of women workers, a relative underestimation of their ability to fight and organise. First and foremost, however, our own coherence as well as that of other people had to be put to the test.

We carried out our first experiment with a special meeting on 12 April 1984. The enthusiastic response of the five main trade union organisations, the Women's Co-ordinating Union and many others comprising a largely female membership, evident in the huge turnout to this event, was a great boost to our outlook and confidence. For a whole day, the CIPAF women, together with men and women union leaders, discussed the information outlined in our study, abandoning the coldness of officialdom to speak frankly about the implications of the kind of data and percentages which had emerged.

One thing was clear from the start: women workers largely perceive their status as workers as transitory, thus placing a negative burden on their self-perception as members of the proletariat, and blocking the development of a definite class consciousness. The statistics collected by *compañera* Magaly Pineda are convincing in this respect: 33% of women workers recorded in our survey had received training in trades such as hairdressing, confectionery, pottery, typing and clerical duties; yet 62% of the total had never gained any social benefits from that training, a fact which

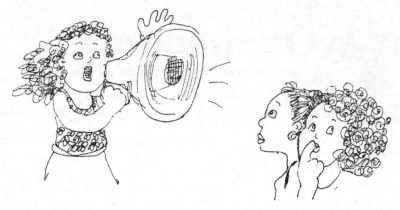

Detail from CIPAF booklet on the need for women to organise for better health services.

has undoubtedly contributed to the build-up of considerable personal frustration.

Furthermore, as Magaly points out, the search for other options dictates that they have a different vision of themselves, merely reproducing the cultural standards traditionally imposed on women, which basically reinforce obstacles against them ever reaching positions of greater responsibility and technical accomplishment.

This subjective rupture of women's links with their class reality is one reason, among many, behind their lack of interest in union organisation. CIPAF's national survey of women workers showed that 60% of firms employing women do not have

CIPAF (as above). Cartoons by Millaray Quiroga.

unions and, in the 40% that do, only 27% of women are even affiliated; except in a few cases, affiliation doesn't presume active participation in the decision-making or in the struggles of the working community. This state of affairs largely stems from ignorance of the above mentioned labour laws which affect almost 90% of the people we interviewed, among them 12.5% women union members.

But women's work does not just end or begin in the work-place. Added to the barriers we have quoted against female unionisation, are all those associated with the completion of a double working day, factors which unions wholly disregard when planning and developing their activities.

Finally, there is a long history of repression by employers in the face of all attempts at working-class organisation. Our study found that in 60% of cases of attempted union organisation the protagonists were sacked; in 19% there were huge cancellations; and 7% ceased production altogether. It is, therefore, hardly surprising that such a large percentage of women (and men) are put off such activity. Especially if we add the 28% or so who didn't respond to our survey, we have a precise picture of the state of mind of women workers when considering the possibility of organising to assert their demands.

All this is not to say that many women don't recognise the importance of trade unionism. CIPAF recorded that over 48% saw it as a primary instrument for achieving 'better working conditions', a need which far outweighed their demand for equal pay, child-care facilities and other rights. It is hard to imagine the levels of degradation in which women work. Quintina Reyes from the research team heard stories which seemed to have come from another capitalist era; stories of squalid conditions, emotional and physical pressures leading to widespread nervous disorders, indicating causes far beyond the nature of the work itself.

Starting from our central focus on the need to hand back the knowledge gained in the course of our research and convert it into a weapon of change, we hope that publicising the results of our work survey will help educate a wider union sector about the reality of women's dual exploitation. The huge turnout of union leaders, members of the Women's Co-ordinating Union and others on our first day of publication is undoubtedly an auspicious sign.

26   A Statement by Domestic Workers in Uruguay

Women of ALESDA

This statement from women in the Domestic Service Union, ALESDA, is translated from the Uruguayan national feminist paper, *Mujer* (No 1, September 1985), which is published monthly by the *Colectivo Editorial Mujer* in Montevideo.

We are women workers without a factory; adolescents who would only be a burden to our families at home.

Our work was inherited when lack of culture and lack of money to pay for our education offered no other alternative for women. Our union, which embraces one of the biggest, and certainly the most exploited, labour sectors in Uruguay is rooted in shared deprivation. In the 1975 Census we numbered 65,000 and today, owing to the economic crisis, the figure has more than doubled, as have the inhuman working conditions and exploitation that we suffer.

We are a union of women workers with a class consciousness and the will to struggle for our dignity, like that of any other worker, despite our condition having always been ignored.

Although they may not know each other or, in some cases, not be recognised as members of domestic service, there are many men in our sector: servants, cooks, chauffeurs and gardeners. But the union is essentially made up of women, something which puts off many of our *compañeros* from joining, though there are a few.

We are fighting for our rights as workers and as people. Women have always been taught and brought up to do domestic jobs, relegated to the social role of being servants in our own homes. However, we're no longer so isolated. Today, in the face of lower and lower family incomes, many so-called housewives go out of their way to search for paid work, only to find their hopes dashed through lack of training and their opportunities for employment reduced to domestic service.

We are also workers from factories that have closed or else reduced their workforce, the unskilled – mainly women – always being the first to go. We have made great progress since adding our own contempt to the general contempt shown by management and bosses for our work. Some *compañeras* still underestimate their worth but we're growing stronger all the time. Things are definitely changing.

We finally emerged as the Domestic Service Union, ALESDA, in the middle of 1984 by which time, after several abortive attempts, we had managed to unite and clearly identify our class line.

Our unionisation has cost and continues to cost us a lot of effort and dedication; on the one hand having to endure harsh and unjust working conditions – 10, 12 and up to 16 hours non-stop with scarcely 24 hours rest a week; and on the other, wages which are way below the national minimum rate. There is little time or opportunity to get together with other women workers. We may be one, at the most two or three, women workers in the same house, isolated from ourselves, all of which makes it difficult for our *compañeras* to join the union. It's a problem which those of us who are organised are trying hard to overcome.

Our general platform and strategy for change is based on the following demands:

- an eight-hour maximum working day;
- a minimum wage;
- Christmas bonus;
- holidays;
- holiday pay;
- pension contributions;
- abolition of the right to dismiss a worker after three months;
- classification of jobs;
- health and accident insurance.

With the help of everyone in the union, and our labour lawyer, we have worked out a bill that has been presented to the House of Deputies for approval. Through this bill we hope to alter current legislation and at least begin to reverse the current situation.

Over the years we have been – and still are – at the mercy of bosses who know full well how to profit from the benefits granted to us by labour legislation against the interests and rights of domestic workers. We are subjected to ill-treatment and abuse, such as the example of a *compañera* who was sacked from her job in a private house because she refused to accept the advances of the 'darling youngest son'. Supported by the union and our labour lawyer, she won the case at the Ministry, showing the power we can have when united. Alone and isolated, we'll achieve nothing but united and organised, let them dare touch us!

Part 6:
Against Violence and
Sexploitation

27 Violence Against Women: An Understanding of Responsibility for their Lives

Govind Kelkar

Dr Govind Kelkar is among a growing number of feminist scholars and activists concerned with campaigning against and analysing the specific nature of violence against women in India.

This is an edited, slightly shortened, version of an article of the same title which was first published in *Samya Shakti* (Vol 2, No 1, 1985), a women's studies journal produced by the Centre for Women's Development Studies in Delhi.

Violence is too often narrowly defined as an act of illegal, criminal force; in reality it can incorporate exploitation, discrimination, the upholding of unequal economic and social structures, the creation of an atmosphere of terror, situations of threat or reprisal, and many other forms of political control and coercion. While these concepts of violence are clearly interrelated, its specific nature in relation to the situation of women demands a closer and critical look at aspects of structural violence, namely acts of violence exercised on the part of the family and society. The state not only tends to overlook these forms of violence but perpetrates them in the name of cultural legitimacy and the maintenance of 'law and order'. At a meeting on Women and Violence in January 1985, organised by the South Gujarat University and Centre for Women's Development Studies, we summed up the specific nature of violence against women as follows:

> The specificity of the gender dimension lies in the fact that while violence against women perceived as a structural phenomenon is indeed part of the general violence against oppressed classes, the forms of control and coercion exercised in the case of women are gender specific and arise out of a hierarchical gender relationship, where men are dominant and women are subordinate. The forms of control exercised over women cover essentially three areas: sexuality, fertility, and labour. Secondly, women become instruments through which the social system reproduces itself and through which systemic inequality is maintained. This is achieved through rules of legitimacy of offspring, through controlling sexual access to women (as for example, in caste-endogamy rules) and in general through the establishment of possessional rights over women which men have as

husbands or fathers or older male relations. Such possessional rights include promise of protection (whether actually fulfilled or not in reality) in return for submission and exclusive use. This is further strengthened and maintained over time by the socialisation process that embeds women strongly within the familial structure and hierarchic gender relations such that they have little or no independent status, and transgressions outside the family and male authority expose them to swift retributions and confirm their vulnerability.[1]

Violence against women, like all other historical phenomena of violence, must be seen in a socio-economic and political context of power relations. It is produced within a class-caste, gendered society in which the male power dominates. For example, women from landless, agricultural wage labour families, particularly from the scheduled castes and tribes, are most vulnerable

From *Voice of Women*, Sri Lanka

violence. Mass rapes are used by ruling-class men for the repression of poor peasants of poor and landless labourers whenever they get organised and demonstrate militancy for higher wages or for the implementation of land reforms. Violence against women in such cases is the result of an attempt to grind women and their men down into submission, as a form of social and political control, ideologically supported in a variety of different ways by the state.

From *Voice of Women*, Sri Lanka

Against this background the specificity of violence against women involves a further analysis of the gender-based inequalities centred in the family and supported by a state ideology of male dominance; the state in India has never tried to effectively outlaw the subordination of women to men, or to change their particular relations of dependence within the family.

Increasing crimes against women

Over the past few years, the phenomenon of women-burning and rape has registered a sharp increase throughout India. In Delhi in 1983 an average of two women died of burns every day.[2] In Bombay, a survey from two police stations indicated that in a period of eight months in 1984, one woman was burnt to death every five days. In Bangalore, suicides and 'dowry deaths' nearly doubled in 1984 as compared to previous years. According to police reports, on an average two women committed suicide every day in 1984.[3] In Madhya Pradesh, records from the biggest hospital show that one woman died of burn injuries every five days. According to various women's organisations an equal number of burning/suicide cases go unreported. This is mostly on account of the refusal of the police to register the cases or when they do register, their tendency to minimise the offence. For example,

We shall not be cremated alive We shall fight for our rights.

TEXT TRANSLATED FROM HINDI

over 90 per cent of the cases of women burnt in Delhi were registered as accidents, only five per cent were noted as murders and five per cent as suicides.[4]

The dowry witch-hunt has taken its heaviest toll in the middle-class urban areas, but the burning of women for more money and domestic goods in the form of dowry is quite widespread in the slums and in the countryside. Investigations have indicated that women-burning is prevalent all over the country, it is most acute in Delhi, Haryana, Punjab, the Western Uttar Pradesh and the Saurashtra region in Gujarat.

In early 1984, serious concern was expressed in Lok Sabha at the increasing cases of criminal assaults on women, gang rapes, molestation, sale of women and kidnapping of female children for the purposes of prostitution. In 1983, United News of India reported 811 cases of 'eve-teasing' (sexual harassment), 68 cases of molestation, and in the first half of 1984, there were 324 cases of sexual harassment and 28 cases of molestation. It was further reported that nearly 5,000 women were made Devdasis every year. According to the figures given by the Bureau of Police Research and Development, New Delhi, in 1972 there were 2,562 cases of rape reported all over India. In 1975, 3,283, and in 1978 3,899. Nearly 435 of the rapes committed in the rural and tribal areas in 1982 were by government officers. It is a matter of common knowledge that the majority of rapists are set free for lack of adequate evidence. In Delhi in 1982, there were 202 cases of rape registered with the police; of these only 27 were convicted.

There is much more to it than crime statistics. These are a manifestation of political malaise in India and malady in the organisation of our socio-economic system. The atrocities committed against women within families have often been hidden from the public eye by a social attitude comprising a mixture of apathy towards woman and an inexplicable sense of privacy. We need to examine to what extent are current family institutions in India responsible for creating and maintaining structures and ideologies of subordination-structures that inherently resist the participation of women in decision-making and ideologies created by a sex/gender system geared to maintaining existing power relations and forms of exploitation.

Women and the family

Violence runs along the lines of power in the sex/gender system. The family, with its basic axis of the sexual division of labour, is its principal underlying institution. The violence of women-burning in the privacy of home has to be examined with regard to its systemic relevance. Details of violence and crimes meted out to women are not necessary in the present context. The focus is on the impact of these type of acts on women. We need to look at the relations of authority within the family around which dowry violence is organised, and at the property relations which this authority realises and maintains. Socio-economic arrangements, sex/gender based disparity, for instance lower wages for women, their under-reporting in the labour force, and the disadvantaged position of women in health and education, have been justified on the assumption that women's employment and physical existence is secondary to that of men. There is, therefore, a close connection between the family and the organisation of politico-economic systems. In other words, the family approach legitimises the subordination of women in policy making and the organisation of the economy.

The Constitution of India has declared sex equality as a guiding principle, thereby acknowledging that a family should basically be a equalitarian unit founded on equal rights and willing choice by its central male/female individuals.[5] In practice, however, the subordination of women to men and junior to senior pervades family life in all classes and castes in India. The ideology of subordination is required by the material structure of production. Women are subordinate to men (and thereby dependent too) because men may own land and hold tenancies while women by and large do not. Customary practices preclude women from inheriting land as daughters, except in the absence of male heirs. This is wrongly justified by the claim that women receive their share of patrimony at the time of marriage in the form of dowry.

Hindu laws of property and ownership of the means of production give women negligible rights, as independent entities, to family income, assets and property. The Hindu Succession Act, which has put daughters on an equal footing with sons in regard to succession to parental property, and the Dowry Prohibition Act, are not a dead letter by any means but they can be appealed to only in certain circumstances: in cases of disputes among families or where land ceiling legal provision makes it expedient for large land holdings to be divided 'on paper' waive male and female heirs. In most of these cases, daughters waive their land rights in favour of their brothers. Otherwise, they would be denounced as 'selfish' sisters and risk alienation or the severance of ties with their natal families. Women's effective exclusion from the possession and control of land is largely the basis of their subordination and dependence on men in rural India.

It is important to point out here that it would be wrong to assume that women in India are passively groaning under an ever increasing oppression within and outside the family. Rape and women-burning have long been major issues for the women's movement. The Supreme Court judgement on the Mathura case drew attention to the efficacy of rape laws,[6] to be followed by a number of forums against rape and atrocities against women in several parts of India.[7] Initial protest in the form of a big demonstration against the harassment and killing and burning of women with inadequate dowries came in June 1979. Ever since, women's organisations have been demanding from the government more stringent, deterrent measures to check crimes against women. Women have organised in protest against rape and sexual harassment. Demonstrations and meetings continue to be organised throughout the country to protest against direct and structural violence on women. For the past few years, in Delhi and other major cities in the country, women's organisations, and housewives, have held sporadic demonstrations against the husbands, in-laws, lawyers and police officers involved in the cases of women-burning and killing by other means. In early August 1982, 30 women's organisations in Delhi, under the name of *Dahej Virodhi Chetna Manch* (Anti-Dowry Consciousness-raising Forum) jointly organised a protest march against dowry, and were joined by several hundred ordinary women and men, including the 'parents of dowry victims'. They questioned police action and tardiness in investigation, highlighting the government's lethargy towards this problem. They demanded that bride-burners or killers be ostracised, and pleaded to legal pundits and legislators to suggest some system of summary trials for such crimes against women.

These demonstrations on the one hand have acted as checks on culpable husbands and in-laws by exposing the real nature of violence or crime (i.e., the protracted harassment and battering of women, followed by killing and/or burning them) and thereby disallowing an easy escape through a facade of suicide or accidental death. On the other hand, they have pressed for effective change: the implementation of laws, the tightening of loopholes in legal procedures and the need for due consideration to be given to women's unspoken experiences of harassment, torture and molestation through proposals for the reorganisation of police enquiry procedures. Further, these demonstrations have opened up areas of female subordination and domestic violence to public attention, empowering harassed wives and rape victims to speak out. The victim's new ability to describe her plight has merged with a resurgence of feminist consciousness-raising efforts, influencing others. Moreover, these groups have particularly suggested critical scrutiny of the family and role of the state in reinforcing the familial structure of domination.

The government, unable to ignore these organised efforts by women, has responded by amending the laws related to rape, criminal procedure and dowry as well as by setting up anti-dowry cells in Delhi and other cities. However, while these laws have sought to improve the existing legal situation, they fail to question women's subordination and dependency on men within the institution of marriage and the family.

Strangely enough, the woman cop in charge of the Delhi anti-dowry cell said in a recent interview:

> It is very difficult to decide whether a burn case is suicide or murder. In both cases the victim is doused from head to toe in kerosene and severely burnt. We feel that 80 per cent of the cases which are brought to our notice are suicides. The husbands and in-laws are certainly culpable because it is their harassment which drives the person to this act.[8]

The social awakening implied by a number of neighbourhood action committees, the emergence of women's wings and front organisations of various political parties, including the increased attention to the woman's question in some radical Marxist-feminist organisations, and by the non-party political associations, trade unions and professional groups, has been a welcome trend. Conscious women activists have been organising *Padyatra* (long-march), made skits, plays and movies on the oppression and exploitation of women, launched protests and set up women's centres, where women in distress can get help, support and legal aid. Feminist magazines and network bulletins have reported on both the problems of women and their attempts at resistance. Some feminist academics have questioned the limitations of social sciences in the study of demographic patterns and female roles in economic production in their own society. A landmark was the report *Towards Equality* pointing out the national neglect of women in development programmes for women in the fields of employment, health and education.[9] Feminist researchers have been involved in studies of women's roles in protest movements and their participation in nation-building. These studies have further pointed out existing inequalities in the socio-economic, political system, and how women's studies offer a new perspective which enables researchers and students to try to build an egalitarian social structure, within the family and community.

Women's protest through their studies and demonstrations has made the crime of women-burning visible as a serious social problem. It has opened a whole new vista by calling attention to the oppression, conflict and violence hidden behind the superficial portrait of love, support and nurturance in the family. Nevertheless it would be simplistic to say that we are on the brink of profound change towards equality and justice in society. In the words of William J. Goode: 'we must never under-estimate the cunning or the staying power of those in charge'.[10]

Besides, there is an absence of satisfactory theory in the women's movement in India, where the family tends to be explained in purely functionalist terms or in terms of certain distinctive cultural features of the sub-continent. Social scientists have been engaged in debate on whether or not a nuclearisation of joint-family structure is taking place but they do not question the complex power relations between gender and generation that underlie the family, the ideology and structure of dependence and sexual division of labour that strengthen the patterns of inequality and the oppression of women and children.

At the same time, however, in recent years the family has emerged as a political issue in India. The government has formulated policies to further strengthen the family, while the women's movement raises questions about family boundaries. Women's organisations have pointed out that the proposed planning, with its women in the family approach, would not lead to greater equality in society but to an increased polarisation between the sexes. As a result of pressure from women activists and scholars, a concession was made by incorporating a chapter on 'Women and Development' in the Sixth Five Year Plan. The chapter admits that women are 'the most vulnerable members of the family' and will continue to be so 'for some time in future'. It further promises to give 'special attention' to the interests of the 'vulnerable members'. Nevertheless, the Sixth Five Year Plan insists that 'the family is the unit for programmes for poverty eradiction'.

The problem of the repression of women in the family was acknowledged, but the family as the basic unit of economic development was maintained, thereby preventing a constructive analysis.

Women and the State

The state in India has never set out to fundamentally restructure relations of authority within the family or to allow women access to property and other resources. Through its construction of the family-centred programme, in its assignments of productive and reproductive functions, and above all in its land/property holding and technology control functions to the (male) heads of households, the state seems likely to erode even further the rights which women earlier enjoyed.

Historically speaking, during the nationalist period under the leadership of Mahatma Gandhi, there emerged a distinct approach to the role of women in society. The leadership realised that women were 'condemned to domestic slavery' and therefore sought to liberalise the family to expand women's activities in the public sphere within politically acceptable limits.[11] Women were urged to participate in the struggle for freedom of their country. Gandhi viewed women's oppression as historic and nearly universal. He lamented over their non-participation in social, political affairs, women's sexual subjection into their role as 'man's plaything'.[12] In Gandhi's view, the qualities of courage, endurance and moral strength made women the 'natural leaders' of a non-violent struggle against an unjust socio-political system. He wanted to 'feminise politics' because women had the potential to give a blow to the established socio-political power structure and could be vanguards of a non-violent struggle for a just and non-exploitative socio-political order.[13]

This seemed a radical stance but the kernel of women's oppression – the sexual division of labour and thereby their subordination in the structure of material production were neither fundamentally questioned nor altered. 'She is essentially mistress of the house. He is the bread-winner, she is the keeper and distributor of the bread'.[14] Women supplement the meagre resources of the family, but man remains the bread-winner.[15]

The traditional glorification of women's role as guardian of Hindu morality and spirituality and their self-sacrifice and endurance are central to the concept of non-violence advocated by Gandhi, while he has frequently referred to women in their domestic roles. He was oblivious of the violence done to women in the notion of chastity. For instance, he believed in moral appeals to the rapist and, failing that, suicide as the only course left to a woman. One must admit, though, that there simply has not been enough research to do justice to Gandhi's views on women's historic role. The dominant trend is, however, ambivalence on women's role.

In the 1930s and 1940s, there was an uneasy alliance between feminism and nationalism.[16] While women's organisations accepted a subordinate and complementary role in politics they repeatedly came into conflict with Congress when it threatened women's issues and alienated women members. At the initial exclusion of women from the Dandi March in 1930, the Women's Indian Association protested against the Congress leadership: 'This division of sexes in a non-violent campaign seems to us unnatural and against all the awakened consciousness of modern women'. The Association demanded, that 'no demonstration organised for the welfare of India should prohibit women from a share in them'.[17]

In the following years, the three basic components of the strategy of planning in India i.e., land reforms, co-operative farming and community development in the 1950s and 1960s, were ridden with class, caste and gender relations. Protagonists of rural development worked to help rural women become 'a good wife, a wise mother' and totally disregarded women's work in the rural economy, specifically their contribution to agriculture and side-line production, cattle-rearing, fishing and weaving.

Most of these wife, mother, improvement programmes have proved a failure because they are irrelevant to the needs of women in subsistence agriculture and have been unable to augment women's income in any way.

Women constitute 48 per cent of the population, while the percentage of women in the total workforce is only 20 per cent. Thus approximately every fifth woman is a worker, as against every second man. Among the 'marginal workers' (those who are engaged in work for less than six months), 84 per cent are women as against 16 per cent men, while of the 'non-workers', more than 61 per cent are women.[18] Moreover, work opportunities and women's participation have been declining over the last few decades. It was observed in a earlier study of mine that Green Revolution technology on the one hand denies women employment opportunities otherwise available to them, and on the other hand stereotypes all those jobs which pay less and require less skill, forcing women to take up jobs which come to be regarded as purely female tasks.[19] As a consequence, the invisibility of women as producers in the economy is enhanced, and they increasingly lose ground in the traditional economic and decision-making roles. There was no attempt to redefine the roles of women; perhaps most important, the division of labour within the family retained all its force. In a report on women's rights, entitled *Inside the Family*, conducted by the people's Union for Democratic Rights, it was stated:

> The treatment of the family as a private area governed by religious and social customs, the regarding of women as peripheral to economic development by the state, the inability of the legal system to recognise their unique unequal status, the bias of the police and courts in relations to crimes against women, are all part of these social values.[20]

While a number of legislative measures were adopted to guarantee legal equality to women, in practice, however, hardly any opportunities were provided for women to learn their new roles; the process of a revolutionary transformation in the social position of women came to an end by being submitted to an anti-participatory, elitist bureaucratic structure of exclusion and manipulation. Attempts to legislate, reform and enforce laws have tended to build on the assumption that society is against such phenomena, so law enforcement would reduce or delegitimise them. The state initiatives were accordingly directed towards making its executive functionaries more sensitive, judiciary more receptive and the law, in words, less sexist. This may create an illusion of progress or improvement, but now it has empowered women to halt the increasing violence and destruction of their lives. We need to know what the state has done to transform its class-caste and gender construction. Has it changed its formal and legal norms for possessional right of men over women, the rules of legitimacy of offsprings, which denigrate and limit women as sexual, sub-human objects? Has it effectively de-legitimised processes which are in agreement with the advocacy and interests of the ruling class and gender-oriented social structure, and made substantive policies for the development and liberation of women? Is the liberation of women crucial to the development of a society?

Women involved in the liberation movement have increasingly realised that the phenomenon of violence against women will not be challenged without a struggle to end the subordination of women, to transform unequal social relations based on oppression and exploitation. We need a radical transformation in the organisation of the economy, along with a radical change in the structure of the family, including the reordering of our most personal and intimate relations.

Notes

1. The three day (January 11–13, 1985) meeting at Surat included 20 activists and academics from the States of Maharashtra and Gujarat, Bombay and New Delhi. The responsibility of summing up the discussion was given to Maithreye Krishnaraj and Govind Kelkar. For a full report, see 'Women and Violence', *Economic and Political Weekly*, Vol. XX. No. 12, March 23, 1985.

2. For details see Govind Kelkar, 'Women and Structural Violence in India', Sangarsh Vimochana, Bangalore, December 1984.

3. *Daily*, 10 January, 1985.

4. *Indian Express*, Editorial, 27 April 1984.

5. For a discussion on the constitutional definition of the family and confusion about the concept, see A. R. Desai, *Urban Family and Family Planning in India*, Bombay. Popular Prakashan, 1980, chapters I and II.

6. The High Court of Bombay had convicted two policemen of raping a 16 year old tribal girl Mathura, from Maharashtra. Mathura had complained that she was raped in the police station in the middle of the night. The Supreme Court reversed the Bombay High Court judgement and acquitted the policemen. They dismissed Mathura's testimony as a 'tissue of lies' because there was no clear evidence that she

actively resisted intercourse with the two men and there was proof that she was not a virgin. The Supreme Court judgement triggered strong reaction from activists and lawyers. An open letter from four distinguished experts of law – Upendra Baxi, Vasudha Dhagamwar, Raghunath Kelkar and Lotika Sarkar – asked the Supreme Court to reopen the case. This was followed by meetings and rallies by women's organisations, and formations of lawyers' collectives and forums against rape in several parts of India. They discussed shortcomings of the law and proposed changes to make it more effective.

7. For a detailed discussion of these forums, see Seema Sakhare, 'Analytical Study of recent Rape Cases in Vidarbha Region of Maharashtra State in India, Paper presented at Workshop on Women and Violence, Surat, January 1985. Chhaya Datar, 'Anti-Rape Campaign in Bombay', Unpublished 1982.

8. *Patriot*, New Delhi, June 24 1983.

9. *Towards Equality. Report of the Committee on the Status of Women in India*, Government of India, Department of Social Welfare, Ministry of Education and Social Welfare, 1974.

10. William J. Goode, 'Why Men Resist' in *Re-thinking the Family, Some Feminist Questions* (ed) by Barrie Thorne and Marilyn Yalom, (Orient Longman, 1982) p. 132. He compares the position of men with that of other dominant groups and to the complex dialectic of men's control and women's efforts to combat and circumvent it, especially within the relationships of intimacy and mutual dependence in the family.

11. M. K. Gandhi, *Young India*, 26 February, 1918.

12. Vina Mazumdar, 'Another Development with Women: A View from Asia', in Development Dialogue, the Dag Hammarskjold Foundation, Uppsala, 1982: 1–2, pp. 67–68.

13. Sugata Dasgupta, 'Emancipation of Women in India'. (Unpublished paper prepared for the Committee on the Status of Women in India.)

14. M. K. Gandhi, *Women and Social Injustice*, Ahmedabad, Navjivan Publishing House, 1947, p.27.

15. *Ibid.*

16. Geraldine Forbes, 'The Indian Women's Movement: Struggle for Women's Right or National Liberation in *The Extended Family, Women and Political Participation in India and Pakistan*, ed. by Gail Minault (Delhi, Chanakya Publications, 1981).

17. R. K. Sharma, *Nationalism, Social Reform and Indian Women*, New Delhi, Janaki Prakashan, 1981, p.65.

18. Census of India 1981.

19. For a detailed study, see Govind Kelkar, *The Impact of Green Revolution on Women's Work Participation and Sex*, Roles, Geneva, ILO, 1981.

20. People's Union for Democratic Rights, *Inside the Family, A Report on Democratic Rights of Women*, March 1984, p.3.

28   Crimes Against Women in Iran

Simin Ahmady

Simin Ahmady is a schoolteacher living in the Iranian capital, Teheran. With the help of funding from the International Women's Solidarity Fund, in 1985 she completed a one-year study on violence against women in Iran, much of which is based on the country's newspaper coverage of anti-woman crimes.

The following is an edited sample from that study, the original of which appeared in the first newsletter of the International Working Group on Women and the Family (November 1985), based in London (see Networks).

A man who suspected his wife's modesty abducted her and took her to the deserts around Varamin, east of Teheran, where he took out her eyes with a knife in order that she never set sight on any man again. The woman's father, Gassem, prosecuted his son-in-law, Tagi Zavarei Tabatabaii, in the No. 13 Criminal Court of Teheran, under the Islamic Code of Retribution. Tagi was found guilty and condemned to the loss of one eye since, under the Islamic Code of Practice, two female eyes are equivalent to one of a man's. In September 1984, reporters from the Iranian newspaper, *Keyhan*, interviewed Maryam, the victim, in the presence of her parents and young brother, Mahmood. This is what she said:

> My husband is 24 years old and has a Do-It-Yourself shop. I was married to him at the age of 12 and have three children by him, aged 12, 8 and 6 respectively. During the years I have lived with him I haven't had one happy day. My husband is a jealous and suspicious man. He used to be so suspicious of me that when he left the house he would lock the door and take the key with him, leaving me inside. When my parents or neighbours protested about his behaviour, his reply was: 'I like to train my wife this way'. He believed that women ought to do all the work in the house, heavy or light. I used to have to shift great big wardrobes and heavy chests of drawers on my own. No one was allowed to help me. He was so suspicious that he wouldn't even let me hang up the washing outside on the roof. He told me I should ask his mother to do it for me, but she refused since she thought it was my job. We would argue with Tagi together. If he saw me wiping the windows we'd have fights because he believed I was only doing it as an excuse to look out into the streets at men.

Maryam cried as she explained her life story. She said she had never committed any sinful act of looking at a stranger, either outside or inside her home.

HAMIDEH

After years of quarrels and fighting and degrading treatment, I decided to petition for a divorce. I first applied in 1359 (1980) to the Family Protection Courts. The judge agreed with me that Tagi wasn't a suitable husband and should divorce me. Under current Islamic laws in Iran a wife cannot divorce her husband so I had to live with my family until he was persuaded to do it. This is where I have been, away from my children, ever since. He would not divorce me, no matter how much we tried to reason with him.

It was in Nour Rooz 1361 (New Year in Iran, 21 March 1982) that he blinded me. I had gone to see my sister along with my brother, Mahmood. I was waiting in queue for the telephone when a woman tapped me on the shoulder and pointed to my husband to see what he wanted. Mahmood came back and told me that Tagi wanted to take me to see the children. Thinking they would be in the car, I went to him immediately but found only my youngest son. Tagi said the others were waiting at home and that I should go with him to see them. He promised to behave himself. He took out a Koran from his pocket and swore not to hurt me. I decided to trust him and, together with my brother, got into the car. I soon noticed that he wasn't driving in the right direction, but he denied it, saying that I had simply forgotten how to get to Varamin after two years of refusing to go to his home. Eventually he stopped the car in the middle of nowhere, got out and opened the trunk. Two men jumped out. Tagi snatched my son away from me and pulled me out of the car by my hair. He then forced me on to the ground, drew out a knife and took out both my eyes. The two accomplices got scared and ran away, as did my brother. Not knowing what to do next, Tagi now tried to blackmail me by saying that if I wanted to get home I had better tell people that I'd had an accident and a piece of iron had caught my eyes. Then he put me in the trunk and drove to Varamin. I guessed we had arrived when I heard

191

the voices of people shouting slogans in the burial ceremony of an Islamic martyr. I started screaming and banging on the lid until people stopped the car and found me there. Tagi told them I was his wife and we'd been in an accident, but they refused to believe him. I was taken to the hospital and Tagi to the Police.

Maryam was resentful of the Retribution Laws which required her to pay her husband the price of his eyes if she was to see him punished by the Islamic Courts – a sum of money beyond her parents' financial means.

We won the case in court, but according to these laws I can claim only one of Tagi's eyes, considered to be worth two of mine. To punish Tagi properly will cost us the price of 2,625 ounces of silver. However, with a lot of effort I've managed to find the money and pay the court so I will see justice done.

A *Keyhan* reporter asked Maryam if she wouldn't forgive Tagi for his 'stupidity and youthfulness', but she refused to even listen.

Tagi must lose both his eyes for him to know how I feel with no eyes to see by. My parents have to look after me all the time. Of course I want my children back and Tagi must pay for their upkeep. My father is only a manual worker with one of the municipal offices and cannot afford to support us all. However, the final decision regarding my children's custody is up to the Islamic Courts. I can only consider it to be my right to have my children with me after all that I've gone through.

My name is Simin. I live in Iran and have been doing research into male violence against women in my country for the last 12 months. I do so by buying all magazines and newspapers published in Iran, nationally and locally. (Oh, no . . . there are no longer any local papers here. Due to censorship laws, no groups or individuals can set up a newspaper, nor even keep a photocopier at home. It is against the law.) I also collect evidence on male violence by keeping a diary on what I see and hear around me, on the streets, at work and at home.

The story above is only one from many of my newspaper cuttings indicating the everyday extent of male violence against women in Iran. I am hoping to show that being a woman in Iran today is the most horrific experience. Not that it was any better under the Shah. Iranian women have been forced to submit themselves to the men in their families for centuries.

The late Shah made a half-hearted attempt at change by giving Iranian women the vote and the right to initiate divorce or have custody of their children, if the courts thought it proper. But it's said that these were partially a response to pressures from the multinational business companies which needed a cheap and efficient labour force. Women are very good, hard workers here in Iran. We work in offices, factories, on the land, as well as doing all the housework and looking after the children. On top of that, since the Islamic revolution we have to spend hours on our feet every day, standing in food queues. Housework in Iran is similar to working in a factory. The boss has the right to discipline the worker if she has not done her duty properly. That is, if Iranian women show negligence regarding household tasks; if they don't complete their chores neatly and on time, the man in the family has the right not only to reprimand them but to take disciplinary action.

Here's an example from a newshort printed in *Etelaat*, one of our two major daily newspapers.

> On 16th Mordad 1364 (July 1985) it was reported that a man was arrested in Ardakan and charged with murdering his wife 44 days previously. He had only been married for one month when he came home to find that his wife had cooked Iranian broth for dinner, despite the fact that she knew he didn't like it. He slapped her on the face three times and she fell to the floor unconscious, whereupon he took her to the basement, wrapped her dead body in a blanket and ran away.

There are no laws or social customs to support or protect Iranian women against these male atrocities. The present Islamic Republic altered whatever meagre legal measures the Shah had provided towards allowing women to have some say of their own. All laws today are in favour of men and their dominance over women. Even when men quite viciously violate women's human rights, the law operates in their favour. In the first story you read that, even though the husband blinded Maryam, she has to pay him before she can see him punished.

Newspaper reporting is also distorted as they inevitably try to put the blame on the woman. In that story the interviewer at one point challenged the blind woman's wish to confront her husband in order that he see how she feels having lost her eyes. His own vicious action is never questioned.

Against this background, as my research evidence shows, woman-killing happens quite often in Iran. Brothers, fathers, husbands feel they have a right to demand that women pay with their lives in order to sustain family honour and generally uphold the family as an institution that maintains Iranian patriarchal society. Such violence is necessary if women are to be kept as slaves subservient to men. We have a saying in Iran that 'if a man really wants to keep his wife under control, he must make sure that he gives her a good beating every now and again'. Iranian men begin exercising their authority over women as children, over their sisters, mothers, no matter how young these future patriarchs may be.

On 25th of Shahrivar 1364 (September 1985), *Keyhan* reported that:

> A 28 year old woman was stabbed to death in front of her own home. Her name was Eshrat Souri, a nurse in Mehere Hospital in Teheran. The police were informed of the murder in a telephone call from neighbours who had gathered around the body in Ladak Avenue. The neighbours told reporters that Eshrat was originally from Bakhtaran, west of Iran, and now lived here alone with her child. After marrying in Bakhtaran she had left her husband on account of marital disputes and quarrels within the family. Today her brother had come to see her in Teheran and they had been quarrelling a lot. Later, when Eshrat came home from work, he stopped her in front of her house and stabbed her to death, taking advantage of the dark to make his escape.

This murder I shall classify as a 'Crime of Honour'. Ask any Iranian about this incident and they will explain the reasons behind it: Eshrat had lived and married in Bakhtaran, most probably where her family and brother live too; they marry her off to a husband with whom she doesn't get on, although she tries hard to make the marriage work. As a result she has a baby by her unwanted husband. Eventually, unable to persuade her husband to give her a divorce, she leaves him and her home town for Teheran where she lives independently as a single mother.

Her chauvinist, prejudiced brother cannot cope with the *scandal* of his sister, not only leaving her husband but moving to Teheran to start a new life. No woman in Iran should live independently of men. Probably his friends keep nagging him about his weakness and easy-going attitude to his sister's behaviour. One day hell breaks loose and in a rush of madness the brother comes to the capital and decides either to take her home or kill her and therefore eradicate this disgrace to his family. Eshrat refuses to go with him, so he does what he's made up his mind to do and stabs her to death.

Family honour is a very delicate issue in Iran and women, and how they behave, are the only elements which keep it intact. No women have the right to determine their own sexuality or sexual partners. Any 'perverted' behaviour is severely punishable by Civil Law. That is, women who step outside their controlled boundaries are accountable both to the male members of their family and to the Iranian Civil Courts, which are mainly set up to reinforce and ensure the social control of Iranian women. Further illustration of this control is shown in the amount of money and other resources which the Islamic Republic is prepared to spend on forcing women to wear the veil, on the streets and at work, and the fact that veiled or unveiled Iranian women cannot walk the streets of our cities without sexual harassment or assault.

This situation will continue as long as Iranian men feel they are superior to women and therefore should be in control. Some say that education will eventually change male attitudes. Although I am inclined to agree with this belief, the evidence I have collected shows otherwise. Many well-educated and highly qualified Iranian men kill and batter their wives. As a schoolteacher, I hear my students talking about the violence their mothers suffer day and night at the hands of their fathers. I have also collected many newshorts from Iranian dailies, describing cases where men of status have murdered their wives. As usual, there is never any proper investigation as to the causes of such violence. I believe that only a team of sympathetic women will find out why it is so widespread and fatal.

Newspapers only mention family problems as reasons for women's killing; we need to specify what kind of family problems. As a woman living in Teheran, who is married with children and also works outside the home, I'd say that vicious acts of violence against women stem from jealousy, prejudice, and the male desire for power and control over women. I can't help feeling that it's my duty to rush home after work and make sure the food is ready, the house is clean and the children are properly dressed. I feel my husband has the right to question me, shout at me and rule over me, even though I work as a teacher eight hours a day and bring home a wage; even though I have to stand in long queues to do my shopping for the evening meal. I don't know why I still feel this way, but I am almost certain it's how all Iranian women feel and see themselves.

My research shows that many Iranian women, young and old, commit suicide, again as the newspapers specify, because of family problems. This I can understand. Quarrels and rows with husbands, brothers and fathers can be nerve-wracking and demand a lot of courage. I have evidence of several women who, in despair, have died by setting themselves alight. Others throw themselves into big rivers or into the sea. There are so few sources of comfort. Take this advice to a young woman who wrote to the Iranian woman's magazine, *Zan-e-Rooz*:

> I am N. Mohammadi. On 5th Sharivar 1362 (September 1983) I went to court and demanded a divorce from my fiancé with whom I cannot get on. The court decided that I had no right to divorce him and that I could only force him to divorce me by demanding my *mahriyeh* (bride-price). My fiancé says he is prepared to pay my *mahriyeh* by monthly instalment, but he won't divorce me. Please let me know what to do. I am not going to his home, ever.

The advice given by the magazine is that she has no right to divorce her fiancé, which is why the court refused to accept her petition. Well, I wouldn't be surprised if this woman had already committed suicide. A potential marriage which is so obviously unworkable should be terminated now.

I've also read a report about a woman killed only six days after her marriage, which took place despite the fact that bride and bridegroom had quarrelled and fought throughout their six month engagement. Having threatened to kill her several times, he merely waited until after the wedding to carry it out.

Such is, and has been, the lot of Iranian women: battered, maimed, murdered and driven to take their own lives, with virtually no one to hear their cries for help. Through my research and writing up of some of these accounts I feel that I'm at least doing something to challenge the overall silence which surrounds the situation and experiences of Iranian women.

29 SOS – Mulher of Rio de Janeiro: An Interview

Maria Laura Cavalcanti (Lalá) and
Maria Luiza Heilborn (Malu)

SOS – Mulher in Rio was one of the first Brazilian women's groups to provide a support, help and advice service for women victims of violence. This interview with two longstanding members, Lígia Rodrigues and Rita Andréa, was recorded in September 1982. Although SOS has changed and matured a lot since then, its basic aims remain the same.

Thanks to Ines Rieder for providing the interview, first published in the journal *Perspectivas Antropológicas da Mulher* (No.4, December 1985), and translating it from Portuguese.

Malu: *First we'd like to know how SOS began and how it sees itself as part of an alternative feminist practice.*

Lígia: Well, violence as an issue was taken up by the Brazilian feminist movement only in 1979. There had already been a few articles about violence against women in newspapers and magazines, including certain feminist demands, but it wasn't adopted as a cause by the movement until the National Women's Conference which took place that year. Despite reluctance from the organisers – during a planning meeting I even heard the old cliché 'in Brazil a woman is beaten because she likes it' – violence was eventually listed in the topics for discussion.

The conference workshop on violence included, among others, two women who are now in SOS and many more who continued the work and then got lost. Basically, this original discussion was so good, so rich and to-the-point, including relations between us, that we decided to carry on meeting to formulate some plan of action.

Out of this grew the Committee on Violence Against Women. In 1979 and 1980 the Committee operated like so many other feminist groups in Brazil at that time; that's to say it was relatively closed, combining consciousness-raising on specific topics with trying to do something more concrete and visible through agitation and propaganda. But we reached only a small number of women. From the beginning, we knew that in order to advance our work, whatever its form, we had to develop a structure and way of working that really involved women. But it took us a long time to get there – to find the courage to actually form an SOS group.

Cover of popular education booklet (Centro de Defesa dos Direitos Humanos, Paraiba, Brazil).

Gradually, however, women who were living in some sort of situation of violence began to come to us. We did whatever we could, sending them to feminists and lawyers for counselling, but it was all very precarious. We were worried about not having the answers, yet when a woman did come to us we became very involved and her problem soon became ours.

Around this time the first trial of Doca Street [a well-known playboy who killed his girl-friend – a rich woman who had left her husband to live with him] took place and he was acquitted. We couldn't organise a demonstration before the trial, but managed to collect 500 signatures in a campaign of protest, published in the daily *Jornal do Brasil*. Then there were the two women murdered, one after the other, in the state of Minas Gerais. A group of women from the capital, Belo Horizonte, organised a series of demonstrations, went to mass and called legal representatives from São Paulo and Rio to look into the case. The husband and murderer of one of the dead women, Eloísa Bellesteros, claimed to have almost 'caught her in the act of adultery' when he saw her talking to an ex-lover in a shopping centre. The defence was based on the argument that Eloísa had been too interested in her professional career and neglected her obligations as 'wife and mother'. [Three years later the husband was sentenced to two years in jail.]

Malu: *I remember, it was covered in the newspapers.*

Lígia: Yes, and there were repercussions in other states. Feminists in São Paulo became motivated to do something about violence and started to consider founding an SOS group, which was finally established in 1981. Meanwhile, we in Rio were in a state of 'mental masturbation', reflecting, reading, writing, feeling desperate and worried without getting anywhere.

What finally changed us was the murder of Christel Johnston. After leaving her husband in December 1978, she was followed by him and molested constantly up until her death. Not one of her frequent requests for police and legal protection were heeded. We knew her well for she'd worked with the Committee for some months and the murder had a great impact on us. We had lived through her situation with her, do you understand? It was something very, very painful. It hurts more than your political consciousness or preoccupations. As a result, Maria Alice, Nilce, Stella, Virginia and I proposed the founding of SOS at a feminist meeting.

Malu: *And how did you become involved, Rita?*

Rita: I had never been a militant and didn't have any experience with the feminist movement. I thought it important but wasn't keen to join a consciousness-raising group. I wanted to take part in concrete action. I went to this meeting in response to a proposal being circulated about starting up an SOS group to tackle the problem of violence. I was also motivated by the proposed method of practice which allowed me to organise around having a small child.

Lalá: *What was the biggest inspiration to create structures like SOS – Mulher here in Brazil?*

Lígia: Many of our ideas about violence were influenced by what was going on in Europe, where quite a few Brazilian feminists had lived. But in reality the situation in Brazil was not the same. To begin with it was thought that here, as in all European countries, the big issue, the major aspect of violence that would persuade women to come out, to denounce and to go to court, would be rape. But it was different: it was the question of murdering women. As far as I'm concerned, this is what lay behind the foundation of organisations such as SOS.

Lalá: *Was it to do with the fact that those murders happened at a particular time?*

Lígia: No. The murder of women in Brazil is a serious problem. It happens all the time. Depending on what newspaper you read, it happens every day.

Malu: *Why were the murders a focus in Brazil?*

Lígia: One reason is that, up until recently, no woman had ever denounced having been raped, let alone reported it to the press or allowed it to be taken up as a cause by the feminist movement. Murder is a public crime, independent of the victim's accusation. It makes newspaper headlines, even when it happens to women.

Lalá: *Is SOS leading feminism here in Rio? Is it the strongest organisation in terms of feminist direction?*

Rita: As far as autonomous feminist practice goes there is only SOS.

Lígia: The group isn't that 'strong' but at least . . .

Rita: We achieve our aims by working regular hours when we can help the women who come to us, from whatever kind of violence they might be suffering.

Malu: *Who does this regular work?*

Rita: There are 15 of us, aged between 25 and 40. We all have university education and all are feminists. Most of us have been in other groups.

Lígia: Almost everyone comes from a background of militancy, either here or in Europe. We have plenty of economists and sociologists. There are physicists, journalists, teachers, psychologists . . .

Lalá: *Lawyers?*

Rita: Not a single one.

Lígia: No, lawyers are lawyers; they are neither militants nor volunteers.

Malu: *How does your schedule work?*

Rita: We have weekly sessions on Tuesdays and Wednesdays from 3 to 8pm. We take turns so that each has her duties every fortnight. At the moment four women work together on one shift.

Lalá: *Four deal with one case?*

Rita: No, that depends. When it's necessary we split up, usually according to the needs of individual women. If someone wants to talk but is intimidated by the presence of so many women we leave the room.

Lala: *What kind of women show up? Who are your clients?*

Rita: All sorts, maybe because we're in the centre of town. Women from the South Zone [wealthy neighbourhoods] come, middle-class students, professionals, women from the shanty towns, many from the suburbs and even from right outside. We see lots of 'low-income' women.

Lígia: I would say the lower-middle class. They are not the proletariat, the manual workers but middle-class women: housewives.

Lígia: If she works outside she may be a public employee, earning the equivalent of, say, US $150 a month, and he a sales clerk earning up to twice that amount . . . or a public employee, too, or a cab driver . . .

Rita: Most of the women who come to us can't afford to pay a lawyer, so we have to find them legal aid. Often women who work, for instance doing occasional cleaning jobs, hide the fact from their husbands for fear they will beat them up. The women who come here are really mixed up.

Lígia: For some reason it's always worst on Tuesdays. Many more women come and with usually the worse problems. Ages range from about 20 to 62. Most are white; I've not seen any black women.

Rita: Oh, I've dealt with quite a few.

Lala: *How is the violence focused?*

Lígia: In our files there are 25 cases of women who are either separated from their husbands, or else want to be, in order to escape being beaten.

Malu: *What motive, besides violence, makes these women want to leave?*

Rita: The man drinks, he doesn't give her any money, she has to support the children . . . beyond necessity there's no sense in staying with a guy who simply doesn't fulfil his obligations. He may have another woman, whatever the case a part of it is always that men don't help out at home.

Malu: *Being a bad provider, is that it?*

Rita: Many come to us saying: 'If he had another woman but still gave me money to keep the children, it wouldn't matter so much – at least he'd be supporting the family.'

Lígia: There's a difference here between poorer women and those from the middle class, who give reasons like: 'We have nothing left in common. I don't like him anymore.' But the guy won't accept the separation.

Rita: He never accepts it.

Lalá: *Is that always the case?*

Lígia: Yes. He never accepts. This is absolutely consistent.

Rita: And he threatens her with death, with what he'll do, what will happen and how he'll take the children away.

Lígia: He tells her she has no rights and that she will lose everything. Men profit a lot from women's ignorance about their rights.

Malu: *How long do women tend to put up with this kind of situation?*

Rita: One, for example, suffered from the start of her marriage. She told me that on her wedding night her husband decided she wasn't a virgin because she didn't bleed. He has beaten her ever since and humiliated her in front of friends, saying he's married to a woman who 'was not a girl'. Her life became hell. She has three children, the youngest of whom is now 36. Only through coming to SOS has she found a lawyer who assures her that she won't lose the roof over her head if she kicks him out. She's now given him an ultimatum to leave.

Malu: *Do her children still live with her?*

Rita: Only the youngest who is very nervous. We sent her for psychiatric treatment. The mother is a typical case: she makes sweets to sell, mends sheets, makes pillows, all hidden from her husband. They live near me. It's a totally mad situation.

Malu: *And he beats her until this day?*

Rita: As far as we know. When she came to SOS we talked to her and the daughter for about three hours. We managed to wake her up for she, too, has made mistakes. The man hardly ever sleeps at home since he has another woman, but when he does appear everything has to be ready – clothes ironed, food on the table etc. Otherwise he beats her and makes a scandal for the whole neighbourhood to hear. It's a long story, very difficult to resolve but at least she's beginning to take charge of the situation in giving him a date by which to leave.

Lígia: A woman we have been in contact with for quite a while, who's now left her husband, put her finger on it when she was talking to another client who had showed up for the first time. 'The problem is', she said, 'that you never talk about it with other women. And because you never say anything you never realise how others live or that they experience the same things. You always think you're the only one. You're ashamed that it's happening to you and have to justify it. Everyone thinks this way. Women don't talk to each other and we all remain isolated.' This is precisely the problem which crops up in all the statements we receive.

It's amazing what women put up with. There's one who works as a maid; she's 35 and has been married for 11 years. Her husband started beating her two days after the wedding. Eventually he forbade her to speak to anyone or leave the house. Their sex life was unsatisfactory. He refused any of her advances and would only have relations with her after watching dances on television which excited him. Otherwise he'd beat the children. She was telling us all this when all of a sudden she said: 'Well, all I can say is that it's because he's a worker and responsible for bringing the money home.'

Rita: Middle-class women don't talk like this. They come up with disguised justifications, like 'he beat me because he was nervous' or 'Ah, he was just drunk'. It's crazy . . . partly a problem of education, how we are taught to see ourselves, that is, if we are battered it must be because we did something wrong.

Lalá: *Are children often beaten too?*

Lígia: Usually men only beat their wives or the woman they are living with. The majority don't beat children; they're not violent men in other situations. Women often say: 'People don't believe me when I tell them. But he's so nice, they say.' He's nice at work, nice in his social relations, nice as a militant, nice in the bar . . . He's not this brute who walks down the street, knocking down anyone who looks at him the wrong way. If he did, it'd be possible to confirm that he batters his wife at home.

Malu: *What provokes such masculine rage?*

Lígia: Often seemingly nothing. For instance, two days before Christmas the wife says to the husband: 'What's happening? You didn't put any money aside for the children's presents.' He turns to her and says: 'Here's your Christmas present right now', and POW!

Rita: Or it can be provoked by a woman's refusal to have sex, although this usually only happens if she is already being beaten for other reasons as well. A man may beat his wife because he doesn't want her to watch television. The quantity and diversity of motives merely show that these aren't the real reasons, which are far more complex.

Lígia: One element is a man's insecurity in his role as dominator and controller; having to keep up the image of macho all-powerful master assigned by society.

Battering is one way for men to keep intact the mechanisms by which they dominate women.

Rita: I also think that society has a role to play. The tradition of marriage is very strong. A man won't leave his wife and when she threatens to leave him, taking the children with her, his reaction is to want to kill her.

Lígia: He kills, he kills the dog, the cat . . .

Rita: There's such pressure to live up to the ideal family model that they feel threatened themselves. They also don't like losing the comfort of having food and clean clothes, in other words the unpaid maid. And women have no idea of their rights. They don't ask for alimony or anything, just the freedom to escape with their children and not to be killed.

Lalá: *How do you take care of the women who arrive at SOS?*

Rita: It depends on the individual woman. We wait for them to speak and it starts from there. There's always more than one helper present to assist the discussion. We ask questions to make them think a little, although in general we know that the first thing they want is a lawyer. We provide technical knowledge about women's rights while at the same time allowing them the security to talk about other things. Sometimes we do it all in one session, sometimes not, especially if a woman just wants a lawyer straight away . . . Often they want a concrete solution.

Lalá: *But also support?*

Lígia: Yes, and they want to be heard. They want someone who will listen although we always combine it with talking about ourselves. I like to do this. She tells me something and I tell her, for example, about my own separation or about my difficulties in finding an apartment. It somehow helps to put the situation in perspective.

Rita: It's hard from the position of psychologist or psychiatrist, being on a pedestal, but we try to avoid establishing a relationship of power between us and the women who come for help. We at least try to be on equal footing. A woman who has had three husbands and is now leaving the third might start asking the others if they've ever been married. I say that I am. 'And you got a separation?' 'No', I reply. 'But how long have you been married?' I tell her eleven years. 'That's impossible. You must live well!' I do.

Lalá: *What aim do you want to achieve with these women you're helping?*

Lígia: That's a good question. One way or another we try to improve their lives by encouraging them to leave their situation and resolve certain problems. But SOS has wider aims. We are a political organisation with political interests, in the sense of feminist politics of course.

Malu: *How are relations among the women working with SOS?*

Rita: We are a democratic organisation in that we all share the work.

Lígia: Horizontally, we all do the same thing.

Lalá: *You mean there's no internal hierarchy?*

Lígia: No, none in the formal sense but it practically always happens. You know how it is. It's part of the crisis we're currently going through. There's always someone who is doing things better, who talks more or is stronger and more aggressive. At a certain point, those who carry the group on their shoulders – and it always happens – say 'enough'. No one in particular is to blame: there used to be a little group leading and then, some time ago, it stopped. Now it's more complicated since we're having to work without someone to push us; to try to work horizontally at best, and I don't think we know how to do it.

Malu: *Do you ever get women coming who you don't consider to be victims of violence? Are there women you don't like or cases that simply don't move you?*

Lígia: All the weird cases come on Tuesdays. Sometime I must change my day to see them. There was a woman married to the doorman of a building. He fell ill and eventually died and she did his work for months, but they didn't want to pay her a salary. It was a question for the labour courts.

Malu: *Why didn't you resolve this case?*

Rita: It was about exploitation and discrimination against a woman living on her own.

Lígia: Then there were the two women who lived together in a relationship. One came to SOS, saying that they were being discriminated against and persecuted in their building. We called a lawyer and went to a meeting in the building, only to find out that it was them causing the problem. They used to argue and beat up the children, but we had a good relationship with them.

Rita: What about the other two women who won't admit that they are living together? They live close by . . .

Lígia: They didn't even want to come out to us.

Rita: Maria finally came out, but only after several long talks. It was also a question of dominance. The older one was dominating the younger, until she finally admitted it. They are a typical couple: one in the house, cooking, washing and cleaning while the other leaves to work outside. They argued with the neighbours; one woman called them 'dykes' and it ended up in a fight.

Lígia: We went crazy. We were prepared to receive women victims of male violence but this was a case of women doing the beating. It all happened in the beginning when we simply weren't ready for it.

Rita: We have had funny incidents too. A woman once telephoned one of us, Rosa, at home and said: 'Is that SOS-Mulher?' Rosa answered: 'No, but I work with SOS. What's it about?' She was Portuguese and her problem was simple. She had a number of children . . .

Lígia: They had all grown up, gone to college and become doctors, engineers, lawyers and architects . . .

Rita: . . . all well-to-do and living in Recife while their mother continued to live in Rio. Now they wanted her to come and visit them.

Lígia: And she wanted a course in manners in order to know how to behave in her son's house! SOS can be lots of fun!

30 Shelter for Battered Women in Thailand

Women's Information Centre

The Women's Information Centre, based in Bangkok, campaigns to improve the situation of Thai women, especially prostitutes working in Thailand and overseas. A recent information sheet describes the Centre's origin and aims:

Due to economic problems and very limited opportunities in finding jobs that generate sufficient income to support children and family, many Thai women decide to search for a so-called 'better life' in foreign countries. But, frequently, the reality which they encounter as aliens abroad is worse than before, since they are stripped of their freedom, lured into exploitative conditions, forced and molested, subjected to racial and sexual prejudices, and restricted to work only in the service sector, particularly in sexual services or outright prostitution.

These unjust conditions gave birth to the Women's Information Centre which is run by a collective of Thai social activists, who have committed themselves to struggle for the rights of women. The Centre started in 1984 with a counselling service for Thai women who intend to go abroad hoping to find a 'better life' there. As members of the Centre know from our own experiences what sort of life migrant Thai women will encounter in alien countries, they provide the most realistic information and, if required, other forms of individual assistance without violating the principle that every person has the right to decide on her own. This service aims at learning more details about the personal background and motivation of migrant Thai women, at increasing their critical consciousness, and at preventing that more sisters fall into this misery and distress.

However, it was soon recognised that written information is of very little value to those migrant women due to their low literacy. Moreover, it became the basic position of the Women's Information Centre that structural changes have to be initiated by organised and conscious women, in order to eliminate impoverishment and exploitation.

Since then, the Centre has extended its programme considerably. The new thrust focuses on the creation of developmental modules for professional skills training, for awareness-building, for organising and for self-determination of women in rural areas, in factories and in poor, congested urban quarters. Appropriate educational media are designed and produced in close cooperation with these women. In order to disseminate more knowledge to the broader public on the productive and emotional life of women, the Women's Information Centre also supports women-related studies and research.

This article outlines some of the Centre's research before opening up a now established refuge for battered women. It is reproduced from a special women's issue of the *Thai Development Newsletter* (Vol 4, No 1, Spring 1986).

The Women's Shelter Programme is another step forward for the Women's Information Centre (WIC). The programme is the outcome of increasing needs felt by WIC staff on the issue of family violence. After long association with women in Bangkok slum areas, WIC staff discovered that Thai women are facing another kind of daily violence – domestic violence. An increasing number of women are being physically and mentally abused by their own husbands.

In a family, a wife already suffers from the economic problem no less than her husband. A wife, however, is obliged to carry a double burden, that is the traditional role of 'wife and mother' in maintaining household chores and raising children, and being a 'sandbag' for her husband. Many wives found themselves becoming objects on which their husbands could vent their frustrations, indignation and tension from work, as well as to attack when drunk.

From the records of *Baan Tarn Tawan* (an emergency home for women and children) and the Children Foundation during the first half of 1985, 25% of children receiving treatment at the two Centres (25 out of 100) come from families where the mother is routinely beaten.

From our conversation with women in slum areas of Klong Toey, we found that 50% of these women are regularly battered by their husbands. Statistics of battered women in general, however, do not yet exist due to the lack of data-gathering mechanism in both governmental and private sectors.

Such an absence reflects the lack of interest among social authorities over the plight of battered wives. The reasons can be threefold:

1. Society considers that a husband is entitled to 'discipline' his wife, therefore battering a wife is categorised as a 'private' problem of each family.
2. Society perceives that it is usually women who stimulate violence and hostility in men: 'She asked for it'.
3. Service agencies, both governmental and private, fail to understand the interrelationships between family violence and socio-economic problems, therefore do not provide specific assistance. Consequently, battered women have no refuge to turn to even in times of crisis which threaten their lives. Most women tolerate all kinds of maltreatment, abuses and violence not as free will, but have no choice.

From our experience, most battered women do need assistance during a crisis. Some women want temporary separation so that they can have time to analyse their own problems and thereby find solutions for themselves. Instead of reconciliation some women want to divorce, but only if they can be economically self-reliant – for themselves and their children.

But without any neighbourhood or social assistance at all, and when the abuse becomes intolerable, a few women return violence with violence. For example, on 12 October 1985, in the Klong Toey slum area, Mrs Moo Intachet stabbed her husband who was always extorting money from her and beat her daily. Once she found that her husband was dead, she thought that her bad 'Karma' with him was over. ('Karma' in the Buddhist belief is the accumulation of good or bad deeds in the past, which influence one's present life.)

We are aware that the issue of battered women is not merely one of 'bad Karma' or a 'private matter' of each individual woman. We see it as a problem imbedded in our social structure, which neglects the fundamental rights of women. Because society has undermined the plight of women, the 'Women's Shelter' was established, to provide needed assistance to women suffering from family violence, and to stimulate public consciousness over this issue.

The Women's Shelter Programme

The aims are as follows:

1. To provide proper assistance to battered women in terms of an alternative 'home', a temporary refuge for physical and mental recovery as well as to provide legal consultation.

2. To organise group therapy in which victimised women can exchange their experiences, ideas and feelings in order to increase their capacity to understand and deal with their own problems.

3. To mobilise public consciousness over the issue of battered wives as another form of violence which any woman, regardless of status or class, can fall prey to.

4. To produce visual aids and educational media for public dissemination, on the whole issue of family violence looking towards public resolution.

5. To encourage the setting up of a 'Women's Shelter' in other provinces.

Survey on public reaction to the Programme: summary of responses

After we decided to found a women's shelter for battered women, we designed a set of questionnaires to elicit public opinions and suggestions about this programme. The questionnaire was distributed to women of various professions so that the response would become useful criteria for setting up the 'Women's Shelter'. The aim of our attempt is to be able to launch the 'Women's Shelter' Programme to meet the real needs of a larger section of needy women.

We conducted the survey during October–November 1985 by randomly sampling 150 women, including housewives, vendors, hawkers, construction workers, factory labourers, slum women, lower-ranking government officials, teachers, Health Department staff, state enterprise employers and college students. The responses can be summarised as follows:

1. About 50% of the informants, especially among women in slum areas and the construction sector, experienced physical abuse. The causes are attributed to economic pressures, drunkenness or gambling. Other causes which ignited domestic conflict are children's problems, sexual jealousy or minor wives.

2. Although the other 50% of informants have never experienced physical abuse, they have witnessed the hostility incurred by their married friends, neighbours as well as in their own families (parents or relatives). Mass media, such as films, television and radio programmes and newspapers, also contribute to their awareness about family violence.

3. The poll indicates that battering of women can happen to any woman, regardless of class or profession. This phenomenon, however, is more apparent among women in the bottom rung of society who have no secure or definite income. They are workers such as wage labourers, vendors, hawkers and low-ranking officials as well as those who were lured into the 'special service' sector.

4. Opinions show that men attack their wives because of men's weakness, male-dominated social values and women's compromising nature. Men have less capacity to tolerate and are usually unable to control their temper; therefore, they exercise their aggressiveness and physical strength not only to cover up their weakness but also as a sure way to overcome women. This habit can be related to early childhood training in families, which emphasises men's role to be strong and the leader of the family. Ironically, women's nature to reconcile and tolerate such oppression encourages men to use violence.

5. The reasons why women abide physical abuse are economic dependency, social expectations for a woman to be a dutiful daughter, a loyal wife and a pious mother. Divorce can be a stigma for the woman's parents as well as for herself, that is, the parents failed to train their daughter to be a 'good wife'. Often a woman tolerates her husband's hostility because of her forgiving nature . . . Her husband is a nice man when not drunk, some day he may quit drinking and behave better, etc. She fears that her children will feel inferior for not having a father. Most of all, women lack self-confidence that they can survive and manage their own lives without their husbands.

6. Battered women tend not to report their cases to the police because of shame and having no confidence in them. Women feel that the problem is private. To report the incident will only spread this 'shameful' problem beyond the family boundary, which may fuel the husband's anger as well as harm the children's self esteem.

7. Violence is mostly initiated by men's mischief rather than women's.

8. About 90% of the respondents think that men do not have any right to batter their wives. The remaining respondents – mainly housewives – approve the husband's right to 'punish' their misbehaviour, but suggested that the punishment should be mild for better understanding rather than violence and suppression.

9. About 40% of the respondents consider that a battered wife is a private, family problem. Another 40% feel that all women share this problem, therefore there should be a dialogue between victimised and non-victimised women. The other 20% think the problem can be either, so one should consider each case individually to sort out which should be disclosed.

10. Almost all the respondents think that there should be a temporary shelter

where battered women can recover, physically and mentally. A few with a higher educational background were of the opinion that a shelter does not tackle the root cause. They, however, agree with the principle that a temporary shelter is necessary for battered women in crisis to find peace of mind and have time to analyse their problems. Such a place enables the victims to exchange their feelings with each other as well as to gain proper consultation from empathetic specialists. In this light, such a shelter can inspire oppressed women to live and take charge of their own lives.

11. Suggestions on the needs of women in crises in addition to a women's shelter are: group therapy (discussion among the victims); proper physical and mental treatment and care; specialists' advice for legal rights and actions against violence. Since economic dependency perpetuates violence, the women's shelter should offer skill training for income generation. The shelter should also produce media which reflects womens' plight by means of films or music in order to conscientise all women about their rights over their own bodies.

Paradoxically, many suggest a shelter for men who are prone to violence to train them to understand and respect the basic rights and dignity of women and of all individuals. A man's shelter could be necessary to stimulate men to be responsible towards their families as well as to teach them to use reason rather than violence to resolve family conflict.

12. According to the poll, an 'ideal' shelter should be a private home in a safe location, with a playground and a space for vegetable gardening, to create an atmosphere of home rather than a prison. House activities such as skills training will not only be a means of mental therapy, but also to equip the women with the

ability to be economically self-reliant in the future. Moreover, the staff at the shelter should be friendly, empathetic and able to nurse as well as provide psychological advice.

13. Suggested strategies towards wider cooperation and public resolution against family violence start with the consciousness of the victimised women . . . family violence is not shameful or private. Non-victimised women should, on the one hand, learn on the other give encouragement and possible assistance to victimised women. This will lead to a collective study and analysis to tackle the root cause of family violence. Some women should start classes, for instance on self-defence or skills training; women should also unite to stigmatise those men who use physical strength to oppress women. As a mother, each woman can inculcate new attitudes and values in her children to exercise reason rather than violence and to respect and honour women.

14. In order to campaign against family violence, battered women should be courageous enough to unveil their real situation to the public. A woman's shelter can be a medium for disseminating their factual data via the mass media. Women should form a pressure group to review laws unjust to women, as well as to campaign for legal action against aggressive men in order to curb family violence.

15. The poll also indicates the need to expand the number of services similar to the 'Women's Shelter' into other provinces and rural areas. In addition, all women's shelters should be part of the network of a campaign on the issue of battered women.

31   Strategies Against Prostitution in Thailand

Siriporn Skrobanek

Siriporn Skrobanek is director of the Women's Information Centre, described above. She is also on the editorial staff of the *Thai Development Newsletter* which published her following study.

Prostitution is certainly not women's oldest profession, but it is a mode of reproduction in a male dominated society, in which women's sexuality is controlled and utilised for male sexual pleasure. To consider prostitution as women's oldest profession neglects the role and participation of women in economic activities – in every mode of production since human history is recorded. Most of the work done by women in production and reproductive tasks like housework and child-care has been overlooked and its economic value hardly been recorded in any official statistics.

In former times, women were usually paid only when they sold their body (and in many cases their labour) for male sexual pleasure. But, they were then considered as 'fallen women' and deserved only negative moral and social sanctions.

Now, as in the past, laws and programmes tackling prostitution are based on this bias against women. Instead of helping or protecting women in prostitution, these measures, especially the laws, tend rather to 'protect' the men from 'bad' women in prostitution. 'Rehabilitation' Programmes are another example of this prejudice against women in prostitution. Their hidden significance is to rehabilitate 'fallen women' to become again 'decent women' in a society where male domination remains unchanged.

In general, most people do not distinguish between the women as individual human beings and prostitution which is an institution. Based on this lack of distinction, the suppression of the institution 'prostitution' is, therefore, synonymous with arresting and penalising women who are prostitutes. Such an approach neglects other elements and factors in prostitution, for instance the syndicates involved in the traffic of women as well as the socio-economic and political transformation in more recent times which are often strongly influenced by multinational companies and agencies.

In the meantime, the institution 'prostitution' is no longer limited to one national boundary, but expanded into 'happiness without barriers' (as advertised by one marriage agency in the Federal Republic of Germany) – in other words:

'Sexploitation without barriers'. To work in this field requires, therefore, national and international cooperation.

In order to understand the institution 'prostitution', some principal factors have to be taken into consideration; namely: the ideology of a male-dominated society; and socio-economic transformation and its consequences for employment opportunities for women.

The ideology of male-dominated society

One element of the patriarchal ideology is the demand that a woman should not allow more than one man access to her body. This ideology lowers the self-esteem of those women who are unable to fulfil this socially determined requirement. As a result, most women consider themselves as 'worthless' after having lost their virginity or after being separated from or abandoned by their husband or lover. Their 'worthless' body is then transformed into an instrument to earn a living. This attitude is the general rule in a male-dominated society and the outcome of the double standard with regard to sexuality. Only by this form of degradation can some women become economically independent from male 'protectors'.

While women's sexuality is considered an object and controlled by this ideology, men are treated as human beings with natural sexual needs. Whereas virginity is imposed as the most important asset of a 'decent' woman, sexual promiscuity is accepted for and practised by men without any negative social sanction.

Socio-economic transformation

The development strategy of Thailand since 1957, aiming at economic growth by the integration of the economy into the world economic system, resulted in the increasing landlessness of peasants and in urban migration. Peasants were transformed into wage earners whose income is insufficient to feed the whole family. Increasingly, peasant women are also forced by impoverishment to migrate into towns to find jobs. But those employments are very limited and based on 'feminine' characteristics. Women are mostly required in the service sector, for instance as domestic servants, maids or waitresses in bars and restaurants, from where it is not far to prostitution.

Those women who find employment in factories, receive lower wages and encounter hierarchical relations with male workers, due to being unskilled. Since women are considered as workers of 'secondary status' in the market-oriented production, they are in the position of 'last to hire, first to fire'. Their wages are considered only as supplementary to men's. For women who are the main or only breadwinner of their family, supplementary income becomes, therefore, compulsory. In many cases women take on prostitution as an additional part-time job.

Due to the increasing number of migrants from rural areas, the urban economy of the country is less and less able to provide sufficient jobs for both male and female migrants. The unequal sexual division of labour also makes it more difficult for women to get permanent employment *outside* the country. Whereas male skilled labour from Asia is in demand on the new labour market in Arab countries, few women, being considered as workers of 'secondary status', have access to jobs on the labour market in a few neighbouring countries. The biggest demand for women from Thailand and from other Third World countries comes from the international sex business.

213

Forms of prostitution

Prostitution can be broadly divided into two categories: forced and free. It is mostly innocent, ignorant, young girls from rural areas who are lured into forced prostitution. The conditions of work are extremely exploitative. For this type of prostitution, legal measures that exist already should be enforced to help those young girls out of their deplorable situation, but penalise only procurers and other agents.

Legal protection is also required for free prostitution. According to interviews with women in this category, none of them wants to stay long in this 'profession'. They see prostitution as a short-term means for their survival. Therefore, solutions like registration of prostitutes would stigmatise them and make it more difficult for them to leave this institution.

'Rehabilitation' schemes

The term 'rehabilitation' expresses strong prejudices against women in prostitution and reflects at least a paternalistic 'top-down' approach. Prostitutes are considered as 'fallen women'. Therefore, having been rescued, they have to be 'upgraded' and prepared for becoming normal members of society again. Of course, the same rule does not apply to any of their male customers.

Due to this misconceived understanding, the present rehabilitation schemes function as punishment for women. Consequently, prostitutes are afraid to go through this scheme, which they understand as a kind of detention for a period of at least one year before they are allowed to return home.

Procurers and brothel keepers can, therefore, successfully threaten prostitutes under their control with the feared conditions of life in the rehabilitation centre. Instead of requesting intervention and assistance from the authorities, prostitutes fall victim to the procurer's arguments by claiming – often contrary to the truth – during police investigations, that they are *not* forced into prostitution, but engage in it by their own will. This answer will largely minimise the danger of their being placed in a rehabilitation centre. Unfortunately, the authorities cannot take legal actions against procurers and brothel keepers.

The skill training programmes provided for women in rehabilitation centres are not very helpful, because most of them reinforce the traditional 'feminine' duties and aim at skills that are not demanded on the labour market. According to one officer in the north, seven out of ten women who passed through the rehabilitation scheme and were, finally, sent home, returned to prostitution because no work was available in their communities.

Towards a new strategy

Since prostitution is an institution reflecting inequality between sexes (gender) and classes, the ultimate goal should be the complete eradication of this institution.

Under the present conditions, however, this may need much more than a lifetime's work until success is near. Therefore, strategies for short term goals are also required.

When working on this issue, it is very important to distinguish between women/prostitutes and prostitution. Otherwise, any solution will worsen the already vulnerable situation of women. The new strategy should include three levels of cooperation: local, national and global; women in prostitution should also take an active part.

Experiences of action groups

There are many projects operated by government agencies to help women in prostitution, such as health services, rehabilitation schemes and vocational training. But, very little has been done to prevent women and young girls from being lured into prostitution. The phenomenal increase of mass prostitution is the result of two major factors: a) the previous US-bases: and b) tourism to Thailand, and has led some government agencies and politicians to plan measures, if not to stop, at least to 'contain' prostitution, for instance by registration of prostitutes, organisation of state-run brothels etc, in order to control and earn taxes from prostitutes. These new control mechanisms of the state force women to become even more dependent on brothel keepers and procurers as their 'protectors'.

Unlike state-run programmes, private action groups have placed more emphasis on raising public awareness of the problem of prostitution and the traffic in women and young girls. These groups have campaigned for legal amendments to the prostitution law which would punish procurers and brothel keepers, but not prostitutes.

Public awareness

In January 1984, five young women were burnt to death in a brothel fire in Phuket, an important tourist spot in the south of Thailand. This serious incident coincided with the plans for a week-long campaign against traffic in women and against prostitution scheduled for 8 March 1984. A two-day seminar was organised by various women's and human rights groups and drew considerable attention from the government and the general public. A set of posters on exploitation in prostitution was distributed nationwide, in order to draw the attention of people at the local level. Another two-day seminar on the same topic was organised in June 1985 for local authorities, community leaders and development workers from eight provinces in the north, where the problem is most acute. Many concrete plans were proposed by the participants to fight against traffic in women and girls.

Aid to women

Besides building up public awareness, action groups also provide assistance to women and young girls such as:

1) Temporary shelter for women and girls, for instance the Emergency Home run by the Promotion of Status of Women Association.

2) Legal aid to women and girls, including their families, in order to take legal action against procurers and brothel keepers. There are many groups providing this service, for instance the Women's Lawyers Association, Friends of Women Group, Centre for the Protection of Children's Rights etc.

3) Financial assistance and accompaniment for women and girls who have been freed from brothels to return home.

4) Information service for women who want to work abroad and/or to marry foreigners, in order to prevent them being lured into prostitution and becoming victims of the 'male order bride' system and other exploitation overseas. This service is provided by the Women's Information Centre, which was set up in 1984, originally supported with a small fund from the Dutch Embassy. The Centre tries to work with women, who have experienced prostitution in a foreign country, and motivate them to speak out.

Local and national strategies

1) Preventing newcomers from involvement in this institution.

2) Disseminating information through the media.

3) Building up awareness, and drawing participation from local authorities, community leaders and extension workers.

4) Organising courses on exploitation in prostitution, for sixth grade children in primary schools (school-leavers).

5) Producing materials and teaching modules for local teachers and authorities concerned.

6) Enforcement of laws to suppress the exploitation of prostitutes.

7) Changing attitudes with regard to sexuality based on patriarchal ideology.

8) Providing more development projects for women, in which appropriate skills training is provided and women are drawn into the mainstream of socio-economic development.

With regard to helping women freed from exploitative and forced prostitution the following measures are proposed:

1) Rehabilitation schemes should not be obligatory for every woman, but participation should rather depend on their own free decision.

2) Government agencies should take a more positive attitude towards private action groups and help in their efforts.

3) Skills training should be in accordance with the economic conditions and the demand on the labour market.

4) Teaching courses should be provided for prostitutes to help them understand the structure and exploitative forms of prostitution, instead of internalising patriarchal ideology with its 'good' and 'bad' women.

5) Persons responsible for 'rehabilitation' should have a better understanding of prostitution and a more appropriate approach to women in prostitution.

International cooperation

1) Building up a solidarity network with private women's and human rights groups and state agencies in other countries.
2) Enforcing legal protection for migrant women.
3) Relief aid to foreign women in prostitution.
4) Solidarity action against all forms of sexploitation, including prostitution, male order bride systems and pornography.

32 Prostitution: A Philippine Experience

Tonette Raquisa

Prostitution in the Philippines, closely linked to the sex tourism and 'hospitality' industry, was more than just tolerated under the 20-year dictatorship of President Marcos; it was actively encouraged as an important source of foreign revenue for a country crippled by external debt.

Sex tourism, based on the sexual and economic exploitation of women (and children), has become a growth industry in certain Third World countries, particularly in South-East Asia. According to a briefing paper produced by the London-based Philippine Support Group, there are around 100,000 Filipinas employed as hostesses, waitresses, go-go dancers, sauna-bath attendants and call girls, many driven by rural poverty to the cities to be advertised and treated as objects which foreign money can buy. Perhaps the most blatant illustration is the advertising in Western Europe of 'brides for sale'. Presented as the 'perfect wife', charming, beautiful, as good in the bedroom as in the kitchen and far more passive and docile than her Western sister, women are literally bought and transplanted to a new country where they remain trapped, socially and culturally isolated and totally dependent on their husband's wishes.

The following article, by a member of the national coalition GABRIELA which links over 45 Philippine women's groups, was written shortly after the fall of Marcos through a popular uprising in February 1986. Only time will tell if his successor, the country's first-ever woman president, Corazon Aquino, will be able to bring about the social and economic changes necessary for the complete banning of sex tourism, prostitution in the US bases and trafficking of women that GABRIELA demands.

The red light district awakens to a pulsating sensual beat. Neon signs advertising love for sale beguile and beckon. Inside sleazy joints, women and men gyrate to blaring disco music; undulating their briefly-clad bodies before leering male audiences. Bare and supple flesh abounds; primed and preened for the picking. The name of the game: quick sex and fast bucks.

In this whoredom, every man of any sexual preference and perversity can have his fill – at a price. For the lovelorn foreigner, pliant and domesticated native brides. Pornography, thinly guised as legitimate art, proliferates in the mass media. Simulated sex and women stripped naked have become staples of news tabloids and

From *Womenews*, Philippines

local films. Even children are fair game in this reputed sex mecca of the Pacific.

This is the Philippines where prostitution comes in different packages. Yet the bacchanalian fête runs only skin deep, for behind the flesh trade lurks a seething desperation that gnaws at the conscience and sensitivity of a people.

Sex peddling is a social evil that comes into being from the mass deprivation and the systematic exploitation and commodification of women. It thrives in a society which has nothing more to offer women than a life of land bondage, tilling the land of another in the name of unpaid family labour; or the life of a wage-slave worker, cloistered in factories that stretch her physical and mental endurance to produce a quota for a meagre pay; or that of a dogged professional whose pay is not commensurate to her long working hours.

The backward agrarian economy of Philippine society has far-reaching repercussions on the plight of women. Sixty-five per cent are of peasant origin. The women absorbed by the manufacturing sector – a mere 25 per cent – are, most often, either self-employed and unpaid family workers or hired hands in small handicraft shops where the minimum wage laws are not even observed.

GABRIELA Convention, March 1985. Photo by Raquel Sancho.

Moreover, women are encumbered by a feudal patriarchy which institutionalises male authority over them in the home and in society. Hence, as they are relegated to a second class status and their labour deemed peripheral to social production, their being is reduced to that of sex objects.

It is thus woman's double oppression – as part of an exploited class and member of a discriminated gender – that the Filipino woman becomes easy prey to sexual exploitation. Because of poverty and slim chances of seeking a better life, more and more women are induced, if not forced, into prostitution to eke out a living for themselves and their families.

This situation is further aggravated by the economic crisis from which the people are currently reeling. As the cost of living soars, as real income takes a deep plunge and job opportunities become scarce, making both ends meet has become a day-to-day struggle that often demands more from women than their labour.

To secure a better life, thousands of women professionals seek employment abroad. Many are forced to work as domestic helpers and chambermaids; accepting menial tasks that promise better pay than the white-collar jobs they left behind. Others still, escape the bleak future that awaits them in their homeland via the commercialised marriage route. The male-order bride business has never had it so good, as scores of Filipino women seek their future husbands and, hopefully, a good life through penpal clubs and introduction service agencies. Germans,

Australians and other Caucasians are the usual takers. (From 1978 to 1983, the number of Filipino women granted finance and spouse visas by the Australian embassy alone grew by 400 per cent.)

Yet, it is usually the women who get burned in what often turns out to be a raw deal. Many find out too late that the contract they had entered has turned them into unpaid household helps and bed partners to virtual strangers – for better or for worse.

Indeed, the options left for women to overcome the crisis exact a dear price. The flesh trade has become the ultimate consumer of many more women. To date, there are some 90,000 registered 'hospitality' girls and an estimated 5,000 child prostitutes in the sex jungles of Metro Manila.

The trafficking of women for profit and for pleasure reached its peak during the autocratic rule of Mr Marcos when tourism rose to become a major dollar-earning industry. A dictatorship had one advantage: the repression of the people's rights provided the political stability essential for attracting tourists. In 1976–77, 13 government-funded five-star hotels were constructed costing $415–545 million (an amount equal to the country's foreign loans for that year).

It was no coincidence that the entertainment business experienced a reciprocal shove. During the same year, for instance, the number of licensed cocktail lounges rose from 93 to 225, all of which featured women as their main attraction. Today, Manila's tourist belt likewise serves as the main arteries of the city. For where the dollars are, so are the women – along with the pimps, sex ring operators, bar managers who live off their women. One glossy Australian-owned bar has as many as 500 women a night and rakes in about $1,875 on bar fees alone.

The two largest American military installations outside mainland USA, Clark Air Base at Angeles, Pampanga and Subic Naval Base at Olongapo, are also the biggest recruiters for the flesh trade. Olongapo City has more than 500 clubs, bars, hotels and other entertainment establishments. In 1980, there were 9,056 registered hospitality girls, a reported 8,000 street walkers and 3,000 waitresses-prostitutes catering to the sexual appetites of US servicemen stationed at Subic for rest and recreation (R&R).

Angeles City, on the other hand, boasts of 450 hotels, disco joints, cabarets and cocktail lounges. Some 7,000 registered hospitality girls service the Clark airmen. The local governments concerned have adopted an open policy toward prostitution, it being the only trade that keeps their communities afloat.

Prostitution in contemporary Philippine society has taken on new forms. For as long as the economy remains heavily addicted to foreign capital, nothing is held sacred in the face of the mighty dollar: the compromise of a nation's sovereignty to foreign creditors, specifically the IMF-World Bank; the sell-out of one's economy to foreign investors; the commercialisation of one's culture to dollar-bearing tourists.

It is thus that GABRIELA and various women's groups have taken issue with the problem of prostitution. For this is no different from the other social ills that afflict women in a society that is semi-feudal and neocolonial. As long as the feudal patriarchy and decadent values prevail, and as long as poverty continues to plague the vast majority of the people, women's social function will remain confined to an acceptance of men's lust and source of filthy profit. Moreover, the dignity of Filipino women will never be truly uplifted in an economy raped and ravaged by foreign powers, namely the US.

GABRIELA, together with other local organisations advancing the women's movement, have undertaken in-depth studies on the plight of their sexually-abused and exploited sisters. Toward the long-term goal of eradicating the flesh trade, they are also working for the implementation of concrete demands, namely: the provision of alternative and decently paid jobs for prostitutes; the punishment of users of and traffickers in women and children; and the closing of establishments, including marriage bureaux which are engaged in sex peddling.

This is a historic moment in the women's and people's movement for national sovereignty and genuine democracy. As the people's collective might have struck a deadly blow to the US-backed Marcos dictatorship and have installed a popularly-mandated government led by President Cory Aquino, women–as well as people–power has acquired new meaning. The people have taken a giant stride in securing their liberation.

Yet much is to be done in the task of nation-building, particularly on the women's front. Just as other progressive groups will actively participate and call for the complete dismantling of all vestiges of the Marcos autocratic state, so will we put forward specific demands and ventilate the interests of women of various sectors. For the establishment of a nation truly free and democratic is an essential prerequisite toward women's emancipation from exploitation and degradation. So, too, a nation truly free and democratic must carry the interests and aspirations of one-half of the total population – its women.

A statement from GABRIELA, 8 July 1986

Stop racist exploitation of Third World women!

We, women of GABRIELA, a national organisation of women's organisations, strongly protest against the latest Nye Philnor-sponsored trip of Norwegian men to the Philippines. The trip, annually arranged and promoted by Nye Philnor, a Norway-based pen pal club engaging in the male-order bride business, has one and only one objective: the pairing of the men to 'pliant, submissive and domesticated' Filipino women. Or as the agency so crudely stated in its ad: to Filipinas who, poverty-stricken as they are, bestow their 'faithful friendship for free'.

Such insulting portrayal of Filipino women has become a staple in ads promoting Filipina male-order brides-to-be in the foreign media. The sales pitch belying a racist come-on: men from the more advanced countries can have their pick of Third World women (Filipinas being a favourite) who because of their gender and of being members of a long colonised people possess traditional 'virtues' like passivity, subservience and blind loyalty.

Indeed, the male-order bride business benefits from the poverty of Third World nations like the Philippines. Given their destitute state, more and more women have opted to enter into an inter-racial marriage-of-convenience to escape the bleak future that awaits them in their own impoverished country. Going by the Nye

GABRIELA

Philnor logic: love, marriage and women in the Philippines thus come cheaper still.

We, therefore, denounce and demand a stop to the practice of marriage bureaux, pen pal clubs and other such agencies which turn the country into a mecca for lovelorn men; more notably, for Norwegian, Australian and German men. We vehemently protest the use of Filipino women as commodities; packaged and marketed by profit-seeking enterprises in the commercialised marriage circuit. With the intention of revving up their income, these marriage bureaux and pen pal clubs are guilty of propagating a distorted image of the Filipina. To wit, some ads and promos even stress the 'passionate' nature of Filipinas; attributing this to our supposed ethnic history of 'free love'.

The male-order bride business is nothing more than a subtle form of exploitation of women. Not a few Filipinas have been victimised as they find themselves transformed into unpaid servants and bed partners to virtual strangers in foreign lands. In the bargain, too, comes the wholesale degradation of the Filipino woman, as our reputation is besmirched to satisfy the macho desires of its predominantly white clientele.

The GABRIELA Network on Violence Against Women and other women's organisations will work, for among other demands the regulation and monitoring of foreign and local marriage bureaux, so-called introductory clubs and tourist agencies in the male-order bride business; and for the protection and promotion of the rights and welfare of Filipino migrant women.

To women, let us push for the eradication of all forms of sexist and racist discrimination and exploitation against women and peoples. Let us join ranks and together with other sectors work for a truly egalitarian, just, free and prosperous society so that our sisters may find a better life in our own land.

STOP THE TRAFFICKING OF WOMEN BY MALE-ORDER!

STOP RACIST EXPLOITATION OF FILIPINO WOMEN!

UPHOLD THE DIGNITY OF WOMEN!

CONTINUE AND HEIGHTEN THE STRUGGLE FOR GENUINE FREEDOM, JUSTICE AND EQUALITY!

CENTER FOR WOMEN RESOURCES

GABRIELA

33 Operation Clean-up

Zimbabwe Women's Action Group, with Ruth Gaidzanwa

In November 1983 the government of Zimbabwe ordered Operation Clean-up, a programme designed to rid the country of prostitutes, beggars and squatters. During this campaign several thousand women, and almost as many men, were detained under the Emergency Clause of the Vagrancy Act of 1960. The government's 'clean-up' campaign targeted the country's most economically and socially disadvantaged groups, those most vulnerable to the coercive power of the state. These groups have been made victims of the country's economic and social ills. Zimbabwe's Three-Year Plan has not incorporated a strategy for providing employment for Zimbabweans, male and female alike, either in the short or long term. Prostitution in Zimbabwe has increased since independence, but the reasons why have not been explored by the government. Instead, a moral stance has been taken. In 1982, the daily *Herald* carried an editorial advocating 'a clean-up operation of the purveyors of these same diseases', and added that the Ministry of Community Development and Women's Affairs should teach young girls 'a sense of self-esteem and a fear of immorality'.

The following article, reproduced from the international feminist quarterly, *Connexions* (No 12, Spring 1984), combines excerpts from an article by the Zimbabwe Women's Action Group and from a paper on the history of prostitution in that country by Ruth Gaidzanwa, member of the group and of the University of Zimbabwe's sociology department. The original piece by the Women's Action Group was published in *Moto*, a Zimbabwean magazine (December 1983/January 1984). A more recent report in another Zimbabwean publication *Speak Out* (September 1986), revealed that government attitudes towards 'cleaning up' the country haven't changed. Women food vendors and others continue to be harassed by attempts to remove them from the streets of Harare, provoking one woman, a secretary, to observe: 'If you are an unmarried black woman you will be questioned and maybe arrested if you have no way to prove you have a job. It is bad that in a free country women must carry some kind of pass, such as a marriage certificate, to prove they are not prostitutes. We are afraid to go anywhere unless we are with a man'.

In November 1983 people were indiscriminately stopped by either the police, army or sometimes the Youth Brigades and informed that they were under arrest. Women were stopped while walking on the street singly, in groups or with men, in public places like cinemas, at parties and even at home. They were detained under the Emergency Clause of the infamous Vagrancy Act of 1960. Under this act they had no access to the courts. Most of the women held, as is well-known by now, were not prostitutes. But in any case, prostitution is not illegal in this country: soliciting and living off immoral earnings, however, are.

Once arrested, people were held in prisons or police station compounds, and released only upon the presentation of marriage certificates or proof of employment. Women had to depend upon husbands, employers or heads of colleges to come forward with such certificates. Women failing the 'screening' were sent to a settlement area in the Zambezi Valley, several kilometres from Mashumbi Pools, [where people were initially incarcerated].

Who was detained? Most women in Zimbabwe are from worker, peasant, or migrant labourer families and so these were the main groups of women picked up. There was even a case of 200 female workers in Mutare who were picked up on the way to work at the Liebigs factory. The manager thought they had gone on strike. Meanwhile, they were being held in the football stadium. But there were also some middle-class women who were seized, i.e. students, nurses, housewives, teachers, women working in ministries, unemployed women and schoolgirls. Middle-class women learned that their class position does not necessarily guarantee them immunity from state violence against women. The lower income women have lived with the knowledge that state violence is part of their lives. Most of the women picked up were black or coloured, although some were white.

There was a lot of frustration and protest from the public, most of whom were appalled by the method of the exercise. People were generally worried by the violation of civil liberties and the freedom of movement and association, since women were no longer free to move on the streets for fear of harassment by the police or the army. Nevertheless, many people, including some women's organisations, who in general approved of the operation, felt that the identification of prostitutes should have been more skilful and discriminating. Those who support the intentions of the campaign do so because they feel that prostitution is the main cause of disrupted family lives. However, decline in family life cannot be blamed on prostitution; the migrant labour system must take most of the responsibility for this.

We of the Women's Action Group not only object to the method, but to the operation in general. It is possible to condemn prostitution as a social evil which degrades human relationships without condemning prostitutes. Prostitution is the evidence of the failure of the Zimbabwean economy to provide the means of earning a living in a dignified and unalienating way, particularly for women. This condition has historical roots, and the conditions that maintained it still prevail. Poverty is the main factor, although depression, racism and other forms of violence, loneliness and feelings of relative deprivation also feature in inducing women to become prostitutes.

The government of Zimbabwe needs to understand the historical origins of prostitution in order to avoid responses such as Operation Clean-up. That operation does not indicate any recognition of history and the situation that women face economically and socially. Without this understanding, these sorts of measures only intensify the destitution of women and criminalise their very existence. Women are being scape-goated for complex social problems. It is easy to blame them, like other groups in weak positions in society, because they have fewer resources with which to 'fight back', and because of long-held ideas about women's 'proper' roles and their 'natures'.

History of prostitution

Prostitution was structurally integral to the development of capitalism in Zimbabwe. When Zimbabwe was colonised, black men as labour migrants were placed in compounds on the farms, mines and households of white settlers. They were paid wages based on the calculation of a labourer's most basic needs for survival. Women and children were supposed to subsist on their own labour in the rural reserves. The compounds, therefore, had huge concentrations of male labour. In such a situation, sex became useful for the settler state and employers as a means of controlling workers.

Women who were marginalised by the loss of land rights, or whose husbands could not support them with wages from farms and mines, gravitated to the compounds where they could practise prostitution in order to survive. At the inception of colonialism, the mines, farms and households did not employ women, thus restricting the spheres in which a woman could earn a living. Only later in the process of proletarianisation of black labour did some opportunities arise for women to make a living in wage employment.

The black women in the compounds prostituted themselves to both black and white men. White settlers, as well as black settlers, did not bring enough women to go around, so they had liaisons, and married black women in some cases. It is in this socio-economic context that we have to examine the response of the Rhodesian state to the phenomenon of prostitution.

Why were prostitutes encouraged to stay in the compounds? One of the main reasons was that prostitutes provided personal services to alienated labour, such as better meals, which improved the health and productivity of the labourers. They also acted as a buffer between black labour and white women. The possibility of blacks, an alienated and sexually deprived labour force, raping or approaching white settler women was abhorrent to the white settlers.

Another even more pragmatic reason for the toleration of prostitution by the settler state was the fact that prostitutes attracted labour initially and helped labour to stay on longer after the initial contracts expired. The stabilisation of labour was a high priority to settler employers, as this cut the costs of recruiting new labour. Officially, the regulation of prostitution became the best solution to the situation. However, there had to be a balance struck between allowing labour some controlled sexual outlet and maintaining their productivity by precluding the occurrence of debilitating venereal disease. Therefore, prostitutes were subject to compulsory medical examinations. It is interesting to note that in the case of Shamva mine, 'African' women were used to examinine any new woman who wished to stay in the mine compound. Here we have a classic example of women being used by the state to keep other women in line.

A similar method was employed during Operation Clean-up. It was reported that the police used prostitute informers to point out other women purported to be prostitutes. It has also been suggested by an official source, in a personal communication with the author of this paper [Rudo Gaidzanwal], that in the next phase of roundups, married women are going to be used to identify women purported to be prostitutes.

Prohibition and the authoritarian state

Legally, prostitution was never a crime in Rhodesia and still is not in Zimbabwe [but soliciting was and is to this day]. The actions of the Zimbabwean government in Operation Clean-up ought to be examined in this light. The government took a prohibitionist stance without the legal right to do so. After the first public protests, an emergency retroactive amendment was attached to the Vagrancy Act in order to legalise the illegalities arising out of Operation Clean-up.

Those who feel that the whole operation is a joke should realise that the implications of the campaign go beyond the question of women's rights. The new clause of the Vagrancy Act can accommodate everyone – the unemployed, the landless, the self-employed, the unwaged, the housewife – anyone who cannot show concrete proof of the work they do. It greatly extends the right of the police to enter and examine any premises without a warrant. The powers of other agents of the state, such as the Youth Brigades, social workers and rehabilitation officers, over other citizens will also be greatly enhanced by such legislative changes. Equally important is the removal of any access to legality, i.e. to lawyers and to the courts. It is mainly middle-class people who have such access. In a country such as ours, which sees itself in transition to socialism, bold steps must be taken to extend these rights to women, workers, peasants, and migrant labourers, not to disenfranchise them further. Prohibitionism's prerequisite is for an authoritarian and undemocratic state, which Zimbabweans fought to oust for 89 years.

Another consequence of prohibitionism, coupled with the lack of better and more productive job opportunities for women, is that prostitutes will be driven underground and marginalised by the criminal nature of their activities. This situation necessarily presents opportunities for the corruption of law enforcement personnel and the super-exploitation of women engaged in prostitution. Prostitutes in such situations seek protection from arrest. Who are the people who can offer protection? The police, business people in the entertainment industry, the criminal underworld, etc. Thus, the prostitute is forced to use bribes in the form of cash or with all she can offer, sex, thus reinforcing her need to further prostitute herself to survive and maintain a clean police record. She is exploited by all.

Clearly, what is needed is educational and socio-economic action to better the lot of women. Women are the part of the population most vulnerable to formal unemployment, although of course most women work very hard as homeworkers and farmers or in the informal sector. But women are often discriminated against in employment and are often less educated than men: women constitute only a small proportion of the industrial work force in this country. They are particularly affected by lack of employment, especially as they often have families to support. In addition, women's access to adequate shelter, to land and other property rights and to services like health and child-care are severely limited. Under these economic circumstances, and given that many men are conditioned to use prostitutes, the social problem of prostitution is bound to increase – even if the current campaign temporarily 'cleaned-up' the country.

In Operation Clean-up, there were no rehabilitation facilities at all. However, segregated rehabilitation merely serves to draw public attention to the plight of prostitutes. This might militate against their reacceptance into society. The case of ex-combatants in post-independence Zimbabwe can be used by way of example. Most employers, particularly in white enterprises, will not hire anybody whom they know to be an ex-guerrilla. As a result, many young men and women actually conceal a significant and important period of their lives in order to get jobs. What prospects would known ex-prostitutes have on the job market if the people regarded nationally as heroes cannot actually make any progress if their past is known?

In Zimbabwe the question of women's liberation was first raised in the struggle for independence. And social changes, especially since independence, have meant that some women, particularly in cities, have been able to acquire a measure of freedom denied to them traditionally (but granted to men) such as the right to live where they like, rights to work, to walk unaccompanied, to choose their own associates and to go about their daily lives without interference. These freedoms and rights have all been challenged by the 'clean-up' campaign.

The campaign attacked the fundamental rights of women as human beings. The rights granted to black women under the Legal Age of Majority Act become meaningless when women are required to produce marriage certificates to avoid detention. In effect this constitutes a new type of pass system for women in which a certificate of marriage constitutes a valid 'pass'. Was the campaign part of a backlash against democratic rights so recently granted to black women? The democratic gains which women and men have struggled for are being eroded. Operation Clean-up is hardly an appropriate name for the sort of unjustified scandal, suspicion and personal distress the campaign has spread. The answer to prostitution is not incarceration, but lies in the provision of employment for all people and the re-education of men to seek real relationships.

Part 7:
Health Touches Every Part of our Lives

34   Women's Health is
Women's Concern

Nirmala Sathe

Women's health status is closely linked to their social status. Even though the 'ideal' woman is supposed to look weak and delicate, she has to be able to perform all the domestic tasks necessary for the sustenance of the family. Her major role in society is that of a reproductive machine. The feminist movement aims at uniting women to raise their voices against the oppression of these stereotypes. In an article in the Indian publication *Socialist Health Review* (No. 2, September 1984), Nirmala Sathe, a feminist-activist, briefly reviews the sporadic activities concerning women's health in her country and strongly urges that women's health issues be taken up more by women's groups.

All of us have a right to good health. The right to health means not only the right to be free from disease, but also to enjoy physical, mental and emotional well-being. Health cannot be separated from political, cultural or economic systems in which we are living. It cannot be isolated from the roles we are playing and the status we have in society.

My grandmother often used to tell us 'Beti, a woman cannot afford sickness. If she does fall sick then she can't complain, but has to bear her illness silently; for who will tolerate a sick slave?' Many of us have experienced this truth in our own lives or through those of our mothers, grandmothers.

Although it is true that in economically poor classes even the men do not get proper medical aid in sickness, it is the women who are the more neglected group. Even among the economically better off, where it is possible for women to afford good care and proper food, they are found to be weak, or rather not as healthy as they could be. This is because of cultural influences. According to the ideal image of women perpetuated in society, a woman is supposed to be weak and delicate. A 'strong' woman thus becomes, in a sense, the victim of cultural norms. Women are traditionally supposed to eat only after the rest of the family have eaten and then only what has been left over, even though in poor families it is hardly ever sufficient to keep body and soul together. It will not be an exaggeration to say that she even gets sufficient rest only on her deathbed.

Menstruation, pregnancy, childbirth, breast-feeding, menopause, all these are considered to be 'women's issues'. In a way society at large has nothing to do with them, because women are not equal members of the society and, therefore,

Credit: CESA.

complaints about these are treated as, 'psychological' or as 'women's sickness' and are not given the serious consideration they deserve. Doctors and medical professionals produced in this male-dominated society are taught to either close their eyes and ears to such complaints or to immediately connect all women's complaints to their reproductive system. A woman is looked upon as a mere reproductive machine rather than as a human being. Politically also, it is a worldwide phenomenon that as drives for population control or population increase, breast-feeding or the baby foods campaign have treated women as reproductive machines. Nowhere have these issues been treated in a manner where women's 'health' is given central importance.

In order to understand the location of women's health issues in the context of feminist movements, it is necessary to broadly define feminism and the feminist movement. Feminism is a new concept in India, a concept not yet well-accepted or understood by the people at large. Broadly speaking, one can say that feminism deals with all the aspects of a woman's life and her role in society – male-dominated society. Feminists are interested in changing a hierarchical society and in creating one in which everybody is equal. In today's society, women are at the bottom of the hierarchical structure. In any class, caste or race, whatever their status, women among them are always at the bottom.

No doubt women of the upper classes have more facilities and opportunities than the lower class males, but in their own class they are the least important. Not only that, but because they are women any man from any class can express his superiority as a male member of the patriarchal society. One example is rape.

So the main role of the feminist movement is to unite women to raise their voices against their oppression in a male-dominated society. In her family life, work place, place of education and in all the aspects of her life, women have a lower status than men. In our health systems too, the status of women is only as a reproductive machine.

In India, we cannot say that there exists any mass feminist movement. But at the same time it is a fact that there are several women's groups – feminist groups – which are involved in activities in various areas of women's oppression, such as rape, wife-beating, legal reforms and so on. Their activities range from cultural activities to demonstrations and 'helping' individual women in distress to fight for their rights and the common cause.

But none of these groups has as yet taken health as the prime issue. Many of them have touched on one or the other aspect of the issue at some point, but there has been no consistency. This is because of various reasons which are rooted in our outlook (such as the cultural and social stigma attached to the discussion of

'Look how he's treating me . . .' (CIPAF).

women's problems about their bodies). Many feminists have inhibitions which do not allow them to freely discuss these issues among themselves.

Some groups have made an attempt to raise their voices against oppression through medical systems. For instance, the Women's Centre in Bombay held a meeting with other feminist groups to discuss the effects of 'amniocentesis' as a sex-determination test, which gave rise to demands and concerted action in Bombay [see following article]. Two of these demands were: (1) Amniocentesis facilities should be allowed only in research institutions with proper machinery and control; (2) the government and the medical profession should be brought under pressure to abolish pre-natal sex-determination. It was pointed out that unless and until major social upheaval takes place regarding the status of women in society, female babies will continue to be murdered.

Recently, another meeting was held by the Women's Centre to discuss the issue of Depo-provera, the controversial injectable contraceptive. Womens' magazines – feminist ones such as *Baija* (in Marathi) and *Manushi* (in Hindi and English) – have given importance to the health and reproductive activity of women by bringing out special issues on the subject. *Baija*'s special issue was on women and health in which the whole problem was discussed from the feminist point of view.

Organisations working in health, such as the People's Science Movement, Medico Friend Circle (MFC), have also touched on the women's health problems. The *Lok Vidnyan Sanghatana*, Maharashtra, prepared an exhibition on women and health which received a tremendous response from various women's groups as well as others working among the toiling masses. This was the first attempt to discuss a woman's body and her health, reproduction and social biases about it. The exhibition was taken to many villages and it was a thrilling experience to find that women are able to relate to one another while discussing their experiences about their bodies from menstruation to menopause. They were all encouraged by the fact that as women, irrespective of educational status, caste or class background, they have gone through the same experiences and feelings of inferiority because of their physiology. The explanations we had received were shrouded in myth, and the actual scientific explanation of the various functions that a woman's body has to perform had been denied us.

The exhibition criticises the social outlook and stigmas attached to the female sex in society, and superstitions about women's bodies and child bearing, especially with regard to producing male children. Mainly the posters about sex-determination and about fertility, entitled 'Who is responsible for not getting a child?' have made a great impact and have very positively put forward the view that a woman is not wholly, not even mainly responsible. The exhibition emphatically argues that a woman is not merely a reproductive machine. In *adivasi* (tribal) areas as well as urban areas like Bombay, Nasik, Pune, Miraj, the exhibition attracted large numbers of women.

This exhibition was shown by women and *only to* women. It is only in this situation that women can become vocal about their problems. It is very important to realise that women can relate only to other women when it comes to health and their bodies because only women can truly understand each other's problems. I feel very strongly that women's organisations should mainly handle the issue of women and health; male activists, although sincerely interested in understanding the problems, are not able to evolve a movement or even a group around the subject.

At Anand, the MFC held an annual meeting in 1983 where many women were called from various groups interested in women and health. The majority of the women, who were educated and working in one or other organisation, found it difficult to discuss their problems in the meeting when men were present, as even with the desire and sincerity to understand the problems, male participants were unable to understand the intense emotional impact of the problem. At the session where only women were present, there was a lively discussion and a free exchange of experiences.

Here, I do not intend to devalue the male activists, who are really helping to raise the voice of women against the medical oppression of women. MFC activists have brought out various articles and debates on the problem. People's Science Movement groups have attempted to make people aware through health exhibitions, posters and pamphlets on anaemia. In both organisations, it is mainly women activists with the help of male activists who have worked very hard for it.

We can conclude that women's organisations should take prime responsibility for women's health issues, and other organisations in the health area can help them in a number of ways. With this mutual cooperation, one can hope for a strong women's health movement.

The Women's Centre in Bombay is planning to start some health activities. They will be mainly: 1) educational – making women aware of their body and its functions, to help them to tackle the social prejudices and superstitions and to create a healthy outlook about themselves; 2) preventive; and 3) curative – with the help of sympathetic medical professionals to help women prevent and cure health disorders.

Most of us have very little control over the health-care system, very little say in the decisions as to what kind of health care is available to us. In all phases of our lives, women face difficulties and become the victims of the health-care system – or lack of it. As potential mothers, as mothers, as housewives, as consumers in order to keep ourselves in accordance with the beauty norms of the society, women are either neglected or misguided by the health-care system. To raise our voices against this, women's groups should start (and are starting) to organise around health issues. Only this can lead to a strong and united fight against all sorts of oppression in male-dominated society.

35 Campaign Against Sex-Determination Tests in India

Sonal Shukla, Sanjeev Kulkarni, Lata and Harpal

This article is made up of extracts from two papers presented at a workshop organised by the Indian Forum Against Sex-Determination and Pre-Selection Techniques on 8 April 1986. The first, written by Sonal Shukla and Sanjeev Kulkarni, discusses the social implications of sex-determination tests, while the second, prepared by Lata and Harpal, outlines strategies for a national campaign, many of which have now been carried out.

The Forum, based in Bombay, is an informal group of individuals and organisations working in such areas as women's liberation, health, people's science and human rights. Their first activity was a poster campaign, mainly concentrating on the railway compartments of suburban trains, designed to counteract advertising by sex-determination clinics. Then followed the workshop, where over 70 activists, doctors, researchers and journalists gathered to discuss and record various aspects of this sinister new offshoot of modern medical technology. After wide newspaper coverage, a sit-in demonstration, the formation of a specific Doctors' Forum, more posters and the production of a 30-minute film in Hindi, this Indian movement for the survival and protection of daughters is rapidly gaining momentum.

The social implications of sex-determination tests

The use of amniocentesis (withdrawal and testing of amniotic fluid from the uterus at around the 16th week of pregnancy) and other tests for sex-determination, leading to the deliberate abortion of female foetuses, is yet another example of how advances in medical technology are used to discriminate against women. Throughout the world ancient medical science has been used to degrade, humiliate and exploit women, as well as other underprivileged members of society. Cliterodectomy, that horrid practice of mutilating the clitoris of a woman so as to decrease her sexual response, has been going on for centuries in African and West Asian countries. The emasculation of poor males employed to guard the 'virtue' of women in the harems of kings again shows how female sexuality, or rather female sex organs, are treated as objects of male pleasure and property. It is women's role to produce children, preferably male; men must have children too, but they also assume the right of sexual enjoyment.

238

In our region of South Asia the obsessive preference for male children is responsible for the misery and death of countless female infants and also of adult women, whether by malnutrition and neglect or by calculated intention. The traditional disregard for a woman's health and life, supported in part by religion and highlighted in such practices as *sati* (widow-burning) and female infanticide, provides an obvious background for the promotion of sex-determination techniques.

Is it a woman's choice?

Nearing the end of the 20th century we see around us some signs of improvement in the status of women. But much of it remains on paper while even newer and more perverse practices against women are allowed to develop. Vast sections of people live within the framework of age-old social norms and attitudes, characterised by poverty, ignorance and religious obscurantism, remaining quite untouched by change. Even today, the life of a childless woman, with a very few urban, upper-class exceptions, is one of untold misery. The life of a woman who only has daughters is hardly different and it is only natural for her to regard anything that might assure her a son, including an abortion to avoid the birth of a daughter, as a blessing. Doctors, too, are usually quite eager to help such a woman out of her immediate predicament. It's not just that they make money out of it, though that is certainly the factor behind the mushrooming growth of sex-determination clinics; many doctors also regard it as helping a woman by providing a legitimate means of family planning. That their attitudes are affected by the insidious anti-woman biases of society is something they are scarcely likely to admit. Doctors, generally coming from the urban upper classes, also reflect the mindless population control ideas of those strata. Population control in practice means preventing births in the unwanted categories: the poor, the minorities, the women, by whatever means available. In the case of preventing the birth of females, the commonest and strongest argument put forth by our righteous and 'socially aware' medical fraternity is: How can we deny help and services when a woman has come on her own asking for it? True, in many cases pregnant women themselves volunteer for amniocentesis or other sex-determination tests. But are these decisions made in a social vacuum? Brought up as they are, right from birth, among male supremacist ideas and placed as they are in the plight of being son-less wives, what alternative is there but for them to submit themselves to the tests? They might as well do it willingly!

A matter of social convenience

It's the very timing of amniocentesis that makes it such a dangerous phenomenon. If a female child, young daughter or adult woman in the family is ill-treated or neglected to the point of misery, malnutrition, sickness or death, at least the neighbourhood, that's to say the outside world, sees and knows what is happening and may criticise it. Not so with amniocentesis and selective female foeticide. When the woman is four months pregnant she's taken to a doctor for a quick test, followed, if necessary, by a quiet abortion, and it's all over. As far as the outside world is concerned she was never pregnant, so the question of criticising or taking action against a crime doesn't even arise. The fact that amniocentesis and selective abortion can be done clandestinely, as a 'hush job', makes it all the more acceptable to our society – tragically, the 'womb-to-tomb' oppression of women becomes literally true.

There is one more facet to the 'hush job' nature of amniocentesis. In our society, the very basis of which is injustice, and where hypocrisy is an accepted norm, a crime is a crime only to the extent that it is seen and known to the outside world, and the same goes for any guilt feelings arising from it. So when a woman gets rid of a female foetus on the quiet, it hardly ever affects the conscience of family members and is quickly forgotten; only to be followed by another series of pregnancy-amniocentesis-female-foeticide, until a son is conceived and makes everybody happy.

The arguments used to justify such a practice apply to a whole range of anti-woman practices. For instance: the son will be a breadwinner for the family, he will be a prop in old age, will ensure salvation, will continue the family line etc., whereas, after all, a daughter gets married and goes to some other household; she is only a burden to be brought up and married off. These arguments are too well known to be repeated in detail here.

The family planning argument

There is also an argument that selective female foeticide may act as a check on the population explosion in India, but the evidence of statistics disproves this theory. India is one of only four countries in the world with an adverse female-male population ratio. This situation has actually worsened over the last six decades, yet it has had no significant impact on India's overall rate of population growth.

As we have already pointed out, population control is quite different from family planning. Selective control of a population, focusing on a category of powerless people, by those wielding social and political power is clearly anti-democratic, to say the least. Gender-based sections of society are harder to divide than those based on race, class, caste or religion. Opposition to sex preselection is, therefore, much more difficult to organise or even to perceive; women, as the victims of gender inequality and oppression, can ever be coerced into supporting it.

Against more than 1,000 female foetuses discovered in a Bombay hospital and later aborted elsewhere, only one male foetus was removed. This was discovered by two women activists in Bombay. The exception was a Parsi woman who already had a son and wanted a daughter. The management of the hospital is deeply religious and doesn't allow abortions to be performed on the premises although, according to one of its leaflets, it does provide the very 'humane and beneficial' services of a sex-determination clinic. The woman concerned was required to inform the hospital after her abortion as to the sex of the foetus in order to supply an institutional record of the test's reliability. Meanwhile, full amniocentesis treatment is not available to women who are likely to give birth to a genetically defective child.

Needless to say, opposition to selective abortion is not to be confused with women's right to free, safe and legal abortion. Women must have the right to control their own bodies. They must be able to seek abortion to avoid unwanted pregnancies; unwanted motherhood cannot be forced upon them. But a woman who wanted fewer children, would terminate a pregnancy irrespective of the child's sex, as unmarried pregnant women usually do. As things go, in many families, especially from communities where large dowries and bride-burning are rampant, any female foetus is got rid of even if the couple has no daughter. Some of the so-called respectable clinics and hospitals piously claim that they perform the sex-determination test only if the woman already has at least one daughter. They are merely reaffirming a couple's right to have a 'balanced' family. They quite deliberately ignore the reality that almost no one ever tries to balance a family in this way when the couple has only a son. There is no question of their having to make it compulsory that the couple has at least one son before a woman has a sex-determination test. Also, they cannot vouchsafe for countless doctors who will always perform these tests without restrictions.

The campaign ahead

The campaign against sex-determination and preselection techniques must consider the issue at multiple levels. Given the inferior status allocated to women in society at large, it will definitely form part of a wider struggle against women's oppression. But to raise one's voice against these practices is also to show a basic concern for human rights and demonstrate resistance to the misuse of science and technology against people in general, as well as women in particular. This multi-dimensional character means that the campaign should attract not only women's groups but organisations involved in health, civil liberties, human rights and legal action, not to mention individuals concerned about the overall issue.

The campaign needs to focus on organising a general awareness drive, concentrating especially on women. Some suggest that this would be a waste of time as women themselves choose to go to clinics for sex-determination and the subsequent selective abortion. This is true, but the behaviour of women doesn't stem from their own free choice. Treated as child-producing machines and subjected to enormous family pressures and training; denied an independent existence and identity, women both submit to and internalise the very male-dominated values which act against them. A well-known example is the mother-in-law's oppression of her daughter-in-law. The vast majority of women who agree to sex pre-selection and female foeticide do it out of submission to the social demand for a male child. If there's to be a change in this mental state of women, as well as in society at large, widespread consciousness-raising among women about their independent identity, alongside a relentless struggle against male-dominated values, is the only alternative.

The above will be a long, slow process. But the rate at which sex-determination and preselection techniques are spreading, and the rate of development of new scientific research, require immediate action. To awaken public opinion against these anti social practices will be the primary goal of our campaign. This will enable us to bring pressure on the Indian government for a ban on all such techniques and a halt to any related research activities.

The following approach and activities are suggested as a beginning:

1. The campaign should attempt to bring together all organisations and individuals who have spoken up against the issue in the past, as well as all those currently expressing concern. Three years ago, a number of mainly women's groups, but also people's science groups, made serious attempts to force the government to ban sex-determination tests. Among reasons for the campaign's lack of success was that the different groups were acting in isolation. A concerted, joint struggle by a variety of interested groups would achieve better results. Efforts must be made to approach as many as possible and co-ordinate the campaign, first at city and then at national level. A nationwide signature campaign could also be undertaken immediately.

2. Exchange of information is vital for the initiation of activities to be successful, in particular for legal action and the raising of public awareness through the press. Some form of national co-ordination for the exchange of information between different organisations and institutions is urgently needed.

3. A primary aim of this workshop is to discuss various myths and biases in an effort to evolve a correct perspective on this issue, including the participation of activists from a range of social groups; this is how pressure groups are born. More seminars, debates and workshops around the country will gradually hasten the build-up of sympathetic public opinion. Detailed articles and special supplements covering all aspects of sex-determination tests must be published in newspapers and magazines. For this purpose we could prepare a full package of articles and photographs.

4. Regional groups need to be set up in order to collect data and information regarding the various irregularities in clinics and in private and public hospitals in their zone. They could also launch their own campaigns, exposing these places and the doctors who perform tests and/or the specific abortion of female foetuses. Street plays, poster exhibitions and slide-shows could be produced to back up their work; and *dharnas* (sit-ins) held at centres to highlight the problem.

5. We also need to launch a wider campaign against the advertising of sex-determination techniques and the clinics performing them. As well as using newspapers and other media, we should deface advertisements, place our posters alongside and do widespread wall-writing.

6. Parents who have only daughters should demonstrate their positive feelings, for instance during the *yatra* (traditional march of schoolgirls carrying flowers).

7. Finally, legal petitions will be filed, and demands for appropriate legislation sent to the Public Health Department, the Department of Women and Social Justice, all Members of Parliament, all political parties, the Prime Minister, President and the Chief Justice of India.

As a long term perspective, we would like to see the inclusion of a special chapter on amniocentesis and other techniques, and their social discriminatory use against women, in the sex-education textbooks which are compulsory for all students in schools and colleges.

36 Tackling Tradition: African Women Speak Out Against Female Circumcision

Adi Gevins

The first of these two interviews by Adi Gevins is with Assitan Diallo of Mali, who went to the 1985 UN Decade Women's Conference in Nairobi in order to discuss her work in fighting the practice of female circumcision. She is involved in research and organising against it at the grass-roots level and is a member of the Inter-African Committee, a multinational organisation based in Dakar, Senegal, which also strives for the eradication of female circumcision.

The second interview, also recorded in Nairobi, is with Stella Efua Graham, a Ghanaian woman currently living in London where she is active in the forefront of the Foundation for Women's Health, Research and Development (FORWARD). An important part of FORWARD's work is the 'Sister to Sister' programme, which was initiated to provide education and information for better health-care for women in Africa, including 'encouragement and support of local action for the elimination of negative social practices affecting the health of mothers and children, for instance the notorious practice of female circumcision'. Stella Graham also works closely with African women living in Britain.

Both interviews are reprinted from the North American international feminist quarterly, *Connexions* (No 17–18, Summer–Fall 1985). They also form part of five half-hour radio documentary programmes based on material gathered at the Nairobi conference and produced by a group called the Family of Women. This material is available on cassette from the Pacific Tape Library, 5316 Venice Blvd., Los Angeles, CA, USA 90010.

What got you interested in female circumcision?

I was circumcised when I was four, so I personally identify with the topic. Moreover, in my society, which is Muslim, our family and elder people have too much power over us. It is not like in Europe or the Western world. We are ashamed to say my own life, my own being, nobody would say that. I don't see myself saying to my father or mum 'that's my life' or 'that's my daughter'. For example, I don't want my daughters to be circumcised. I know, though, that it's not enough for me alone to decide, because my aunt can do it or my grandmother. They won't ask me. When I'm at work and my husband is not at home, they can do it. What can I do? Put them in jail? So every woman must say 'I'm against female circumcision and I don't want to circumcise my daughter and I will fight against it'. The best way to be

'Useless Pain'. Poster used in African/Arab campaign against female circumcision (*Connexions*, USA).

sure it won't happen is to fight for its eradication. So that's my goal.

Until I was 24 years old, I knew that female circumcision involved cutting, and I knew that it was painful, but that was it. Then there was a French lady teaching at my school, and she wanted to find out about female circumcision. She kept asking us questions. I was the only girl in my whole class, so she harassed me with questions about female circumcision. Fortunately I had an old grandmother, she was 108 at that time. The older you get, the more democratic you get in our society. So when my teacher asked me a question, I would go back to my grandmother. I knew if I went to my mother she would say, 'God, you are disgusting'. So I would go to my grandmother who likes to talk. In fact, you have to stop her once she begins. I made her talk about it and then would go back to my teacher. In the end my teacher said: 'You know so much about female circumcision, can't you write a paper about it?'

That's how I began. And as I read more and more, from doctors, etc., I began to learn about its harmful aspects.

Islam has nothing to do with it. The meaning given to it in traditional society cannot be given to it now because the specificity of the operation has changed. It has no social meaning now. I have become convinced that it has no purpose. That we don't need it. That we are just doing it mechanically. It was something that once had a role in the traditional world, but now that we are much more modern, it doesn't have a place.

What sort of work are you doing to eradicate female circumcision?

As far as my work in Mali is concerned, most of my activity so far has been academic. In 1978, I did the first survey on female circumcision in French-speaking West Africa. It was mostly quantitative but also an attitudinal study. I interviewed people and also recorded some 200 songs on circumcision. Through these songs I show how our people express their norms, their rules, their education. I also show what the meaning of female circumcision is through these songs, what message is given in traditional society.

One part of my work was to interview people to show what their attitudes are toward female circumcision, how they understand it, and what the difference is between the type of female circumcision they have been subjected to and the traditional type expressed through songs. My conclusion was that there are no initiation rites attached to it anymore, and education is no longer provided. I also found that a lot of people are against it, but nobody wanted to be marginalised by standing out as an example. So they will say 'We are against it, but we will do it'.

There are a few ways I am trying to make more people in my country aware of the practice. I am a teacher in a professional school. Every four years, at the end of their study, the students must present a paper. We teachers can propose topics, and this year I suggested three subjects dealing with excision [of the clitoris]. We have at least 15 ethnic groups in Mali, and each ethnic group is almost a country in itself. I wanted to have a comparative study of the practice in my country.

The other thing that I'm doing is helping to put together a special magazine issue on female circumcision. We only have one magazine in all of Mali; we have many different newspapers, but only one magazine and it's more academic than political. I will contribute to this special issue when I return from Nairobi. It will be sold throughout the country.

Also we are currently setting up a network of women from different countries working on female circumcision, called the Sister-to-Sister Programme. We want to take a new approach on female circumcision, a sexual approach. It's so easy to talk about health, health, health. Before I came here my mum said: 'Are you going to talk about your crazy stuff again? Female circumcision, sex, sex. You should be ashamed to talk about sex among all those people'. I told her it was important, but she asked, 'What do you have against it?' I mentioned all the health inconveniences. She said, 'You didn't die, I didn't die. How many people can you cite who have died?' 'Well, I don't know, but do you know that people have infection, and leaking?' 'But', she said, 'people who haven't been circumcised have that. Even white women have that'.

It's that kind of statement which gave us the idea that we have to tackle the problem from another angle. Our project will include very deep research into sexuality and sex education in traditional Mali and Mali today. And through this we'll show how traditional sex education supports female circumcision. They tell us that sex is dirty, taboo, you should be discreet if you talk about it. They also say that it is important to be faithful in marriage.

Now, what is the justification of female circumcision? They think it diminishes sexual desire, so that means you will be faithful. They say also that female circumcision purifies women, that means our sex genitalia is dirty. So we want to show the ideas which are in our society and the way the society sees women's sexuality and sexual life. To them, female circumcision is very necessary to support their view of women's sexuality. When we understand all this, we can suggest how to change this view, and be able to provide adequate sex education for our young people.

We know it will be hard because people don't want to talk about this part of sex. It is easier to tackle the problem with health, but it is not enough. There is a cultural part and sexual part that's important.

What do you think about Westerners getting involved in the fight against female circumcision?

You know, it is easy to see that something is wrong with the system when you are outside of it. Easier than when you are inside. We should keep in mind that many Westerners have more experience in dealing with the subject than we do, because they were the first to talk about it. And now we are also talking about it. As we said in social science: don't overlook previous work if you want to do good work. So in our relationship with the Western world, I will say we need them. But again, life is complex. We have been colonised by this Western world and we have, let's say, something against them. That means we don't want them to overwhelm our lives anymore.

For my part, I want their help. I want to collaborate with them. But I don't think I can be in the same group with them to fight something in my own country, because I will feel, 'Here they go again, colonisation'. But I love being asked by people working on female circumcision, 'What are the specifics in Mali?' And suggesting to me, 'Why don't you do that in Mali?' Suggesting means that I can say no, or yes. That's different from, 'Do that in Mali, do that in Senegal'. So in my view, they can be like advisers. They can also say to me, 'You know, people do circumcision in France and we French people want to fight against it'. I want them to allow me to say, 'I'm suggesting you do it this way, because these people are from my country, and I think this will be better'. Again, I'm suggesting something, not imposing it on them. That's the kind of working relationship I want between white and black women on the topic of female circumcision.

Stella Graham: We recognise that excision is a very deep-rooted practice and has a ritualistic aspect to it. It also has a deep psycho-sexual aspect to it, so you simply can't legislate against it and then expect it to stop. People who practise female circumcision feel strongly about it and there are many factors that force women to give in. For example, women are worried about whether their daughters will be able to marry. African women living in London are very concerned about whether their daughters will be accepted back into their communities. So we want legislation to be combined with intensive educational programmes.

The challenge that remains for us is to find an alternative to certain parts of our social structure. We need to find a replacement, but we need to maintain certain structures. For example, the secret societies and the initiation rites (led by women) are very positive things, and we must recognise the fact that in Africa women's power has been eroded with modernity. Because of that, quite a lot of societies' structures are breaking down, and people do not know where they are. I think that the challenge for African women is for us to look at the positive aspects of our culture and to build upon them. And there are many positive things.

The secret societies are an extraordinary power base for women. When we hear about secret societies, or initiation rites, maybe our first reaction is that this is primitive behaviour. But actually it is not. It's an advanced kind of social structure which gives people a definite place in society, which socialises people to recognise their roles and responsibilities.

In the secret society, women, such as those who have been circumcised together, have the possibility to bond together as a group for life, like blood sisters. So wherever they are, if they are in trouble, they can help each other out. I think that when a lot of African women say, 'What right does anyone have to interfere in excision', they are not talking about excision *per se*. What they are talking about is the goodness in women being together, the identity of bonding.

So the challenge is not to say that these initiation rites are backward, but to discover how we can take away the actual excision without destroying the women's power base. A group of women as a secret society can have the power to influence the politics of society as a whole. They could come together as a group in a male-dominated society to put pressure on politicians to do something positive for women. In fact, during this Decade, the feminist struggle in the West is to get women together, to get the bonding, and already in Africa we have the bonding, we have the structures, all we need to do is direct the power of these structures.

One good example is that if the secret society is really brought up to date with present developments, we could overthrow our governments if we wanted to, because we know that in African society women outnumber men. We need to use the power of the group to initiate change for our benefit. So the work of the women's activist network is not to condemn but to replace what we have: we've got to build on it. We want to have the resources to further research the structures that exist at the moment and find entry points into them. We want to confer with powerful women leaders about how not to destroy the structure, and how to project it internationally so that other women can see the benefit and use it for themselves.

Were you initiated?

Unfortunately, I wasn't. I went to school without having gone through the initiation ceremony. I come from a matrilineal group and fortunately excision is not part of our initiation. In the tradition of my society, during the initiation period we learn about child-care, about relationships with other people, about religion in our society, and how the society operates. The girls also learn how to recognise their feminity, their sexuality, and sex education was not purely biological, it was also psychological. Our society recognised the sexuality of women as important to the totality of the group. They taught women what sex involves and it was taught in such a way so that she herself would enjoy sex with her partner. They did not encourage promiscuity, but sex as part of marriage and part of life was recognised as important.

I understand from my grandmother that they even made wooden dummies which the teenagers used as part of the whole process of sex education in the initiation ceremony. So when they came out of this ceremony, they were really well informed about themselves, about the menstrual cycle and other aspects. Women were encouraged to have more control over their own sexuality. But unfortunately, with colonisation and the introduction of Christianity into our communities, these ways were regarded as pagan. It is now a remnant of our culture found in very rural areas. But we would like to recapture what we were losing. We want to develop new forms of sex education for our youngsters that are different from the traditional ways in that they take into account the urban modern sector. We are hoping that through our network and research work, we will be able to bring these issues out.

37   What the State Neglects

Mercedes Sayaguez

Mercedes Sayaguez is a Uruguayan journalist and one of the founders of her country's feminist paper, *La Cacerola*. This article, reproduced here from the newsletter of the Women's Global Network on Reproductive Rights (April–June 1986), was first published in *Breaking the Silence* (Canada, Vol 4, No 2, Winter 1985).

One chilly morning I walked through one of the women's wards in the Pereira Rossell Hospital in Montevideo, Uruguay. The cots are aligned facing each other across the long room. A grey light filters through windows that have been covered with newspapers to prevent drafts. It was chilly outside, and not much warmer inside. The women wear thick old sweaters while they huddle under their thin grey blankets.

Some sit on their cots, some lie hiding their faces, some stare blankly at the roof. Some heat water for tea at a kerosene stove at one end of the room. Next to it is a toilet and cold water shower, both of which are filthy and emit a nauseating stench. There is no toilet paper, no soap, and no telephones. Not a nurse is in sight. At night, cockroaches roam.

As I walk down the central aisle, watching the women, some watch me. Some are fat, some are thin. Some are young and frail, others look mature. Some have gaps in their teeth, some show signs of malnutrition. They sit or lie quietly, wrapped in solitude, waiting for visits, for the pain to subside, for the time to leave. For some it will be two or three days, or a week or a month. As I retrace my steps back to the entrance, a woman, probably the eldest, asks in a loud voice, kindly, 'Are you looking for somebody, girl?'

Yes, I think to myself, I am looking for you. I am a journalist doing an investigative report on abortion in Uruquay. I am looking for my story. I have found my sisters, thin and fat and toothless and in pain. Yet, this morning, I won't intrude on their solitude. I say I'm in the wrong ward and leave. With me I carry the silent gaze, the silent suffering of these women.

Of the 54 beds in the women's ward, this month 27 are taken by these women, the victims of clandestine abortion. Every year the hospital treats over 1,000 women for infections and other complications from these abortions. The Pereira Rossell Hospital is a public hospital, serving mainly the poor. A recent UNICEF study

Graphic from the Uruguayan Women's Association.

established that 40% of the population of Montevideo lives in poverty. They cannot afford unwanted pregnancies; they cannot afford good medical care.

Yet these women are the 'lucky ones'. The next morning I visit the 16th floor of the Hospital de Clinicas, the largest public hospital in the city, one that is equipped

'Holy Saints! What will I do if my child dies?' (CIPAF).

with intensive care units and dialysis equipment. This is where women are brought who are in danger of dying from clandestine abortions. From all over the country they come, some to die, some to be saved. They arrive with severe sepsis and peritonitis. One doctor says that in the last year he performed surgery on six women who had been severely harmed by botched abortions; four of them died. The other two survived but all their reproductive organs had to be removed. Some of these patients undergo severe bouts of major surgery and are hospitalised for months. Last week, a 16-year-old girl went home after 6 months in the hospital. The doctor who first saw her says that she arrived bleeding, her womb filled with three litres of blood. She had been aborted during the sixth month of her pregnancy in the back yard of a Montevideo sports club.

The investigative report I undertook for the news weekly *Busqueda* in 1983 looked at the issue of abortion in Úruguay for the first time in 20 years. A 1963 study had found one of the highest rates of abortion in the world, some 150,000 per year, about three for each live birth. The study also concluded that over 100 women died annually as a result of clandestine abortions.

Although the 1963 statistics may be somewhat questionable, it would appear that the number of deaths has diminished since, owing to the introduction of the contraceptive pill, antibiotics and intensive care units. I was not able to ascertain the exact number of deaths in 1983 because during the 1973 to 1985 period of military rule, data and statistics like this were always kept secret. The employees at the morgue knew the number of women who had died of abortion-related complications but they wouldn't tell me. I managed to learn that in Montevideo it was more than 10 but less than 20 per year. In the new democracy, these figures should soon be available. The evidence also suggests that the number of abortions has declined since 1963 thanks to the increased use of contraceptives. Some studies have pointed at a number somewhere between 20,000 and 30,000 abortions per year. Dr Morel of the Uruguayan affiliate of the IPPF (International Planned Parenthood Federation) did a study showing that of the 28,000 women seen between 1965 and 1975, the percentage admitted for an abortion went down from 70% to 40%.

My investigative report brought the severity of the problem to public attention. The treatment of septic abortions is a substantial drain on the public health system – one study calculated that between 1973 and 1978 the cost of treating a patient ranged from $880 to $7,500. These are staggering sums in a developing country where the per capita GNP is only $2,560. The report found that treating a septic abortion cost as much as 12 uncomplicated caesarians, 24 normal births or 36 uncomplicated abortions.

'How can we find out more about our bodies?' Answer: 'the Mothers' Club'.
(Centro de Defesa dos Direitos Humanos, Paraiba, Brazil).

From *Brujas*, Colombian feminist magazine.

It was impossible to find out exactly what percentage of the national health budget was taken up by treating victims of clandestine abortions because of the secrecy of the military government. But figures available from other Latin American countries can help us draw a picture. In Bolivia, for example, the Ministry of Public Health estimates that treatment of botched abortions accounts for more than 60% of the obstetrics and gynaecology budget. In El Salvador, a study in the maternity hospital estimated that this kind of treatment took 13.3% of hospital staff and budget.

This has to be seen in a larger context. In the 1970s and 1980s the Uruguayan military authorities did not consider culture, education or health as high priorities. The amount allocated to health in the national budget was reduced to 9% in 1974 and 6% in 1982 while military expenditures soared to 40% of the country's budget. And of the amount allocated to health, the lion's share was used by the military and their families. A UNICEF study showed that 75 pesos of every 100 spent on health went to the military.

Compounding this was the economic collapse brought about by monetarist policies adopted by the military government which resulted in a sharp drop in earning power and lowering of the average Uruguayan's standard of living. When the foreign debt ballooned from $600 million to $4.5 billion in 1984, problems we thought we had left behind – like child mortality and child malnutrition – reappeared, and so did unsafe abortions.

In my study, I learned about many cheap and dangerous methods that women were forced to resort to. For $5 a midwife will insert a tube in a women's uterus. When the bleeding and cramps start, the woman is supposed to check into a public hospital, where the doctors will complete the abortion and treat her. In the rural areas, a woman might insert parsley stalks or peacock feathers into her womb, or drink tea of *ruda*, a weed that has abortifacient properties. At one point in the 1970s, abortions were performed in a station wagon parked near the Hospital de Clinicas. If a problem arose, the woman was quickly admitted and the abortionist would disappear without trace.

While doing my report for *Busqueda* I interviewed a 28-year-old woman named Mirta. When Mirta, a student, found herself pregnant, she and her boyfriend, both with very little money, searched for a doctor to perform an abortion. They ended up with a medical student in a house just outside Montevideo. When the student discovered that Mirta was asthmatic, he refused to use anaesthesia because of the risks involved. He performed a D&C without it. Her sister grabbed her ankles, her boyfriend her shoulders. The abortionist warned her not to cry out because of the neighbours. Mirta bit a handkerchief so she wouldn't howl.

The stories are similar everywhere. In Uruguay some have raised their voices against this situation. But more than a quarter million women still lack access to contraceptive methods, which are also expensive. There is no sex education in the schools. It is not surprising that the unscrupulous and well-meaning alike take into their hands what the state neglects – women's lives.

38   Building Politics from Personal Lives

Carmen Barroso and Cristina Bruschini

This extract, from an essay of the same title, tells of a popular sex-education project developed by feminists from the Carlos Chagas Foundation in collaboration with small groups of poor women from the outskirts of São Paulo, Brazil. Their discussion, which evolved over one-and-a-half years from 1981, eventually led to the production of a series of booklets entitled *Esse Sexo que é Nosso* (This Sex of Ours) that continue to be distributed among schools, women's groups and some government health agencies in Brazil.

In echoing the Mexican experience described by Gisela Espinosa Damían in Chapter 4, this account confirms that sexuality is becoming an increasingly popular political focus for consciousness-raising and organisation among working-class women in Latin America.

The origin of the project was tied to the demand for discussions on sex education and gender relations voiced by women in the grass-roots movements, and to the political contradictions surrounding the history of feminism and population policies in Brazil. The aims were to construct a collective knowledge about sexuality and to share immediately this knowledge among all the participants. Participant methodology was chosen in order to help small groups of women discuss the meaning of sexuality in their intimate relationships, as well as in the broader social context. Their discussions served as a basis for a series of booklets to be used both as discussion guides for similar groups and as a reference for all interested women.

The project was developed by the Chagas researchers with the *Mothers' Club of Diadema*, whose members are low-income housewives, most of them in their 20s and early 30s, some of them older, who take care of their homes and small children. Most of their husbands are unskilled workers in the neighbourhood factories or have other manual occupations in the service sector.

Their club has weekly meetings, sewing, painting, and knitting courses. They read and write with great difficulty. They are the recipients of free distribution of food provided by government agencies. When asked about group discussions on sexuality, they showed great enthusiasm. Although they had had previous experience in group activities and courses in infant care, they had not had any experience of the kind suggested.

Teaching while learning

In the first meetings they asked many questions about body functions and anatomy. At times it was difficult to avoid lecturing as we tried to provide all the information requested. One way was to start from drawings women made in their small groups. If the aim was to help critical thought, understanding, and reflection on daily life, the starting point had to be aspects of daily life. But we also had to go beyond them to reach the real connections among these apparently chaotic elements. Thus, while each person's individual experience was valued, we also tried to locate sexuality within the context of social relations.

Five booklets were created from these discussions. The first booklet describes male and female bodies in a simple and direct way. Photographs of naked people were used to avoid the coldness of schematic drawings. The idea is to link physiology with flesh and blood, in a body that not only ovulates, but also desires and is able to feel pleasure. Pictures of ordinary people were used to counteract dominant aesthetic standards, and help women to accept and love their own figures.* The production of the first pictures were not easy for, at the beginning, inhibition resulted in rigid positions and artificial smiles. Furthermore, in searching for non-professional models, at first only young, beautiful and middle-class friends were willing to be pictured. After a while we found a wider range of volunteers including a middle-aged physician and a black domestic worker.

The second booklet presents information on birth control and a discussion of the social and political conditions of child-bearing and child-rearing. The third one is geared to helping mothers accept and respond positively to the sexuality of their children, in order to avoid the reproduction of the ignorance and shame of which they themselves were victims. The fourth booklet teaches how to self-examine breasts and genitals, and at the same time encourages the fight for the right to good quality public medical services. Similarly, strong criticism of the authoritarianism of the medical profession is presented side by side with an acknowledgement of the bad work conditions of doctors in the public system. In the last booklet sexual pleasure is integrated with the whole gamut of life's pleasures. Issues discussed include the role of fantasy, similarities and differences between men and women, the variability of individual preferences and behaviour. We have made a concerted attempt to avoid the presentation of ready-made recipes, or the imposition of new patterns of right and wrong. Rather, what is aimed at is the respect by each woman for her own experiences and values and for those that differ from hers.

In dealing with pleasure, we discussed the difficulty of enjoying sex in situations where the whole family lives in a single room or in which the couple is threatened by unemployment. At the same time, it was stressed that pleasure and sexual fulfilment are threatened not only by material conditions, but also by the ignorance, shame, or distaste for their own bodies that women have been taught since early childhood.

* In this we were not entirely successful. Some women, instead of broadening their concept of beauty, were happy to verify that those pictured were 'as ugly as we are!' In any case, the identification made learning easier.

corpo de mulher

SOS CORPO
GRUPO DE SAÚDE DA MULHER
Poster by women's health group, Brazil

Problems with the gynaecological examination were discussed in relation to authoritarian attitudes from doctors and our repressive education about our bodies and sexuality in general.

We also discussed how women's subordination within the family reproduces the power structure of society as a whole, and thus how the family becomes a mechanism for developing submissive individuals.

The need for women to organise to fight for their rights was discussed, although timidly.

In helping the group to arrive at a critical understanding of their own situation, as being part of a structure of social relations, we too were learning, and had a chance to change our minds. We were convinced, for instance, that contrary to neo-malthusian teachings, the most important thing about birth control was that it could not be used as a solution to economic problems. Although we still believe that the most important cause of poverty is structural, the women's resistance to our arguments and their daily behaviour gradually convinced us that information about and access to contraception are also important elements for the improvement of their living conditions on a short-term basis. This improvement is clearly quite limited, both because the structural causes of poverty may remain unchanged, and because inadequate health care renders high-technology contraception particularly risky. Given these limits, however, contraception is perceived as an immediate need to which women attach great priority, and which they do not see as incompatible with the struggle for a better health system and against the roots of poverty. What may seem obvious from the outside, was, in fact, an arduous learning experience for

Por que queremos ter o corpo igual ao das modelos?

'Why do we want to have models' bodies?' From *Esse Sexo que é Nosso*, no 1.

us, given the whole history of heated political debate over this issue in Latin America.

Between indoctrination and neutrality

We tried to avoid both false neutrality as well as the authoritarian imposition of our

From *Esse Sexo que é Nosso*, no 2.

values. Laura, one of the participants, said, 'In other courses, we remained quiet, listening to the teachers. But you don't come to give lectures'. Their active participation gave them greater self-confidence to speak, because they knew they would be listened to. This does not mean that the researchers were romanticising popular knowledge and experience, nor expecting to find a pure, absolute truth among the participants. These women's discussions reproduced to varying degrees the ideology that ensures their domination.

Since the values of the dominant class are internalised by every class, and given that there is no pure and entirely autonomous popular culture, we had to ask ourselves about our role as participant researchers. When they said, for instance, that 'a woman is a woman when she becomes a mother', 'abortion is a crime', or 'homosexuality is sickness', it was impossible to remain quiet. We felt that they had a right to information about what our opinions were, and that attempting to disguise them would be neither very effective nor ethically justifiable, since it did not seem fair to expect them to be candid, while we withheld our own candid expressions.

In dealing with controversial values, we gradually came to the point where we could state our point of view, with no fear of imposing our opinions. In the groups we came to respect each other's convictions, and agreed that a point of view is nothing more than a point of view: to be accepted if it makes sense, to be rejected if it does not.

The most important thing is that they were always at ease to disagree with any one of us. They are not defenceless, naïve beings, ready to swallow any new value mentioned, as one would believe from the over-concern about preserving working-class values, supposedly endangered by the exposure to middle-class feminist values, as voiced in some quarters. As long as it was made explicit that we did not claim to be the guardians of truth, and that our opinions were the result of our personal histories which differed from theirs, this exchange of ideas seemed to help their autonomy, much more than their previous lack of access to knowledge in the area.

We also found that these women disagree among themselves; for instance, when Ana said she thought it was her duty to have sex any time her husband wanted, Suely disagreed immediately, and a heated discussion followed. It did not take long for the naïve researchers to discover that the mythical 'Poor Woman' did not exist. Their shared common experiences and opinions did not exhaust the richness of their different lives and ideas.

New challenges

After one year in which the Chagas researchers had given a series of seminars on the booklets to groups of feminists, grass-root communities and women in Left parties, requests started to come from civil servants – mostly women – in the education, welfare and health systems. These came mostly from the lower echelons at the local level: for instance, nurses of a city health clinic, facing the needs of poor women every day, asked for seminars to learn our methodology in order to replicate it with their clientele. It soon became clear that women doctors, nurses, teachers and social workers came to the discussion groups with the same histories of doubts, fears, hopes and strengths we found in militant and grass-root groups. This 'womanity' had difficulty emerging in some groups when there was a rigid hierarchy in the work-place, an authoritarian personality in the leadership. But on the whole, it was surprisingly easy for women to share their common concerns and intimate experiences. Of course these groups, who called upon themselves the extra responsibility to develop activities in sex education with their clientele, are not the typical civil servants settled within a system that breeds inertia and gives no recognition to special efforts. Although not typical, these groups are growing in number: by June 1984, we had worked with 33 of them (as compared with 35 non-state-related groups).

The transition to democracy presented new opportunities and new risks for Brazilian feminists. A growing crisis of legitimacy, and a deepening economic collapse brought a gradual end to the military regime, starting with the election of opposition state governors in 1982. The coalition now in power is a blend of disparate political forces, including some progressive sectors. Some feminists have entered party politics and are lobbying from inside for gender-specific issues. Others are very reluctant to do so, either because they have joined the other progressive party which has remained in the opposition, or because their view of feminism attaches no relevance to state policies. Some of the 'opposition feminists' work in middle-level posts of the government bureaucracy where they have been trying to implement items of a feminist agenda. This has been facilitated by the need of the current regime to maintain its broad social basis of support, and the resulting courtship of the women's movement.

When, in 1983, state policy papers on women's health were drawn up for the first time, the reproductive rights discourse of the women's movement featured prominently in them. Regardless of that, many feminist groups voiced strong opposition to them. This opposition expressed several trends: a generalised mistrust of government rhetoric, more often used to disguise inertia or unpopular policies than to set guidelines for policy implementation; an unclear conceptualisation of opposition-government relationships and the resulting fear that support for any specific policy would imply loss of independence and weakening of the opposition; an incipient development of the theory of reproductive autonomy and its relationship with state-provision of sex education and family planning services.

Continuing discussions and further developments at the institutional level dispelled some of these fears. It became clear that, while the post-authoritarian regime was not immune to rhetoric, this could now be used to support popular demands and organise to press the government to live up to its lofty declared intentions. Also, feminists became increasingly convinced that the crucial differences between population control and support for women's reproductive rights did not lie in policymakers' hidden motivations, but in the actual practices of health services. In the post-authoritarian regime the greater threat to women's autonomy lies more in the lack of good quality health services than on coerciveness. (Under the military regime, the proposal for the establishment of population control policies constituted a real threat; therefore the fight against them went so far as to downplay the other side of women's right to control their own bodies. With 'redemocratisation', the demand for access to birth control methods came to order.) So the women's health policies ended by gaining the support of the women's movement. Our main criticism now is the slow pace of implementation and the low priority accorded to participatory sex education.*

The programmes of the Ministry of Health and two State Secretaries of Health have included in their activities the distribution of a small number of Chagas

---

* See *Carta de Itapecirica*, a manifesto coming out of a national meeting of 80 women's groups, in October 1984.

booklets. Although small (20,000) this number is much larger than what could be distributed directly through the women's groups. This has not occurred without resistance, of course. A conservative deputy has made a speech against the leaflets' 'immorality' and other similar episodes have also occurred. On the whole, however, they have been well received and this is largely due to the replication in its distribution of the small group methodology.

The project is now over. It was funded by the Ford Foundation which, in Brazil, has supported many progressive initiatives, including some of the most radical feminist groups. During the early period of military dictatorship in the 1960s the Ford Foundation had established a liberal reputation for supporting professors who had been expelled from the universities under the accusation of being Leftists; in spite of that, in the 1970s, most feminists were hesitant to approach the Foundation fearing that the motives behind their interest in the women's movement were to act as an intelligence service or as an attempt to control, co-opt or neutralise the movement. In recent years, these doubts have given way to a more pragmatic approach. Given the fact that Ford officials have made no attempts to intervene in the groups's policies and practices, and that the information collected through grantee's reports is public anyway, feminist groups felt that there was no reason not to accept the Foundation support for projects that otherwise would not be feasible. In later phases of this project, The Pathfinder Fund picked up the tab.

Conclusion

From the enthusiastic evaluations, we know that the discussions have been providing women with information and with a forum to critically question certain values. The warm contact we keep with an extended network is both worrisome and gratifying. On the one hand, it is clear that they considered it very positive for their personal growth, even if conflicts and contradictions in their daily life might have been exacerbated. On the other hand, the degree to which this new awareness is translated into commitment to collective efforts for change is not clear.

Nevertheless, some facts are reassuring. First, these women are taking the initiative of holding discussion groups all by themselves. Second, the booklets generated from the discussion have been shared with thousands of women, assembled in small groups throughout Brazil and other countries. Third, their asserted interest in sexual politics is part of a movement that is spreading in all of Latin America. By 1985, in Brazil, the issues of female sexuality and reproductive rights have come out of the closet. Several groups (SOS Corpa, Recife, Women's House, Sexuality and Health etc) have chosen them as their central concern. National meetings have come up with specific proposals for better health-care systems and methods of promoting women's autonomy. The linkage with general social conditions is presented as mutually reinforcing realms of change, not as excuses for paralysis. All of this was possible because the women of the poor peripheries of the cities asserted their needs, with no respect for the hierarchy of needs established by the well meaning but misguided 'bread first' school of thought.

Part 8:
Resources

1. International and Regional Networks
2. Women's Organisations
3. Suggested Further Reading

1 International and Regional Networks

The number of women's networks operating at national, regional and/or international levels has more than doubled in the last decade. Created in response to the needs of some of the hundreds of women's groups and organisations that have sprung up during this period, they reflect a growing consciousness that women today, both in Third World countries and in the so-called developed world, remain discriminated against and oppressed no matter how enlightened government policies may claim to be. In a paper entitled 'Networking in the Global Women's Movement' Marilee Karl, co-founder of Isis, one of the first-ever international feminist networks, sums up their purpose as follows:

> Networks have been created to fulfil the need for groups to break their isolation and share ideas, information and experiences in ways of working, organising and taking action . . . They give strength to women's efforts by linking up women around the globe in support and solidarity and enabling them to achieve more than any single group or organisation can achieve on its own.

All the networks listed below – and this is only a small selection – operate on either an international or inter-regional scale. They are divided by country or region, according to the location of their main co-ordinating point(s). Many thanks to Isis International from whose publications much of this information has been taken.

Africa

Association of African Women for Research and Development (AAWORD)
BP 3304
Dakar – SENEGAL

AAWORD was created in 1977 by a group of African women researchers who felt the need to organise themselves in order to meet, share experiences and discuss priorities and methods of research. In keeping with their first meeting, entitled 'African Women and the Decolonisation of Research', they are dedicated to the need for African women themselves to study their own societies and formulate their own theories, analyses and development programmes. They have also formed a number of working groups to focus on specific themes, such as reproduction,

267

employment, the media, feminism and research methodology.

In an effort to promote communication and establish new contacts, especially in Africa, AAWORD launched a quarterly newsletter, *Echo*, in 1986, in English and French.

Asia and the Pacific

Committee for Asian Women (CAW)
CCA–URM
57 Peking Road, 5/F
Kowloon   HONG KONG   Tel: 3 682187

CAW aims to improve the situation of Asian women workers through consciousness-raising, organisation and the promotion of solidarity among local groups of women workers in the region. As Teresa Dagdag, a Filipina Catholic sister of the Maryknoll Congregation and long time member of CAW, explains in the introduction to the Isis International Journal *Industrial Women Workers in Asia*:

> In Asia, work for the education and organisation of women workers started as a concern of Church people. As early as 1977, the Asian Women's Forum underlined the importance of responding to the needs of labour and particularly of women workers.

Further groundwork was laid by Church women from Japan, the Philippines and Korea who dedicated themselves to visiting groups, facilitating programmes and raising support for the plight of women, mainly in the industrial sector. A workshop for women garment workers was held in Manila in 1980; for women electronics workers in Malaysia in 1981; and for women textile workers in Manila in 1984. In addition, various newsletters and books were published to raise the consciousness of concerned individuals and groups, among them: *Struggling to Survive* (1981), *From the Womb of Han* (Stories of Korean women workers, 1982), and *Filipino Working Women* (1984).

To quote Teresa Dagdag:

> As more and more women began to see the need to support the struggle of Asian women workers, the idea of CAW was born . . . in December 1982 the organising committee meeting was held in Bangkok, Thailand.
>
> Today CAW is composed of women from different countries in Asia. At a recent meeting in Hong Kong CAW reaffirmed its thrust to be in support and to facilitate response to the struggles of women in Asia, particularly those working in manufacturing industries, as unskilled and semi-skilled labour in the production lines of transnational corporations. In CAW's considerations, Asia is sub-divided into three regions: South East Asia (Philippines, Singapore, Malaysia, Thailand and Indonesia); East Asia (Japan, Hong Kong, Taiwan and South Korea); and South Asia (Sri Lanka, India, Pakistan and Bangladesh). The further sub-division was agreed upon due to the observed commonalities in the

situation of women workers in the same sub-region. Capital flight takes the route via East Asia, then South East Asia and then South Asia. This is evidenced by earnings which show that East Asia offers the highest wages while in general women workers in South Asia receive the least.

CAW produces the quarterly *Asian Women Workers Newsletter* as a forum for news and debate on issues such as legislation, sexual harassment at work, and the latest industrial action being taken by Asian working women.

Pacific and Asian Women's Forum (PAWF)
623/27 Rajagiriya Gardens
Rajagiriya   SRI LANKA

PAWF is an informal network of women activists, researchers and other women concerned with and working on women's issues. It was set up in 1977, by women who met at the Asian and Pacific Centre for Women and Development, with the aim of building a network of women's organisations and activities in the Asian and Pacific region to enable them to keep in touch with each other, co-operate in developing future programmes, and provide mutual support in the search for solutions to common problems.

PAWF brings out (at irregular intervals) a newsletter, *Pacific and Asian Women's Network*, which contains articles on specific issues as well as news and information about groups, activities, conferences and resources in the region. It also maintains links with like-minded groups in other regions of the world.

Third World Movement Against the Exploitation of Women (TW-MAE-W)
769 Aurora Boulevard
Quezon City   PHILIPPINES

TW-MAE-W was formed on Human Rights Day, 10 December 1980, as a Third World initiative to mobilise groups in the Philippines and elsewhere towards the liberation of women 'from all kinds of oppression and exploitation based on sex, class or race'. Much of its campaigning has been concentrated on improving the situation of women workers in agriculture and industry and, more especially, against their abuse as 'commodities in the international flesh trade'. At the Movement's first regional meeting in 1985, attended by 15 participants from five Asian countries, the following principles of unity were established:

1. to do networking among individuals and groups:
   * make known issues and problems of women's exploitation and oppression;
   * share strategies to be taken;
   * enlist support through signing of letters, petitions, etc.;
   * support issues raised by other groups;
   * solicit actively other groups with the same persuasion;
   * give talks, run workshops and seminars;

2. to undertake research on:
   * international migration including migration of professionals;
   * feminist ideologies;
   * women and child prostitution;
   * men who solicit Third World women as prostitutes or as brides through the marriage market;
   * women's services in Asian and other Third World countries;
   * refugee centres or organisations that will help migrants in trouble;
   * information that would be helpful to prevent girls from entering the hospitality services and to enable those who wish to get out of the mess they are in;

3. to empower women using the following means:
   * a manual giving the dynamics of conscientisation regarding women's issues;
   * exposure of sexual stereotypes seen in children's literature, adolescent literature, films and advertisements;
   * video and slide presentations;
   * alternative literature for children and adults;
   * a collection of songs of Third World women and their struggles.

Caribbean Association for Feminist Research and Action (CAFRA)
Language Laboratory
University of West Indies
St Augustine   TRINIDAD and TOBAGO

CAFRA was formed in April 1985 at an official launching meeting in Barbados. The idea to establish the association was born in Puerto Rico in 1980, when women activists and scholars from all over the Caribbean came together for a study seminar on Women and Social Production in the Caribbean, organised jointly by the University of Sussex Institute of Development Studies, England, and the Centro de Estudios de la Realidad Puertoriqueña, San Juan, Puerto Rico. According to CAFRA:

The need was felt to strengthen regionalism by working towards establishing proper links between research and action programmes. Underlying this need is a shared feminist approach, which recognises the exploitation and oppression of women and its relationship to other forms of exploitation and oppression in society and the commitment to work actively towards changing this situation.

From this perspective, CAFRA aims at developing research priorities which respond to the needs of the women's movement in the region, providing a Caribbean marketplace for feminist encounter in this regard. The Secretariat was established in Trinidad and Tobago.

The Steering Committee is comprised of a General Coordinator, a Secretariat, and National Representatives. The National Representatives coordinate at national levels and liaise with the Coordinator in Trinidad. Members meet regularly at national levels, discuss workplans and liaise with the Secretariat which monitors and administers coordinative action.

Europe

Isis International
Via San Saba 5, int. 1
00153, Rome **ITALY**

Isis International grew out of Isis Women's International Information and Communication Service, founded in 1974 to promote communication and networking among women around the world. In January 1984, Isis was transformed into two new organisations: Isis International Women's Information and Communication Service, based in Rome and Santiago, Chile (see under Latin America), and Isis-WICCE (Women's International Cross-Cultural Exchange) in Geneva, Switzerland.

Among Isis International's stated general objectives are:

● to promote and facilitate the exchange of ideas and sharing of experiences among women, women's organisations and others working for greater justice in society at all levels: local, national, regional and international.

● to promote networking and communication channels that enable women, especially at the grass-roots level, to obtain access to needed information, to make their voices heard, and to take action.

● to build awareness of the situation of women around the world, especially in the Third World, contributing to education about and for development.

These objectives are achieved through:

● resource centres in Rome and Santiago which incorporate computerised databases of information compiled from over 10,000 contacts in 150 countries, as well as thousands of magazines, journals, newsletters, books and studies from all over the world.

● the publication of a regular news supplement, *Women in Action*, a twice-yearly journal produced in co-ordination with Third World women's groups, and resource guides such as the latest, *Powerful Images: A Women's Guide to Audiovisual Resources*.

● the organisation of meetings on different aspects of women and development.

● the provision of training courses on new technology for women's resource centres.

Of all the growing number of international feminist networks, Isis undoubtedly has the longest history. This experience and a dedication to mobilising information, not simply collecting it, together with giving consistent priority to making it accessible to Third World women (the bulk of Isis publications are distributed free to groups in Third World countries), have made Isis an important source of inspiration and support to women involved in communication all over the world.

Isis-WICCE
C.P. 2471
Geneva 2   SWITZERLAND   Tel: (022) 33 67 46

Sharing much of the same objectives as Isis International, Isis-WICCE is also a resource centre providing information and materials on issues as wide-ranging as health, peace, sexuality, tourism, media, development, new technology, and violence against women. In addition a large part of its energy is taken up by a yearly cross-cultural exchange programme that offers an opportunity for women active in women's organisations and projects to spend time in another cultural context with a group involved in similar work. The purpose of the WICCE programme is to:

● strengthen the existing women's network through personal contact, direct sharing of knowledge, experience and skills.
● develop and expand the women's movement internationally in order to co-ordinate the actions of women against unjust situations.
● help women to develop themselves, their own culture, and their own positive alternatives.

Each programme takes a different theme, so far: health, communication and, planned for 1987, appropriate technology. The participants, numbering around 15, are all women activists sent to take part in the programme by their particular group; receiving groups are organisations involved in women's issues willing to undertake the responsibility of welcoming a participant and providing a programme of activities and work experiences based on the mutual needs of all concerned. The exchange can take place between Third World countries and/or between Third World and more developed countries.

Isis-WICCE also produces a series of quarterly documents related to the theme of each programme, including a detailed report by participants.

International Working Group on Women and the Family
245A Coldharbour Lane
London SW9 8RR   ENGLAND   Tel: (01) 737 6713

Formed in Britain in 1984, this group focuses on working towards the eradication of violence against women by male relatives within the family.
    In their own words:

> The International Working Group on Women and the Family is a network of women from Third World countries, both those living in their own countries and those living as part of ethnic minority groups in Western Europe and North America. We are individual women and groups of women who believe in working towards achieving a real change in the situation of Third World women, and we specifically want to work to end violence against women and the existing values that condone male oppression of female members of the family. This group will serve as an umbrella organisation for existing groups of Third World women.

The group's main function in Western Europe and North America is to raise funds and so provide the financial backing that women inside Third World countries need to carry out their programme of action. Money is needed for:

Publicity Groups, to ensure publication not only in the majority language, but also in as many minority languages as possible, and to distribute publications as widely as possible in each country, and to visit localities where it is thought likely that women may not have had the necessary education to enable them to read and write, and to undertake oral and/or visual publicity appropriate to this situation.

Research Groups to study the extent of the problem of domestic violence against women, and to understand women's attitudes towards their inferior position within the family, which is mainly used to justify this kind of violence.

National Networks of women to devise strategies suitable for any particular community to prevent violence against women and support women currently suffering from violence.

Support Groups for the women concerned, so through discussion and sharing they will re-establish their self-esteem and gain the strength to assert their equal human rights even within the family.

The International Working Group on Women and the Family believes that traditions and practices that are anti-women are so pervasive and deeply entrenched in all our cultures – both First and Third World – that the attitudes of women towards themselves make the problem of offering support and suggesting possible solutions a highly sensitive issue.

Each group in each country has absolute autonomy to make decisions regarding the best way to support women who suffer domestic violence, as well as deciding what should be done about the problem within their particular cultural, regional, or national community.

As the women in or from the countries concerned, we are the ones who have the most right to take a fresh and objective look at the position of Third World women within the family and the wider social context that sustains it. We will not be influenced by the preconceptions or commitments to values and standards of outsiders, whose criticisms are too often based on a lack of knowledge and understanding of the society they are making judgements on. This lack of awareness too often leads to an analysis and resulting solution whose implications are racist.

The group considers that all the groups have to be *Women Only*. Because of cultural and religious practices in many Third World countries, it would create impossible social and political difficulties if men were to attempt to enter women's circles, homes, or communities to ask questions or attempt discussion as part of this work. Women would also be put in a potentially dangerous situation if they were seen talking with a man, let alone seeking shelter in a house or refuge which was run, even if only partially, by men. It would do more harm than good for any interviews or research to be carried out by men as it would possibly increase the violence, not only within her family, but within the immediate community.

The group believes that it is the shared awareness and natural sympathy that women have for women's situation within the family that entitles them to be the ones to form and direct the work of groups investigating and working towards the ending of violence against women.

Women Living Under Muslim Laws
34980 Combailleaux (Montpellier)   FRANCE   Tel: (33) 67 27 59

Women Living Under Muslim Laws is an international network of women whose lives are shaped or governed by laws, both written and unwritten, drawn from interpretations of the Koran closely tied in with local traditions.

The network was formed in response to three situations requiring urgent action during 1984–85. They were: the case of three feminists, arrested and jailed for seven months without trial in Algeria for having discussed with others the profoundly anti-women Family Code; the case of a Sunni woman who filed a petition in the Supreme Court of India, arguing that the Muslim minority law applied to her in her divorce denied her the rights otherwise guaranteed to all citizens by the Indian Constitution (see interview with Marie-Aimée Hélie-Lucas); and a woman in Abu Dhabi who was charged with adultery and sentenced to be publicly stoned to death after delivering and feeding her child for two months.

Taking the opportunity of meeting at an international feminist gathering on reproductive rights in Amsterdam (July 1984), nine women from Muslim countries and communities came together to form a committee in support of these struggles. The ensuing campaigns, launched with full backing from other women living under Muslim laws and from progressive and feminist groups abroad, led to the formation of the present network.

The main objectives of the network are:

● to create links between women's groups and women prevented from organising within Muslim countries and communities;
● to increase knowledge about their common situation in various contexts;
● to strengthen their struggles and encourage their international support from within the Muslim world and outside.

This work is done through the collection and dissemination of information on all aspects of Muslim laws relating to women, the organisation of meetings, where possible, and the mobilisation of campaigns.

Marie-Aimée Hélie-Lucas, currently the network's central co-ordinator, is anxious to stress that this is not only a north-south process, in other words 'Western feminists supporting us'. The network, which includes women from India, Pakistan, Sri Lanka, Nigeria, Egypt, Sudan, Algeria, Morocco and Tunisia, has long been supporting a group known as 'the Five Mothers from Algiers', five French women whose children were taken away by their Algerian fathers after divorce (see Chapter 1).

WISER Links
Women's International Information Exchange/Resource Centre
173 Archway Road
London N6   ENGLAND   Tel: (01) 341 4403

WISER (Women's International Self-Education Resource) Links is committed to the promotion of greater awareness of women's importance in economic, political and social development, both within Britain and on an international scale. The organisation states among its further aims: to challenge racist, ethnocentric and sexist ideas, institutions and practices; to encourage learning through active involvement and information exchanges, self-education and the learning of skills; and to encourage solidarity with women and their organisations internationally. This work is carried out through correspondence, the provision of research facilities, audio-visual aids and organisational support, such as facilitating speakers, presenting joint events and workshops with other groups, and the production of a bi-monthly newsletter covering women's struggles worldwide.

The resource centre houses a library focusing on women from an international perspective and including both published and unpublished works/grass-roots material, much of it written in original mother tongues. A co-ordinating group of paid and volunteer workers is currently putting together a comprehensive catalogue of these resources, plus a series of information packs and an international directory of women's self-help activities, especially in the areas of health and violence against women.

Women's Global Network on Reproductive Rights
PO Box 4098
Minahassastraat 1
1009 AB Amsterdam NETHERLANDS   Tel: (020) 923900

The Women's Global Network on Reproductive Rights is an autonomous network of groups and individuals in every continent who are working for and support reproductive rights on a national and international level. The co-ordinating group provides the following description:

Our Aims
- Women's right to decide if, when and how to have children.
- The right to safe, effective contraception.
- The right to safe, legal abortion.
- Safe, woman-controlled pregnancy and birth.
- Access to treatment for infertility.
- Health services that meet women's needs.
- Freedom from abuses and discriminatory practices.
- Women's control, not population control.

Our Campaigns
- Some of the issues we have been campaigning on since 1978 include:
- dangerous and illegal abortion, a major killer of women;
- population policies that encourage some women to have children while preventing others from doing so;
- not giving women full information about benefits and risks of methods and treatments, so that they are unable to make informed choices;
- prosecutions and imprisonment, abuses and restrictive laws, all violations of

women's right to control their own bodies without fear;
● testing and promotion of drugs in the Third World based on different standards from those required for use in 'developed' countries.

What We Do
● Build links and exchanges between new and existing groups and individuals who support our aims;
● organise international solidarity;
● collect and share information on the situation in each country, and what campaigns, activities and work women are involved in, including work done by clinics and health workers;
● build international action on the issues which are priorities of members of the network;
● organise conferences and meetings on a national, regional and international level;
● publish and distribute a newsletter four times a year;
● monitor research on reproductive issues;
● work with other organisations on issues related to women's health and reproduction.

What You Can Do
● Become an active member of the network;
● support solidarity requests;
● let us know if you need solidarity;
● send us information about the situation in your country and what women are doing about it, and about all reproductive rights issues;
● initiate and support national and regional networking;
● publicise the information you receive and raise the issues;
● get involved in international actions;
● help to fund-raise for this work.

Women's Global Network on Reproductive Rights is one of eleven organisations which sponsored the Fifth International Women and Health Meeting, held in Costa Rica in May, 1987.

Latin America

Development Alternatives with Women for a New Era (DAWN)
Instituto Universitario de Pesquisa do Rio de Janeiro
Rua Paulino Fernandes No 32
Rio de Janeiro – RJ   BRAZIL 22.270   Tel: 246 1830

DAWN emerged as a loose formation of committed and experienced individuals, organisations and associations, brought together in a rather *ad hoc* fashion to develop a common analysis for the Nairobi Conference. Its goal was a

mobilising one – to provide the women's movement with a platform to politicise the current development debates. DAWN has gained momentum as a non-governmental global network, and its process has offered a forum for an ongoing and ever-widening debate of development alternatives.
(General Report, Third Advisory Council Meeting and Plans for the Future, 1986–88, p. 9.)

DAWN's contributions to the NGO Forum in Nairobi included the organisation of workshops on women and development and a book, *Development, Crisis and Alternative Visions: Third World Women's Perspectives* (see Suggested Further Reading), which was enthusiastically received by participants as a very useful basis for discussion.

DAWN's current plan of action, conceived at a meeting in Brazil in February, 1987 concentrates on six areas of activity: research, training, advocacy, publications, communications and international relations. According to the General Report:

Alternative methodologies for empowering women's organisations will be designed and alternative development policies promoted. A key element of DAWN's perspective aims at linking global problems to local issues. Two major research topics emerged as priorities: 'The Food, Energy and Debt Crises in Relation to Women' and 'Women's Visions and Movements in the Third World'. The research programme will provide the basis for training trainers in both short and long-term efforts addressed to activists, researchers and social policy-makers. DAWN's strategy of networking will underscore the priority areas of work and help to realise the dissemination of the initial collective work. (p.7)

DAWN is co-ordinated by experienced women activists from Jamaica, Mexico, Fiji, Bangladesh, India and Brazil. It is clearly too early to try to assess the practical impact of their programme of action on the daily lives of Third World women, but in seeking to implement a much-needed feminist approach to development it can only be welcomed.

Isis Internacional
Casilla 2067
Correo Central
Santiago   CHILE   Tel: 490 271

This office shares the same aims and activities as Isis International in Rome except that the two main publications, *Women in Action* and the *Journal*, are produced in Spanish. In addition, the women in Santiago co-ordinate the Latin American and Caribbean Women and Health Network.

Created in 1984 at the First Regional Women and Health Meeting in Colombia, it provides information and materials on health and women's health groups, a referral service putting women and women's groups into contact, and a communication channel for sharing experiences. This work is carried out through the building up of a computerised data bank of organisations and resources concerned with women and health in Latin America and the Caribbean; the production of an excellent bi-monthly informational bulletin in Spanish and English; the promotion of campaigns against medicines, contraceptives and other products and practices harmful to women's health; and the establishment of a team of women who are specialists in specific areas, such as health and population control policies, sexuality, nutrition or contraception, and can train further women in the region working in these fields.

Unidad de Comunicación Alternativa de la Mujer
(Women's Alternative Communication Unit)
Casilla 16-637
Correo 9
Santiago   CHILE

Since its formation in 1981, as part of the Latin American Institute for Transnational Studies (ILET), the Women's Alternative Communication Unit has been instrumental in building up an international network through which Latin American women can share experiences and ideas for organisation. Together with ILET, it helps to provide alternative media to counteract the perpetuation and dissemination of traditional stereotypes of women. Information is distributed through:

Mujer-ILET – a monthly publication of newsclippings and features from Latin American newspapers, magazines and bulletins on issues related to women, co-ordinated and produced by the information service.

FEMPRESS – which has correspondents in Argentina, Bolivia, Brazil, Colombia, Costa Rica, Chile, Ecuador, Mexico, Peru, the Dominican Republic and Uruguay. Distributed to women's alternative media, women's organisations and study groups, *Mujer-ILET* gives regular updated information about events related to the women's movement.

Mujer-Especiales – quarterly dossiers compiling articles on specific issues of interest to women. Topics have included: work, abortion, motherhood, politics, Central America, rural women, sexuality, machismo and legislation.

Colección Comunicación Alternativa de la Mujer – a series of booklets focusing on the work of different women's alternative media projects in Latin America. Groups featured include the publications *Mulherio* (Brazil), *Nueva Mujer* (Ecuador), *Maria Liberacion del Pueblo* (Mexico), *La Mala Vida* (Venezuela), Isis Internacional, and the radio station *Club Mencia de Radio Enriquillo (Dominican Republic)*.

   Radio Network – recognising the importance of radio as a means of reaching a wider number of women, the Women's Unit has recorded selections from some of the best radical women's programmes to be further distributed in the region. All the above are available in Spanish only.

Middle East

Arab Women Solidarity Association (AWSA)
25 Murad Street
Giza   EGYPT   Tel: Cairo 723976/738350

AWSA is an international non-governmental, non-profit organisation aiming at the promotion and development of the social, cultural and educational status of Arab women, strengthening the ties between Arab women working in this field. In a leaflet produced for the 1985 Nairobi Forum the Association states:

> Today, more than at any other moment of our recent history, we need to create an association for solidarity between women. The voices raised in a sustained clamour for the 'return of women to the home' are part of a general regressive movement, not only nationally but also internationally. Everywhere and on all fronts we are being called upon to face the challenges, the dangers, and the increasing complexity of problems by a collective and patient intellectual and organisational effort. At every moment we are required to overcome resignation, indifference and even despair, to build up hope and enthusiasm step by step.

Strongly supported by the writer and activist, Nawal El Saadawi, AWSA states among its aims:

● Active participation of women in the political, social and intellectual life of the country as being an essential condition for the evolution of a truly democratic society.
● Social justice within the family and in society and non-discrimination between the sexes in different areas of public and private life.
● A continuous and persevering effort to reach those wide sectors of the female population represented by 'working' and so-called 'non-working' women in urban and rural areas, in order to ensure that the thought and actions of the Association be closely linked to the problems of women belonging to different classes, categories and professions, and that ideas remain integrated to practical activities.
● Programmes and activities oriented towards raising the social consciousness of Arab women and abolishing illiteracy.
● Establishment of a library composed of historical and modern books, studies and documents representing the creative efforts and thought of women in the Arab region, Africa, Asia, Europe, the two Americas and Australia.
● Field studies and research carried out by specialised women members of the Association concerning working women in urban and rural areas, and in the publication of booklets and pamphlets which can assist in evolving practical solutions to some of the crucial problems faced by women.
● Ensure international solidarity between women and encourage fruitful relations with different women's organisations in all parts of the world.

2 Women's Organisations

This is mainly a list of those local and national women's organisations represented in the book. I have also included updated addresses for some of the groups listed in the first volume of *Third World – Second Sex*. Readers seeking information from other parts of the Third World are advised to get in touch with the relevant international or regional network.

Bolivia

Centro de Información y Desarrollo de la Mujer (CIDEM)
Casilla de Correo 3961
La Paz   Bolivia

Centro de Promoción de la Mujer 'Gregoria Apaza'
Casilla 21170
La Paz   Bolivia

Brazil

Centro Informaçao Mulher (CIM)
Caixa Postal 11.399
05499 São Paulo – SP   Brazil

Fundaçao Carlos Chagas
Av. Prof. Francisco Morato, 1565
00513 São Paulo – SP   Brazil

SOS–Mulher
Rua Marquesa dos Santos, 10
Laranjeiras
22.221 Rio de Janeiro – RJ   Brazil
Tel: 225 5419

Chile

Centro de Estudios de la Mujer
Purisima 353
Santiago   Chile

Colombia

Centro de Información y Recursos Para la Mujer
Calle 36, No. 17-44
Bogota, D.F.   Colombia

Dominican Republic

Centro de Investigación Para la Acción Femenina (CIPAF)
Benigno Filomeno Rojas 307
Santo Domingo, DN   Dominican Republic

Fiji

Ofis Blong Meri
Box 623
Nadi   Fiji

Guatemala

IXQUIC
Apartado Postal 27-008
Zona Postal 06760   Mexico D.F.

India

Centre for Women's Development Studies

B-43 Panchsheel Enclave
New Delhi 110024   India

Forum Against Sex-Determination and
  Pre-Selection Tests
c/o Women's Centre
B-104 Sunrise Apartments
Near Vakola Church
Vakola
Santacruz   Bombay 400055   India

Saheli Women's Resource Centre
Unit above Shop 105 to 108
Shopping Centre
Defence Colony Bridge (south side)
New Delhi 110024   India

Jamaica

Sistren Theatre Collective
20 Kensington Crescent
Kingston 5   Jamaica

Mauritius

Muvman Liberasyon Fam
Lakaz Ros
Antelme Street
Forest Side   Mauritius

Mexico

Comunicación, Intercambio y Desarrollo
  Humano en America Latina
(CIDHAL)
Apartado 579
Cuernavaca
Morelos   Mexico

Namibia

SWAPO Women's Council
SWAPO Provisional Headquarters
P.O. Box 953
Luanda   Angola

Nigeria

Women in Nigeria (WIN)
P.O. Box 253

Samaru Zaria   Nigeria

Pakistan

Simorgh Women's Resource and Publica-
  tion Centre
P.O. Box 3328
Main Market
Gulberg II
Lahore   Pakistan

Women's Action Forum
P.O. Box 3287
Gulberg
Lahore   Pakistan

Palestine

Union of Women's Work Committees
P.O. Box 20576
East Jerusalem   Via Israel

Papua New Guinea

East Sepik Women's Development,
  Documentation and Communication
  Programme
P.O. Box 69 Maprik
East Sepik Province   Papua New
  Guinea

Peru

Asociación Amauta
Apartado 167
Cusco   Peru

Centro de la Mujer Peruana 'Flora
  Tristán'
Parque Hernan Velarde 42
Lima   Peru

Movimiento Manuela Ramos
Av. Bolivia 921, Brena
Apartado 11176
Lima 14   Peru

Philippines
GABRIELA
Room 221
PCIB Building
Greenhills Commercial Centre
San Juan Manila   Philippines

South Africa
The Women's Centre
16 Ecumenical Centre Trust
20 St Andrews Street
Durban 4001   South Africa

Thailand
Friends of Women
49 Phra-athit Road
Bangkok 10200   Thailand

Women's Information Centre
113/9 Charansanitwong Road 46
Bangkok 10700   Thailand

Uruguay
Grupo de Estudios Sobre La Condición
    de la Mujer en el Uruguay (GRECMU)
Juan Paullier 1174
Montevideo   Uruguay

Venezuela
Circulos Femeninos Populares
Apartado 4240
Caracas 1010-A   Venezuela

Zimbabwe
Women's Action Group
P.O. Box 5
Harare   Zimbabwe

3 Suggested Further Reading

Books

Afshar, Haleh, (ed.), *Women, Work and Ideology in the Third World* (London, Tavistock, 1985).

Asia Partnership for Human Development (ed), *Awake – Asian Women and the Struggle for Justice* (Sydney, Asia Partnership for Human Development, 1985). Available in Europe from Trocaire, 169 Booterstown Avenue, Blackrock, Co. Dublin, Ireland.

Barrios de Chungara, Domitila, *Let Me Speak* (London, Stage 1, 1978).

Bronstein, Audrey, *The Triple Struggle – Latin American Peasant Women* (London, War On Want, 1982).

Burgos-Debray, Elisabeth (ed.), *I . . . Rigoberta Menchu – An Indian Woman in Guatemala* (London, Verso, 1984).

Carr, Marilyn, *Blacksmith, Baker, Roofing-Sheet Maker – Employment for Rural Women in Developing Countries* (London, Intermediate Technology Publications, 1984).

Davies, Miranda (ed.), *Third World – Second Sex: Women's Struggles and National Liberation* (London, Zed Press, 1983).

Deighton, Jane *et al*, *Sweet Ramparts – Women in Revolutionary Nicaragua* (London, War On Want and Nicaragua Solidarity Campaign, 1983).

Eck, Diana and Jain, Devaki (eds.), *Speaking of Faith: Cross-Cultural Perspectives on Women, Religion and Social Change* (London, Women's Press, 1987).

El Dareer, Asma, *Woman, Why Do You Weep? Circumcision and its Consequences* (London, Zed Press, 1982).

El Saadawi, Nawal, *The Hidden Face of Eve – Women in the Arab World* (London, Zed Press, 1980); and *Woman at Point Zero* (London, Zed Books, 1984).

Eisen Bergman, Arlene, *Women and Revolution in Vietnam* (London, Zed Press, 1984).

Huston, Perdita, *Third World Women Speak Out* (New York, Praeger, 1978).

Isis, *Women in Development: A Resource Guide for Organisation and Action* (Geneva/Rome, Isis, 1983).

Isis International, *Powerful Images: A Women's Guide to Audiovisual Resources* (Rome, Isis International, 1986).

Jain, Devaki, *Women's Quest for Power* (India, Vikas, 1980).

Jayawardena, Kumari, *Feminism and Nationalism in the Third World* (London, Zed Books, 1986).

Kali for Women (eds.), *Truth Tales – Stories from India*, (London, Women's Press, 1986).

283

Khalifa, Sahar, *Wild Thorns* (London, Al Saqi, 1985).
Kishwar, Madhu and Vanita, Ruth (eds.), *In Search of Answers: Indian Women's Voices* (London, Zed Books, 1984).
Kumar, Radha, *The History of Doing – An Illustrated Account of the Women's Movement in India* (New Delhi, Kali for Women, 1985).
Kuzwayo, Ellen, *Call Me Woman* (London, Women's Press, 1985).
Liddle, Joanna and Joshi, Rama, *Daughters of Independence: Gender, Caste and Class in India* (London, Zed Books, 1986).
McDonnell, Kathleen (ed.), *Adverse Effects: Women and the Pharmaceutical Industry* (Penang, IOCU, 1986).
Mernissi, Fatima, *Beyond the Veil* (London, Al Saqi, 1985).
Mies, Maria, *Patriarchy and Accumulation on a World Scale: Women in the International Division of Labour* (London, Zed Books, 1986).
Minces, Juliette, *The House of Obedience – Women in the Arab World* (London, Zed Press, 1982).
Morgan, Robin (ed), *Sisterhood is Global* (London, Penguin, 1985).
Mukhopadhyay, Maitrayee, *Silver Shackles – Women and Development in India* (Oxford, Oxfam, 1984).
New Internationalist (ed.), *Women: A World Report* (London, Methuen, 1985).
Randall, Margaret, *Sandino's Daughters: Testimonies of Nicaraguan Women in Struggle* (London, Zed Press, 1981).
Seager, Joni and Olson, Ann, *Women in the World: An International Atlas* (London, Pan Books, 1986).
Sen, Gita and Grown, Caren, *Development, Crises, and Alternative Visions: Third World Women's Perspectives* (New York, Monthly Review Press, 1987).
Sibal, Nina, *Yatra (The Journey)* (London, Women's Press, 1987).
Shirazi, Manny, *Javady Alley* (London, Women's Press, 1984).
Sistren, *Lionheart Gal – Life Stories of Jamaican Women* (London, Women's Press, 1986).
Tawil, Raymonda, *My Home, My Prison* (London, Zed Press, 1984).
Thomson, Marilyn, *Women of El Salvador – The Price of Freedom* (London, Zed Books, 1986).
Touati, Fettouma, *Desperate Spring* (London, Women's Press, 1987).
Vukani Makhosikazi Collective, *South African Women on the Move* (London, Zed Books, 1986).
W.I.N. (Women in Nigeria), *Women in Nigeria Today* (London, Zed Books, 1985).
Young, Kate, Wollkowitz, Carol and McCullagh, Roslyn (eds.), *Of Marriage and the Market – Women's Subordination in International Perspective* (London, CSE Books, 1981).

Regular Publications in English

Connexions – An International Women's Quarterly: 4228 Telegraph Avenue, Oakland, California 94609, USA.
Isis International Journal and supplement, *Women in Action:* Via San Saba, int. 1, 00153 Rome, Italy.
Manushi: bi-monthly *Journal about Women in Society* (also in Hindi): C1-202 Lajpat Nagar 1, New Delhi 110024, India.
Outwrite: monthly *Women's Newspaper:* Oxford House, Derbyshire Street, London E2 6HG, UK.